D0848513

WOMEN AND POWER
IN NATIVE NORTH AMERICA

WOMEN AND POWER IN NATIVE NORTH AMERICA

EDITED BY
LAURA F. KLEIN AND
LILLIAN A. ACKERMAN

UNIVERSITY OF OKLAHOMA PRESS
NORMAN AND LONDON

This book is published with
the generous assistance of
Edith Gaylord Harper.

HOUSTON PUBLIC LIBRARY

. R01030 13251

SSCCA

Library of Congress Cataloging-in-Publication Data

Women and power in native North America /edited by Laura F. Klein and
Lillian A. Ackerman.
     p.   cm.
     Includes bibliographical references (p.   ) and index.
     ISBN 0-8061-2752-X (hardcover : acid-free paper)
     1. Indian women—North America—History.   2. Indian women—North
America—Social conditions.   3. Indian women—North America—Eco-
nomic conditions.   4. Sex role—North America—History.   I. Klein,
Laura F. (Laura Frances), 1946– .   II. Ackerman, Lillian, A. (Lillian
Alice).
E98.W8W657   1995
306.48′897—dc20   95-5903
                                                                   CIP

Text design by Cathy Carney Imboden. The typeface is Goudy Old Style.

The paper in this book meets the guidelines for permanence and durability
of the Committee on Production Guidelines for Book Longevity of the
Council on Library Resources, Inc. ∞

Copyright ©1995 by the University of Oklahoma Press, Norman, Publishing
Division of the University. All rights reserved. Manufactured in the U.S.A.

1   2   3   4   5   6   7   8   9   10

CONTENTS

v

CONTENTS

PREFACE

The chapters in this volume are the result of a symposium presented at the December 1988 annual meeting of the American Anthropological Association in Phoenix, Arizona. In an effort to bring together some of the diverse studies of gender undertaken in North America, north of Mexico, scholars, both women and men, gathered to present their descriptions of these Native worlds. All the chapters challenge the stereotypes of gender relations and replace them with a much more complex reality that includes real respect and usually power for Native women within their societies. One goal of the colonization that Native North American societies were forced to endure was the reduction of the cultural valuation of women. But success varied widely. The views of the contemporary roles of Native women presented here will challenge many readers' assumptions. Significantly, this collection disputes not only the popular and academic generalizations of Native North American cultures but also some of the long-held theories of human gender relations.

The original prospectus for this symposium focused on the question of gender status in Native North America. Authors were sent the following statement: "The question of whether men and women have equal status in most Native North American groups north of Mexico has never been resolved. Ethnographies describe both gender stratification and gender equality in Indian societies in the past and present. While there is no doubt that both kinds of society occur, we hope in the symposium to determine which kind of gender status is prevalent among North American Indians. Scholars who study gender in each of ten cultural areas in North America will present papers on this problem discussing power, authority, and prestige in such cultural spheres as politics, economics, domestic life, and religion."

The premise, then, was in part a return to the "original question" of anthropological gender studies but at a later stage. Both of the editors have worked on the question of status and power in specific Native American cultures and are familiar with many more. Clearly women had power and authority in many Native American communities, and clearly this was true historically and at present. What was missing from the literature was an academic presentation of this reality. Many popular books and summary articles (e.g., Niethammer 1977; Terrell and Terrell 1974) have been published, but nowhere have scholars come together to look at this phenomenon in a structured way. A major goal, then, was simply to bring together people who have been working on the same set of gender issues to discover the similarities and differences between cultures in North America in their concepts of, and rules for, gender.

Since the symposium, the authors have added data that broadened their descriptions to illuminate or question concepts raised by other authors. Additionally, Daniel Maltz and JoAllyn Archambault provided a concluding, analytical chapter. It was decided not to create an outline of topics and/or theoretical orientations to be followed in each chapter. We believed that spontaneity and flexibility would result in more readable contributions, which would ultimately be truer to the situations involved.

ACKNOWLEDGMENTS

This volume traces its genesis, as many things do, to an informal discussion at a meeting of the American Anthropological Association. It was obvious to many of us there that understandings of Native cultures were impossible when viewed through the lens of one gender to the exclusion, or at best, loss of focus on the other. It was equally clear that Native cultures defined gender relations in a variety of ways that differed just as other aspects of these cultures differed and that these definitions were often at variance with the expectations of Euro-American colonialists and scholars as well. Finally, it was apparent that these truisms were not appearing in the general literature on Native North America. In this discussion, one of us (Klein) commented that she had always assumed that Eleanor Burke Leacock would be the person to organize a critical rethinking of the role of Native women in the first nations of North America. Despite her untimely death, she did play a role that she often assumed in life: she pushed people to action. We therefore owe her a debt of gratitude.

We would like to thank the contributors to this volume for their diligence and patience in seeing this book through to completion. The efforts of the readers and editors of this book have also tightened and clarified our work, and we deeply appreciate their thoughtful contributions. We must thank our departments and universities for their support with staff, equipment, and time. The encouragement of our colleagues has also been of great value. Our appreciation goes to Sarah

Moore of Illustration Services, Pullman, Washington, for her work on the map. We must especially thank Peggy Jobe, of the Pacific Lutheran University (PLU) Division of Social Sciences, who typed and retyped the manuscript, and Margaret Worley, of the PLU Computer Center, who repeatedly coaxed segments of the manuscript out of the jaws of predatory computers. Both restored prose and sanity more than once.

Finally, we wish to give personal thanks for the support of our families and friends and, most centrally, to the Native women who nurtured us throughout the years with their wisdom and kindness.

WOMEN AND POWER
IN NATIVE NORTH AMERICA

Native North American groups discussed in this volume.

1

INTRODUCTION

LAURA F. KLEIN AND LILLIAN A. ACKERMAN

Silence surrounds the lives of Native North American women. The goal of this book is to explode that silence, which has concealed the roles of Native women in the thicket of ethnographic literature. The wives, sisters, and mothers of the Native nations do appear in traditional ethnographies but only where they are expected, and the meanings of their lives are left to the readers' imaginations. We never hear their voices and are never told their tales. The readers, then, write into this quiet their own cultural expectations for the "natural" role of women. As seen by non-Native readers, the image of American Indian women becomes a reflection of self, according to the standards of the times. Through the secondary and tertiary literature, these images become truth.

In an academic period when the urge to deconstruct all texts overwhelms the literature, we have been offered little help. While critical reading of the earlier ethnographies is crucial, deconstructing their gender messages leaves us with little, because the traditional literature is superficial in the discussion of women. We may conclude that the ethnographer created a text filled with his or her own messages, but this insight does not illuminate the important questions. What were and are Native women like? What were and are their lives? How did they construct their lives, and how did others define their barriers and opportunities? How did and do Native women, along with others, create Native America?

The silence must not be ignored or regretted. Instead, we must ask what the silence means. In the preface to her recent book, Ruth M. Boyer speaks about the silence of the power of Apache women (Boyer and Gayton 1992:xii), and this concept is valid far beyond the Apache. There is a silence of familiarity. People do not have to assert "Our women are powerful" any more than they need to argue "Our children are playful" or "Our men are productive." In the many societies where these characterizations are true, they are also obvious. There is a truism in ethnography, commonly traced to Max Gluckman, that societal rules become clear in times of dispute. The appropriate role of women has been in public dispute in Western culture for at least the last century, and the question of power and gender is, therefore, an issue. In societies where no such dispute is prominent, silence would be expected. The tendency to fill in this silence with powerlessness is the Western bias. In fact, the silence tells us nothing but the lack of dispute. Our informants may agree about the power or powerlessness of one gender or group and have no need to defend that concept. They may even assume that we agree and assume the same.

The chapters in this book give voice to the silences. The roles of power, influence, and authority that may be obvious in their own societies are exceptional elsewhere. The story of Native North American women as players in their own societies needs to be told to allow a full description of the traditional lifeways of Native peoples that is dictated less by the structure of Euro-American culture. The changes that have taken place in those societies that have redefined gender roles need to be recorded. This enterprise also illuminates again the complexity of the damages that the colonial mandates of "civilization" brought. For scholars, it additionally challenges the views of cultural life and gender that have so long controlled the field and questions the responsibility of these scholars in repairing damaging stereotypes. For students and interested readers, it offers challenges to rethink the images promoted by popular culture and to search for an understanding that involves new concepts of gender.

NATIVE NORTH AMERICAN WOMEN
IN POPULAR CULTURE

If women in Euro-American cultures have sometimes been characterized either as whores or as ladies, then the equivalent for American Indian women must be "squaws" or "princesses." While this observation is far from original (Albers 1983:3; Jameson 1988:762; Mankiller and Wallis 1993:19), it is important to the understanding of the place of Native women in American popular culture. The concept of "squaw" belittles the lives of Native men and women alike. The squaw is a drudge who is forced to endure hard work while her husband swaps hunting stories with his friends. As Eleanor Burke Leacock has pointed out, any such interpretation of women's work is a double-edged sword. If a woman does not work—that is, add labor and input to her society— she rarely has societal worth (see Friedl 1975); if, however, she actively labors within her society, the Westerner judges her abused and debased. By this logic, the Native woman appears to have no social input, no choice in spouses, and no respect. She is an inferior to her husband and necessary only for her labor and for her sexual and reproductive duties. Her sexual favors can be sold by her husband while she meekly acquiesces.

These images appear in the popular literature from the earliest colonial reports to the present in both adult and children's books. Marla N. Powers (1986:8–14), for example, traces this imagery in descriptions of the Oglalas by early travelers through reports of George Armstrong Custer and into the twentieth century. Euro-American writers stressed the savagery of Native life for women. In contrast, Rayna Green (1984:706) points out that "American Indian people remember that, on many occasions, white women captured in battle by Native peoples refused to return to their own communities when offered the opportunity."

The second, more romantic, image is that of the "Indian princess." Vine Deloria, Jr. (1969:3–4) maintains that this is the Indian from whom most Euro-Americans claim descent, reflecting the Euro-American misunderstanding of Indian culture and the self-deceptive lure of royalty. Certainly, the quintessential Indian princess of American lore is Pocahontas. According to Nancy O. Lurie (1972:29), "Whether the legend is exact or not, Pocahontas is important to white folklore and to the pride of many white Americans who boast of Indian ancestry." The legend of Powhatan's daughter who saves the life of one English colonial and marries another is one of the standard childhood stories of the United States. She is presented, in European terms, as royalty and, in European terms, as rejecting the standards and traditions of her people for European views of morality and romantic love. In "Pocohontas Perplex," Green (1975:704) asserts that for the princess figure "to be 'good,' she must defy her own people, exile herself from them, become white and perhaps suffer death." In other words, the "good Native woman" cannot be perceived as truly Native. Pocahontas's death in England in 1617 is rarely part of the story, perhaps because it presents the undeniable reality that contact with Europeans and Euro-Americans did not benefit the Natives but in fact often killed them. When Clara Sue Kidwell (1992:99–101) reexamined Pocahontas as a woman, a different person emerged. Kidwell presents an assertive and culturally appropriate woman behind the European facade.

It is the myth of Pocahontas, rather than the woman, that is widely presented to contemporary American children. Along with myriad other national and local legends, she represents the princess. While she is not a drudge and certainly not sexually promiscuous, she is nevertheless submissive to men. She is not as much an independent actor as she is a maternal protector and helpmate to the male European actors.

Stereotypically, then, Native women could be viewed as demeaned drudges who followed, or were mired in, the backward traditions of their cultures or as picturesque ladies who took on the virtues of upper-class European society and left Native American traditions behind them. Asebrit Sundquist (1987), in her study of Native women in nineteenth-century fiction, concludes that the idealized women of these novels, influenced in part by the legends of Pocahontas, became the generic ideal woman of European culture. Green concludes,

6

My review of the literature has left me with the conviction that Native American women have neither been neglected nor forgotten. They have captured hearts and minds, but, as studies of other women have demonstrated, the level and substance of most passion for them has been selective, stereotyped, and damaging. (1980:249)

It is fair to note that there have been popular books that represent Native women positively. Perhaps, at long last, the divide between fantasy and reality is closing. In 1930, Flora Seymour wrote a small book for the Woman's Press entitled *Women of Trail and Wigwam* whose purpose was to tell the stories of "heroic Indian girls and women" (15). She included sixteen chapters highlighting famous women, ten of whom were wives of Euro-American men.[1] One other heroine was Appearing Day, who married the man she loved rather than the husband chosen by her family. The standard of heroism was European. By 1954 when Carolyn Foreman wrote *Indian Women Chiefs*, that standard was less obvious, but the state of the data was still seriously deficient. Looking for women who held positions of authority in their cultures, Foreman gathered a series of vignettes of people and cultures that lacked thematic coherence. The sources were largely incomplete or anecdotal, and very few of the women could reliably be classified as chiefs. In 1993 when Gretchen Bataille collected more than 240 short biographical sketches in *Native American Women*, the result was vastly different. These women are distinguished artists, healers, politicians, activists, and anthropologists. While many prominent women could be added to the list, the picture that emerges from this volume is one of diverse and talented Native North American women.

It is wise to note that even at this level of recognition the lives of most Native women remain silent in popular literature. Those Native

---

1. The lives of the Native wives of Hudson's Bay men and other traders have been recorded in Van Kirk 1983 and Brown 1980. Certainly the Hudson's Bay Company protected the image of the "daughters of the land" who married the highly ranked Hudson's Bay Company employees and differentiated them from the common sorts of women (squaws) with whom laborers would consort. These recent works about these women of the fur trade have revised the history of such trade in important ways.

women who were freed from the squaw imagery remained invisible to the average reader. Patricia Albers and Beatrice Medicine's book on Plains Indian women is aptly entitled *The Hidden Half* (1983).[2] The Native people who most often are described in explorers' reports are those the Europeans saw as leaders or troublemakers. The image of "the Chief" becomes central. The occasional female "chief" is introduced in this literature too. For example, Hernando de Soto reported a regional leader, the "princess of Cofachiqui" (Irving [1869] 1971:215–238), but the concept of chief is largely kept as a male stereotype. Women who were viewed as being powerful or strong advisers were often dismissed as oddities, or the men in their societies were labeled in Leacock's (1972:34) pointed prose as "henpecked." Ordinary women, like most ordinary men, failed to appear in much of this literature.

NATIVE NORTH AMERICAN WOMEN
IN ANTHROPOLOGICAL LITERATURE

The ethnographic reports of the first half of the twentieth century followed a similar pattern in regard to women. As Leacock noted in 1981,

> To handle women's participation in a given society with brief remarks about food preparation and child care has until very recently met the requirements for adequate ethnography. . . . Women are commonly stated or implied to hold low status in one or another society without benefit of empirical documentation. (134)

Certainly some ethnographies rose above this level. Robert Lowie's 1935 ethnography, *The Crow Indians*, reported the roles of women in religion, entertainment, community work, and property ownership. He concluded,

> Socially, the women enjoyed a good deal of freedom. Even in the matter of sex relations failure to aspire to the ideal implied no ostracism. A wife had definite property rights. In buying specimens I repeatedly noted that no

---

2. This is not any historic artifact. Witt (1974:29) points out that "present stereotypes are also male. . . . The drunken Indian, the Cadillac Indian, Lonesome Polecat—facelessness still characterizes Native American Women."

husband ever attempted to influence, let alone coerce, a wife in the disposal of her own belongings. To offset their domestic work, women could indulge in a variety of amusements, such as ball and dice games, sometimes among themselves, sometimes in the company of their husbands or lovers.

Altogether Crow women had a secure place in the tribal life and a fair share in its compensations. (Lowie [1935] 1956:61)

While Lowie's work hardly qualifies as a feminist tract or a complete balanced ethnography, there is, at least, a record that the lives of Crow women were not mere reflections of those of their Euro-American sisters. Ruth Landes, in her 1938 ethnography, *The Ojibwa Woman*, provided a volume that focused on women, although the orientation was not dissimilar to other ethnographies of the day. A more powerful trend in the description of Native women at this time was the production of autobiographies. Early in the century autobiographies of Native women began to appear. Truman Michelson (1925, 1932, 1933), Robert Lowie ([1922] 1967), Ruth Bunzel ([1929] 1972), Frank Linderman ([1932] 1974), and others recorded the lives of women who described their lives in times of change and development. The strengths and weaknesses of these autobiographies are described well by Gretchen M. Bataille and Kathleen Mullen Sands in *American Indian Women: Telling Their Lives* (1984). To recent times (see, e.g., Lurie 1972; Blackman 1982, 1989; Mankiller and Wallis 1993) these biographies and autobiographies of Native women have presented compelling accounts of real people.

During the 1950s and early 1960s, a few works appeared which challenged the conventional viewpoint that the roles of American Indian women were similar in all cultures. Laila Hamamsy (1957) criticized the impact of modern Euro-American society in lessening the status of Navajo women and increasing the difficulty of their lives. Eleanor Leacock (1955) challenged the contemporary interpretation of Montagnais-Naskapi culture by demonstrating how determined missionary effort reduced the social status of women. Carma Smithson's *The Havasupai Woman* (1959) focused on the impact of culture change on the gender roles in that society. Louise Spindler's (1962) work on

Menominee women presented a similar conclusion with a culture and personality methodology. Thus a number of scholars questioned their predecessors on the generalizations and primary data regarding women's roles.

Since the mid-1970s, the growth of anthropological interest in women's roles has expanded exponentially, and this is echoed in Native North American studies. Beatrice Medicine's pioneering bibliography, "The Role of Women in Native American Societies," in *Indian Historian* (1975), listed 99 items. Eight years later, Green's annotated bibliography, *Native American Women* (1983), covered 672 items in one hundred pages. Eight years after that, Bataille and Sands's (1991) annotated guide to research contained more than four hundred pages. During these years, dissertations on gender had become acceptable and articles and books on Native American women publishable. As the 1980s came to an end, Sandra Morgen's *Gender and Anthropology* (1989) was published under the sponsorship of the American Anthropological Association and contained a defining article by Patricia Albers, "From Illusion to Illumination: Anthropological Studies of American Indian Women" (132–70). Albers there, as formerly (1983), presents, evaluates, and orders a wide selection of new resources and offers challenges for needed work.

GENDER STUDIES

This introduction is not the place to fully review the growth of gender studies in anthropology. Several reviews have recently been published (see Atkinson 1982; Moore 1988; Morgen 1989; Mukhopadhyay and Higgins 1988; Rapp 1979). All demonstrate the growth in depth and breadth of the gender literature in the short time that this has been an active subfield in anthropology.

While the "original question" (Mukhopadhyay and Higgins 1988: 461) of gender studies concerned the status of women cross-culturally, it assumed a universal subordination of women. Many contemporary anthropologists count Michelle Z. Rosaldo and Louise Lamphere's classic reader, *Women, Culture and Society* (1974), as their first introduction to an anthropology of women. A major assumption of that book was the universal subordination of women in all cultures and stages of history, and the major goal of that book was a search for the reason for that assumed reality. These simple questions and assumptions have given way to a more diverse theoretical universe that allows questions on the very unity of the category "women" and emphasizes variations in time, class, age, culture, and colonial status in gender investigations.

The person and writings of Eleanor Leacock (1955, 1975, [1978] 1981) have affected the scholarship of many of the authors in this book. Her focus on band societies and her interpretation of the relative autonomy of women and men in these societies have been widely influential. In this she also stressed the use of ethnohistorical resources to understand the changes that alter the definition and roles of each gender in specific societies. In *Women and Colonization* (1980), Mona Etienne and Leacock presented a number of cases in which women clearly lost power and authority in the process of colonization or modern development. One study in that collection showed that colonial pressure for female submission could be present but still unsuccessful (Klein, 1980). Examples of both successful and unsuccessful colonial pressure to re-create women's roles are included in this volume.

Jane Atkinson (1982:245–46) cites a "strong commitment to historical analysis" as one of the trends of recent work in feminist studies in anthropology. In Native American studies this has been a constant theme for both better and worse. American anthropological studies emerged from classic ethnographies that recorded the recollections of elders of previous generations ("memory culture") but neglected the more immediate data on their contemporary lives. Contemporary work involves careful archival and ethnographic analysis of data. There is no search for "real Indian culture." The cultures that modern ethnographers study are as real and valid as those of the cultures of the past; but they differ. Since all American communities are encapsulated within myriad changing national and international institutions, the comprehension of modern Native communities requires an understanding of colonial history and the diverse cultures of the region. Modern ethnohistory is searching not for the pure cultures of the past but instead for an understanding of how cultures and the roles of people change over time.

As Carol C. Mukhopadhyay and Patricia J. Higgins (1988:486) concluded in their recent summary,

> Gender must be studied with reference to historical, economic, social, and conceptual context; understanding gender requires more than exploring its relationship to biology and economics. In addition, gender theorists must be alert to how androcentric and Eurocentric folk views influence scholarship. Finally, the concept of homogeneous "woman" must give way to the diversity of "women."

The chapters in this book follow this edict.

GENDER AND POWER IN NATIVE NORTH AMERICA

Power rather than status became the key concept that unites the focus on gender in this book, and individual authors were encouraged to define the term as it best explicates their cases. Consequently, power appears as the multiplex concept it is in both emic and etic terms: some authors have emphasized cosmology, others economic control, others formal hierarchy, and others a combination of factors. All, however, assert power as a process rather than a status. Power, here, is an active reality that is being created and redefined through individual life stages and through societal history. The predilection to label women as a class as powerful or powerless that marked the feminist anthropology of the 1970s and early 1980s is minimized here. A second agreement is that power is a concept that can be discussed apart from a formal political structure. In this, most echo the concept that Leacock referred to as autonomy. The question becomes whether, or to what extent, individuals are autonomous in the living of their own lives and exert control over aspects of the lives of others? Power, in this definition, is found as profoundly within the family as it is in the community council.

Choosing the culture areas as a framework might seem inappropriate at this time, but this framework was chosen for descriptive rather than theoretical purposes. It is a pattern known to students, and it mandates a wide geographic and ecological spread. While it clearly does not cover all the possible variations in gender definition, it does present a broad span of variation. The cultures represented in this volume are, further, not selected because they are representative of a particular culture area: they should not be used to generalize too widely. In other words, there is no claim that each chapter represents the gender categories of a particular culture area. With these caveats in mind, these chapters represent eleven different Native North American cultures whose gender definitions allow a consistent respect for individuality and ability.

It is worthwhile to provide an introductory look at the agreements and disagreements among the contributions. Clearly there are some very basic assumptions that informed the work of all the authors. First, no one assumed that there would be one status of women that would be true universally or even throughout any one culture. All deal with gender as a highly variable concept that could and did change over time and between cultures. Likewise, no authors limited their analysis of gender status to one aspect of any culture. Power is not restricted to the political realm. Analysis of the interaction of religious belief and the behavior system, the family and household concepts, the economic rules, and the public political realm is central to all the studies.

Three issues are important to each author in the analysis of their cases: first, the role of colonial contact and national intervention; second, the concept of gender reciprocity, most often, balanced reciprocity; third, the nature of kinship within the culture and the interaction between the kinship and gender systems. Given the enormity of the colonial experience on all Native cultures and institutions, it is no surprise that this is a key issue in gender questions as well. That there was a conscious effort by Western administrators and missionaries to change gender roles in many societies is clear, and that the fact of colonialism regularly was a disturbing force on gender definition seems certain. What is also clear from these chapters is that the Native societies' reactions to colonial pressure varied. Joy Bilharz argues that the general status of Seneca women differed widely during the period of colonization, but they have now come full circle to their original position of gender reciprocity. Mary Shepardson finds a similar pattern among the Navajo. Martha C. Knack and Laura F. Klein, similarly, find Southern Paiute and Tlingit women in positions similar to their original status, but the road to this end was much smoother than for the Seneca and Navajo. Lillian A. Ackerman finds that the ideal of Plateau women as equal to Plateau men is as true today as it was historically, but the nature of this equality is quite different. Sue-Ellen Jacobs concludes that the autonomy of the women of San Juan Pueblo may have slowly increased over time. Henry S. Sharpe reports a history so unclear that any answer may be "unresolvable."

A more uniform theme is that of balanced reciprocity. The authors in this volume conclude that the worlds of men and women were, and are, distinctly different but not generally perceived as hierarchical. In other words, while there are different roles expected of men and women, neither men's roles nor women's roles are considered superior; the efforts of both women and men are acknowledged as necessary for the well-being of the society. The balance between the two necessary units creates a harmonious society in many cases. Accounts differ on the degree of exclusivity allotted to aspects of each gender role. While it is a truth of American jurisprudence that "separate but equal" is intrinsically unequal, the radically different societies presented here seem to make "separate but equal" work. A major exception to this observation is the world of the Muskogees in the Southeast. Richard A. Sattler describes the Muskogee gender arrangement as inherently unequal, with women's roles clearly subordinate to men's. The existence of distinct men's and women's roles, then, does not indicate in itself either an equality of genders or a superiority of one gender over the other. The complexity of these situations makes the classical dichotomies of private/public or domestic/jural domains too confining.

The issue of family, or domestic life, is treated quite differently in different cases. The centrality and importance of the family in Pueblo, Tlingit, and Inuit lives, for example, molds the behavior of men and women alike. The family is not defined as women's domain or work but as the heart of society. The role of mother, sister, daughter, brother, or

14

son is not innately subordinate but instead is the function of serious and active individuals who are working for the welfare of their people. The family is not found to be an insignificant domestic side of life in Native North America. By and large, the family is not solely women's domain, nor is it an inferior subordinate institution.

Two other issues reappear with important but slightly varied meaning. One is the significance of women in religion. It is interesting, for example, that the importance of the vision quest to women can take different forms. Among the Blackfoot (Alice B. Kehoe), the innate power of women makes the vision quest unnecessary for them, unlike for the men, while in the Plateau (Ackerman), women have the same religious experiences and rituals as men. A second important issue is that of landownership in agricultural societies. While Bilharz shows that the ownership of land is overestimated as indicative of the status of Seneca men and women, Sattler demonstrates how landownership can be differently valued in Muskogee and Cherokee societies. The richness of this collection enables one to make comparisons of this kind on a great number of issues.

CONCLUSION

The chapters in this book speak out loudly on the roles of women in eleven Native nations. They are loud for emphasis. Many contemporary anthropologists have worked with Native communities in this latter part of the twentieth century and have understood that women's roles are as much in need of explanation to a non-Native audience as are the roles of men. In this the authors in this volume have been prominent but not alone. What has been lacking, until now, is a single source that brings together data from the great variety of Native cultures.

A strength of this volume is the consistent emphasis on ethnographic and ethnohistorical depth. It is hoped that these data will be used to propel further study and to criticize the existing work.

The gender stereotypes of Native North Americans held by Europeans and Euro-Americans may simply be an extension of the gender stereotypes they hold of all non-European peoples. Warriors were always the first individuals to be noted by Europeans at contact with new societies. That narrowness of perspective has not yet widened to include the lives and roles of women. In this collection, we have endeavored to place Native North American women in their proper social context. Most of the chapters describe groups that treat women as integrated members of their societies, give almost religious respect to them as wives and mothers, and listen to their advice seriously. A reassessment of the roles of women in all non-Western societies, continent by continent, is in order. It may be that in some cases, the old formulations of women's power and authority are valid; in other cases, we may be surprised.

2

THE ARCTIC

GENDER IN INUIT SOCIETY

LEE GUEMPLE

This chapter explores gender relations in Eskimo (Yuit, Inuit) society with particular reference to equality in power, authority, and prestige. It is a factual account of traditional gender relations, setting aside any consideration of changes that have taken place since the early contact period. Although theoretical discussion of the concepts involved here is beyond the scope of this inquiry, such terms as "equality" and "power" are certainly outgrowths of contemporary Euro-North American interests in gender relations and so express cultural values and sentiments that can be "exported" to other cultures only with some care.

Lillian A. Ackerman (1990:209–212) points out that general accounts by nonspecialists generally allot Eskimo women low status relative to men, whether one looks at such popular writings as those of Peter Freuchen (e.g., 1935:188) or at the characterizations produced by nonspecialists (e.g., Friedl 1975:43; Murdock 1934:213) writing in general terms about the "Arctic." The early literature is sprinkled with accounts (some of them based on myth and folklore) of the beating, mutilation, sexual coercion, abduction, and murder of women; of their hardships during times of shortage; and of their burdens as overworked drudges. These incidents color the assessment of their status relative to men.

One may speculate that the portrayal of Arctic women as under the relatively total domination of their male relatives was early generated by explorers, missionaries, and others—the overwhelming majority of them men—whose general attitude toward "the primitive" was dominated by a more or less Hobbesian view. That is, they saw Arctic life as little more than an interminable struggle to survive. Consequently, social life was necessarily simple and brutish, with men totally dominant because of their "naturally" superior strength and ferocity. That popular impression has faded only slightly, and few have bothered to address the issue of gender status in measured terms.

Studies that focus directly on questions of status equality—the relative power, authority, and prestige of males and females—are of very recent origin, with two exceptions: an excellent treatment of the subject in Margaret Lantis's (1946) monograph on the Nunivak Eskimos of the Bering Strait region and some worthwhile comments in Diamond Jenness's (1922) study of the Copper Eskimos. More recent sources that make possible an assessment of male-female equality are Ackerman's (1990) paper on gender-based authority relationships among Yup'ik-speaking Eskimos; Ernest Burch's (1975) comments on the social position of females in his monograph on the North Alaskan Eskimo;[1] casual allusions to gender roles in Asen Balikci's (1970) descriptive work on the Netsilingmiut; Jean L. Briggs's (1970) sensitive and personal account of Utkuhiqhalingmiut socialization[2] and another (1974) on the place of women among Central Inuits; Bernard Saladin d'Anglure's (1986) analysis of Central Inuit gender as a ternary system in which shamans appear symbolic as a mediating gender; Jaarich Oosten's (1986) examination of the role of women in Arctic shamanism; Joëlle Robert-Lamblin's (1986) study of the influence of education on sexual identity in Greenland; and my inquiry (1986) into the relation between gender, sex, and the division of labor among East Hudson Bay Inuit.

---

1. The Burch study has the added advantage of distinguishing between the "traditional" (to ca. 1890), "transitional" (1900–60), and "modern" (since 1960) periods, which makes it possible to measure some of the changes that have taken place in family and community organization over time.

2. The focus of this work is on the enculturation of children but contains much of relevance to authority relationships because of the differential manner in which boys and girls are socialized.

EQUALITY IN WORK

Eskimos themselves tend to characterize the relations between people in terms of the allocation of work, a characterization that includes not only what one should do but also what one is and in what terms one should be valued and respected by others (Guemple 1986). The literature containing descriptions of traditional task allocation between males and females has been handily summarized by Naomi Giffen (1930) and hence need not be reviewed here.

As both Burch (1975:85-86) and Balikci (1970:104) have pointed out, the marked complementarity of work responsibilities between men and women result in their being together for limited amounts of time, mainly for meals, to perform routine domestic chores, and for sleeping and procreating. Men are occupied with hunting, gathering and hauling food and heavy raw materials, and constructing and maintaining hunting equipment—work that takes them out of the household for long periods on a daily basis. Women's apportioned responsibilities lock them into domestic routines that are populated primarily by other women, girls, and young children of both sexes. Cooking, cleaning, processing and sewing skins and other materials, fishing, and gathering fuel, berries, grass and moss along with child-bearing and child care constitute their primary tasks. Jenness's comments may apply to the entire Central and eastern Arctic: "Marriage involves no subjection on the part of the woman. She has her own sphere of activity, and within that she is as supreme as her husband is in his. . . . Both within and without the house she behaves as the equal of the men" (1922:162).

Neither gender infringes on the world of the other's work, even though the separation is only occasionally supported by repressive sanctions that prohibit invasion of the other gender's sphere of activity. The record is clear that neither sex lacks the requisite skills to perform the other's work. Both men and women have a good working knowledge of the other gender's tasks and, when necessary, can perform the work of the other with considerable skill (Guemple 1986).[3]

---

3. This may be a slight exaggeration. In my experience women *never* make kayak frames

It would be difficult to measure with any precision the amount of strength and/or skill required for each gender's tasks. Men's work is physically more dangerous and may require more brute strength than women's and probably accounts for men's somewhat lower life expectancy. Women's work is probably equally exhausting overall, however, and perhaps a bit more tedious.

Praise for individual conduct is generally expressed in terms of exemplary work performance; statements about the desirable qualities in a potential consort are often expressed in terms of skills and productive potential as well. Hunting is unquestionably the cynosure for males and the community at large; and men's reputations within the community are closely linked to their productive capability. Hours are invested each day in discussing hunting, and no public gathering is complete without some allusion to hunting in general or the day's adventures in particular. Women's worth is equally couched in the language of work performance—particularly their skin work and their ability to organize a smoothly running household—both by other women and by men. Women's tasks do not appear to be thought more onerous than men's, just different. Neither is the work of one more estimable than that of the other.[4]

EQUALITY IN DOMESTIC RELATIONS

Regional variation in the composition of domestic units probably exercises some influence on how the relations between men and women are conducted across the Arctic. Western Eskimos favor extended family organization with matrilocal postmarital residence rules so that males reside in the community of their wives' families after marriage.

---

or repair them, though they sometimes hunt, make and repair their own tools, operate a dog team, and construct an igloo when necessary. Similarly, men *never* process animal skins—though they will sew, cook, and tend children if they have no available female to do this work.

4. If the question of equality of work is addressed in terms of access to and control of the means and products of production, the same situation obtains. Men make most of the work tools used by either sex as part of their allocated work. But tools, like tasks, are complementary; and each is "owned" as personal property and could be disposed of at the option of the owner.

This may limit husbands' ability to control their wives' affairs since they are more or less under the scrutiny and control of her relatives for much of the time. But this may mean nothing more than that a woman's comportment is more closely monitored by her father and brothers than by her husband. It is also true that in parts of this region men spend most of their time in the "men's house," or gazgi: they work, take their meals, and socialize there, returning to the company of their wives only for sex and for socializing with their families (Balikci 1970; Burch 1975).

In the Central Arctic, family organization is more nucleated and residence rules are not clear-cut. They range from an emphasis on virilocality—among the Netsilingmiut (Balikci 1970), Iglulingmiut (Boas 1901), and Tagagmiut (Graburn 1964)—to what I have elsewhere termed "practicolocal" residence (Guemple 1972:92). Here husbands spend more time in the domestic unit, there being no separate men's house. On balance, husbands have more say in the conduct of domestic life—in some groups, a great deal more. Even so, women's reputations rest primarily on their work skills and productivity, and since they work jointly and socialize largely with each other during most of the day while the men are afield hunting, their public standing rests to a large extent on their status among women. Likewise, men's status relies on the esteem of other men.

In Greenland—with the possible exception of the Smith Sound region—residence rules favor patrilocal residence, with the result that married women reside with their husband's kin and are more or less continuously under their supervision.[5]. In that area, the evidence suggests, males tend to have somewhat greater authority over women than elsewhere in the Arctic so that decision making is largely a process to be undertaken between males, without the involvement of females.

---

5. Information on the actual relational structures of Greenlandic Eskimo communities has never been available so that it is impossible to determine if these rules were ever followed. The one detailed demographic profile we have comes from Ammassalik in East Greenland (Holm 1916) and betrays an actual structure not different in detail from that found among Central Eskimo.

Everywhere in the Arctic men and women alike are socialized to be cooperative, pliable, polite, generous, and acquiescent (Briggs 1970). On balance, the relations between men and women are amicable — even decorous. After the age of six years boys and girls tend to play separately, and their relations become more distant and formal. After age eight boys gradually take up men's work and girls women's; and the two will have little time for each other until they are eligible to marry (always couched in terms of work readiness). Boys' socialization differs from that of girls in that, from about six years of age, they are allowed and in some cases encouraged to be more assertive, audacious, and demanding than girls and are somewhat more privileged than girls as family members. [6]

In interpersonal "politics" the general rule is that younger answer to older and females answer to males. Men exercise ultimate control over decision making in domestic matters, if measured in terms of who can issue something akin to "orders" to others or who is most prone to defer to the wishes of others. Such "dominance" is mediated by the entrenched customary division of labor, so that men seldom have reason to interfere with the women regarding their conduct of household routines as long as they perform their work satisfactorily. But women of any age remain "on call" and subject to periodic reprimand by men of the household and in some measure even by those who are not members of the domestic unit. This answerability is cushioned by age to a large degree so that old women do not answer to younger men or boys and only rarely to mature males. Indeed, most men defer to the opinions and wishes of a "grandmother" as they will to no one else.

In adulthood men are more vocal and willful than women and are more likely to resort to physical aggression to enforce their wishes, although such conduct is condemned by the community at large.

---

6. Differential male/female infanticide and adoption rates in the Arctic have often been cited as evidence of a preference for male over female offspring (e.g., Balikci 1970; Dunning 1962:163–67). I have argued elsewhere (Guemple 1980) that the exposure of infant females and the adoption of children depends to a large degree on the stage in the developmental cycle of the family into which the child is born or adopted. Early in the cycle boys are preferred; later in the cycle girls are frequently preferred.

Women may sometimes employ aggressive measures in defense of their honor or when pressed to perform tasks they believe are beyond their responsibility (Balikci 1970;177; Jenness 1922;162). Jenness's comments on the Copper Eskimos are diagnostic for most of the Central Arctic.

Sex is judged by all authorities to be the single most important source of friction, particularly in those Arctic locations where female infanticide rates are relatively high and where, consequently, eligible females are in short supply as consorts. Marriages are generally arranged by families.[7] Failure of the negotiating process might result in abduction; and in extreme circumstances men who covet the wives of others might sometimes resort to murdering the husband so as to appropriate his wife.

Under normal circumstances, however, no woman is forced to take a husband she does not want. Abduction is frequent but seldom as coercive as the term suggests: all Inuit women are expected to be coquettish and, therefore, might appear reluctant to marry.[8] Most authorities agree that "abductions" are matters of pretense, usually preceded by elaborate arrangements on the part of both families with at least the passive cooperation of the bride.

After marriage a woman exercises little personal control over the allocation of her sexual and procreative capacities, these being subject to the consent of her husband. He might share her sexuality with a friend or trading partner—even arrange a temporary or permanent exchange with another man—without consulting her. Such exchanges can result in permanent marital rearrangements; and a husband might choose to take a second or, rarely, even a third wife without seeking his wife's permission.

Women exercise no such personal authority. Women might request

7. Of those communities in which childhood betrothal is customary, only some adopted a mandatory rule that the betrothed must marry on reaching maturity. On the west coast of Hudson's Bay, for example, the betrothed must later marry; on the east coast, they need not.

8. This reluctance is sanctioned by the "Sedna" myth in which a woman is reluctant to marry (or, in other versions, to stay for long with any one "husband"). In desperation her father marries her to a dog by whom she bears a number of dog-children whose progeny found the Inuit race.

that their husbands share them with other men, or they might seek sexual liaisons with someone other than their husbands. In the former case a husband is not obligated to honor his wife's request; in the latter case a woman must arrange to meet her lover secretly—and expect punishment if found out.

Arctic divorce may be a better measure of equality than marriage. Both women and men can institute divorce simply by packing up and leaving, provided they have somewhere else to go. Divorce for a woman, particularly one with small children, is more problematic than for a man because she must first find another household willing to take her in. The usual choice is to seek temporary shelter with a close relative until such time as another suitable consort is found. Divorced men are usually welcomed anywhere if they are good providers; and in some cases a man may temporarily share another's wife until a suitable consort can be located. Furthermore, marriage relations are never completely abrogated or compromised, either by divorce (Heinrich 1972), spouse exchange (Guemple 1961), or polygamy (Burch 1975). A woman and her children retain a "claim" on her ex-husband and on his close relatives for life.

EQUALITY IN THE PUBLIC ARENA

Lantis's comments on Nunivak Island in Southwest Alaska state best the position of women in public life everywhere in Eskimo society:

> A woman did not openly and alone perform any function toward the community as a whole, that is, she had no role directly in relation to community affairs. Hers were relationships with individuals. Primarily she was identified with her husband, the identification becoming more complete as they grew older. She assisted him in the performance of ritual, in his duties toward such individuals as his serious partners and toward the community. . . . [A] woman might be influential in the community through her gossip, her industry and maintenance of high standards of workmanship or of generosity, or her domination over some important man; but all this was unofficial, indirect, and variable. (1946:246)

With the exception of public rituals in which women may assume authoritative roles (see below), mature women enjoy no public "offices." The leaders of Arctic communities have always been men, and the task of formulating collective opinion and organizing any kind of collective action has invariably been left to them.

Freuchen's (1935, 1961) jovial accounts of his relations with his Inuit wife, Ivalu, and particularly of her indirect way of offering advice on politically sensitive matters are probably representative of how women participate in policy making everywhere in the Arctic. Women tend to maintain a strict silence when men gather to discuss matters of concern to the community at large. When a discussion of this sort is afoot in her own household, a woman takes her place on the sleeping platform and proceeds to occupy herself with some routine task such as sewing. Should her husband say something very disagreeable, she may hazard a personal opinion—usually spoken in an innocuous tone of voice and addressed to the wall next to her. Mostly, however, she will bide her time.

When other males are not present, wives discuss issues of public concern openly with their husbands. In my experience, husbands take seriously the opinions of their wives, perhaps for the reason that they can best articulate the collective opinion of the women of the community, since a man will seldom have access to the candid opinion of any females other than those belonging to his own household.

Men ignore such expressions of opinion at some peril. Men of importance in an Eskimo community maintain a demeanor of dignity and pride—one easily shattered when struck by ridicule. In public gatherings, where numbers provide protection from immediate reprisal, women, especially older women, are likely to anonymously voice remarks to the assembled body concerning the stupidity of policy decisions; and they may sometimes hazard a comment on the self-importance of its formulators. These remarks are usually tinged with derogatory humor and would merit retaliation—even physical assault—if articulated by another man or a younger woman. Position in the age hierarchy protects old women from recrimination and retaliation so that they are in a position to insinuate the "women's vote" into what would otherwise be an all-male "caucus."

EQUALITY IN RITUAL LIFE

Shamans are important ritual practitioners in the North, curing illnesses through divination and prescription. Through ritualized séances they also mediate between the corporeal world and the spiritual realm of the principal Inuit deity who dwells under the sea and who controls the weather and the comings and goings of the principal sea mammals on which Inuit depend for their sustenance. These latter rites are public and involve the entire community, which assemble in a specially constructed house for the conduct of the rite. The diagnosis of community ills from the divinatory ritual often leads to therapeutic sessions involving confessions on the part of the community's membership and often lead to spouse exchanges, adoptions, and other social reorderings (Hall 1879).[9] The status of shaman carries as much authority and prestige as any customary role in Inuit society.[10]

Oosten (1986:115-31) quotes widely from the Arctic literature in an effort to show conclusively that men and women are equally eligible to become shamans, angakkut, in Inuit society. In spite of efforts by some authors (e.g., Thalbitzer 1928:419; Weyer 1932:421-22) to force a distinction between males as shamans and women as mere diviners, qilanit, the evidence seems clear that women share the role of spiritual intermediary equally with men everywhere in the Arctic. Saladin d'Anglure (1986) explains women's easy and equal access to this important spiritual role as traceable to the fact that the position of shaman is symbolically neutral in terms of gender.[11]

THE EQUALITY OF MEN AND WOMEN IN INUIT SOCIETY

This last point brings us conveniently back to the matter of "exporting" conceptions germane to the conduct of our own social relations to societies organized on principles very different from our own. Tradi-

---

9. An often cited description of this rite is contained in Rasmussen 1929:123–29.

10. A possible exception is the "whaling captain," or *umealiq*, a status that was restricted to the western Eskimo (Spencer 1959:177–82).

11. Saladin d'Anglure, a student of Lévi-Strauss, tends to see all relationships in structural terms. In his dialectal analysis, the shaman becomes a figure who mediates between male and female in a gender-neutral role.

tional Inuit could likely make little sense of the sort of inquiry I have conducted here for the reason that in *their* ontological formulation of humanity, maleness and femaleness are only transitory states of being occasioned by the entry of a relatively indestructible spiritual substance, a "soul," into a very ephemeral human body at the time of birth. In their view, humans are essentially ongoing "personalities" that cycle between the spiritual world and the corporeal world under the control of the Inuit principal deity, a female spirit called nuliayukj.[12] These personalities are identified by their names, and a newborn child receives this name together with the associated identity shortly after birth and retains it throughout its life.[13]

The significant point for this discussion is that Inuit names are gender-neutral. That is, identities formerly associated with now deceased (or living) men in previous incarnations might equally be conferred on males and females. The reverse is also true. Since the Native theory holds that the inheritor of a name assumes the identity of the spirit associated with it—*and becomes that person in adulthood*—there can be no fundamental difference in the statuses of individual Eskimos, because gender is not an *essential* attribute of being as such.

My judgment is that on the social level men and women in Inuit society enjoy relatively equal status, power, and prestige and that this equality is intimately connected with the independent social roles assigned to them through the division of labor and is also intimately linked to their gender-neutral cultural formulation of personness.

---

12. I use the eastern Hudson Bay Inuit term here. In Baffin Island, Boas (1888:583) noted that this female is called "Sedna," but no known Inuit group has since been reported as identifying her by this term. The source of this term thus remains a mystery. In Iglulik, she is called *takanaluk anraluk*, which Rasmussen (1931:63) translates "mother of the sea beasts." In Smith Sound, she is Nerivik, and in western Greenland, Arnarquagssaq (Kroeber 1899:317). The barren-ground Padlirmiut called her Avilayoq *(aviliayuq)* (Boas 1901:163). She is called by other terms elsewhere.

13. See Guemple (1965) for an analysis of eastern Hudson's Bay name inheritance. Elsewhere the usage is more complex (e.g., Stefànsson 1914: 363ff.) but not very different in principle.

3

MOTHER AS CLANSWOMAN
RANK AND GENDER IN TLINGIT SOCIETY

LAURA F. KLEIN

The Northwest Coast of North America is unique in both culture and environment. Ranging from southern Alaska to Oregon, the islands and mainland west of the Cascades and the Coast Mountains are among the richest in the world. Before the extensive exploitation by humans in this century, the temperate, evergreen rain forests of the region sheltered a wide variety of plants and animals. While the abundance of the land, especially the wood, was extensively utilized, the focus of the inhabitants of the region was largely toward the sea. The people of the coast are known in popular culture as the people of totem poles, war canoes, and salmon and in the anthropological literature as the creators of one of the most luxurious nonindustrial cultures.

The Tlingit, Haida, and Tsimshian, who live in Southeast Alaska and northern British Columbia, are the three major northern nations of the Northwest Coast. Before European contact the people of this area lived in beachfront villages in large matriclan-based wooden houses. A typical summer fishing season could provide enough salmon and other seafood to be preserved for year-round use. Additional foods from land and sea mammals and from plants allowed for a freedom from concern for subsistence needs. The forests also provided cedar and spruce that were used for housing, baskets, tools, and boats.

Within this economy bounty, the people created cultures in which wealth, obtained through extensive trade with other nations on the coast, was key to social status. This wealth was converted to social rank through the celebration of potlatches, great giveaway feasts hosted by kinship units. Wealthy, highly ranked individuals could distribute pieces of great art, furs, tools, and even slaves to announce their status. All individuals, other than slaves, were individually ranked and treated according to their social rank and kinship standing. Thus these coastal people created a highly unusual culture area of hierarchical societies, based on the exploitation of wild plants and animals.

European contact with the people of this coast did not come until 1741 when the ships of Vitus Bering explored the coast of Alaska for Russia. By the 1790s, when George Vancouver plied the waters, the fur trade had begun. News of abundant furs, particularly the sea otter pelts so popular in Asia, brought ships from Russia, France, England, and the United States. The Russian American Company and Hudson's Bay Company were the leading organizations in the region, with the independent Euro-Americans (Boston Men) providing competition. While the traders brought social disruption with diseases, new sources of wealth, and new weapons, the second wave of colonialism in the late nineteenth century brought most of the cultural changes so obvious today. Gold rushes, external political control, and permanent settlement by the Europeans and Euro-Americans began during this latter period. The earlier traders had little to do with the villages, and local-level sovereignty had been maintained.

In the 1880s, tourism, commercial fishing, external government, and missionization became factors of everyday life that could not be escaped. In the midst of this new pressure, the expertise of the Native people in trade and in the use of the local environment helped them cope and, in some cases, prosper. Northwest Coast art was valued in the tourist trade; Native skills in fishing and preservation were used in the fishing industry. Although the environment discouraged outside settlement and the area remains sparsely populated, the mechanization of the fishing industry and the growth of the forestry industry allowed the disastrous overutilization of resources, which endangered the economic core on which Northwest Coast cultures were built.

Native reaction to these new pressures came quickly. Modern political action groups in the region can be traced to the establishment in 1912 of the Alaska Native Brotherhood, and soon Sisterhood, which campaigned for improved living conditions and basic civil rights (see Worl 1990:153–58). The midcentury actions of the Alaska Native Federation led to the 1971 Alaska Native Claims Settlement Act, which created regional corporations to administer the substantial land and monies allotted by the act (see Olson 1991:66–72). Sealaska Corporation and several smaller village corporations represent the Tlingit and Haida in Alaska. The Haida's active defense of their forests on the Queen Charlotte Islands is heard worldwide.

The tradition of assertive competition as a skill of both women and men on the Northwest Coast continues. Outsiders, reflecting Euro-American cultural expectations, often notice that Native women in this area hold social and professional positions that they expect to be held by men. Tlingit women are found in the highest offices of the Alaska Native Claims Settlement Act corporations, government, social action groups, businesses, and cultural organizations. Native women can be found as traditional orators (Dauenhauer and Dauen-hauer 1990:14, 81) and as commercial artists. The cultural hierarchy of both traditional and Western cultures merge. Only a few people can hold prominent statuses in these systems, but in Native culture, both men and women are expected to be eligible for those roles.

THE QUESTION OF EQUALITY

Up to the late 1970s when I and other anthropologists went to the field to study the role of women in societies around the world, the general question was, why are women everywhere subordinate to men? During the last decade, however, this general wisdom that men are everywhere dominant over women has been radically modified in anthropology. Many anthropologists now argue that gender egalitarianism, or at least gender autonomy, can exist and has existed (see, e.g., Leacock [1978] 1981; Lee 1982:37–59; Sacks 1982:65–95; Sanday 1981:xv.) Even today, however, many of these scholars would insist that such a situation would be confined almost exclusively to small, nonranked band societies. This new wisdom is commonly traced back (Sacks

1982:20–21) to the late nineteenth-century ideas of Friedrich Engels (1972) that essentially assert that with the development of rank and/or class systems, along with the evolution of private property, gender becomes an organizational factor with women subordinated in a nuclear family context while men, or some men, are accorded power and authority along societal lines. Certainly the ideas that have developed from this base are, in the best tradition of anthropology, constantly being challenged from many directions. For example, doubts have been repeatedly thrown on the reality of true egalitarianism in bands (Lee 1982:37). From another perspective, a number of case examples that do not clearly fit a "nonclass" category (with notable ones existing in Native North America and in some of those societies presented in this volume) suggest that in fact there are such societies in which individual autonomy is not highly affected by the issue of gender or in which separate gender accomplishments are respected and/or empowered.

THE TLINGIT

The precontact Tlingit of today's southeastern Alaska are a key example of a ranked society in which the issue of gender is not the primary consideration in issues of power and authority. At the very least it is not a negative consideration in gaining power or authority for either men nor women. As I have written elsewhere (Klein 1975, 1980), traditional Tlingit society focused on kinship and wealth as criteria for individual rank, respect, and authority, and those factors would be equally valued and perceived in both sexes.

The culture of the Tlingit presented here represents that of the colonial period of the mid-nineteenth century, which was recorded in Euro-American sources by early explorers, traders, missionaries, and government officials and later by anthropologists through the memory culture of Tlingit elders. Contemporary Tlingit sources on this time period remain the elders who look back on it, in their wisdom, as one of freedom but not perfection. These sources all reflect the biases of their times and social positions and can only be used with discretion. The period examined is a century after the "discovery" of Alaska by the

31

Russians in 1741. This first century of contact was marked by an emphasis on the largely maritime fur trade with most Russians in the Tlingit area isolated in Sitka (Fort Archangel), the Russian capital and headquarters of the Russian American Company. It was only after the purchase of Alaska by the United States in 1867 that full-scale efforts to change the culture reached throughout the Tlingit communities.

It is clear that certain themes run throughout the varied literature with differences of emphasis, and one of these is the strength of the Tlingit women in their culture. To some, including many traders, this strength is a curiosity and an inconvenience; to others, such as the missionaries, it often was a sign of chaos and family stress; to still others, notably, many of the Tlingit informants, it was a thing of pride and superiority. Traders complained of deals done and undone by women's objections: "No bargain is made, no expedition set on foot, without first consulting the women" (Wood 1882:333). Missionaries, both Russian Orthodox (Kamenskii [1906] 1985) and Presbyterian (Condit 1926; Jones 1914), noted the strengths in often less than enthusiastic terms. Father Anatolii Kamenskii ([1906] 1985:50) notes, "A Tlingit man's wife is neither his slave nor simply a worker, as is common among savages. She is more in command in the house and family matters than her husband." The Presbyterian missionary Livingston Jones (1914:51) complained about Tlingit women in 1914, "Some consider it a mark of weakness to yield to the demands of their husbands, and for this reason they often oppose them. In fact, instead of being drudges of their husbands, they do no more than they feel disposed to do; and with some this is very little." Today many look back on the autonomy underlying these characterizations with an understanding that the Euro-American teachings countered a strength of their people.

The Tlingit, who are categorized in traditional anthropology as the northernmost of the so-called Northwest Coast Indians, are a highly stratified fishing society with a focus on the foods of the sea and the raw materials of the evergreen forests. Ecologically, as noted above, the Northwest Coast is about as far from the American stereotype of "Indian territory" as one can get. The Tlingit live on the narrow strip of land in southern Alaska between the high mountains of the Coast

Range and the Pacific Ocean. In this area villages were, and cities today are, built along narrow beach areas backed by the mountains and facing the sea. Large numbers of islands off the coasts offer shelter for residential sites and create a protected inland passage that permits long-distance travel and communication by water. The climate, as well as the topography, runs counter to the stereotype of Alaska. The warm, wet Japanese Current brings rain and moderate temperatures to the region, making the climate more like the climate of Seattle than that of Anchorage. The seemingly constant cool rains and rarer snows help nurture a dense, temperature evergreen forest of hemlocks, spruce, and cedar. Few level fertile regions exist which could support agriculture. The mountainous, forested land, then, directed the people of the region toward the sea, which provided food and communication.

The subsistence economy among the Tlingit followed the common pattern of the Northwest Coast. It was highly seasonal, with a clear, but not rigid, division of labor by sex. The major resource around which the economy revolved was the salmon, five species of which came in heavy runs during July, August, and September. During this period collecting and preparing the salmon was the major preoccupation of all adults. Families moved out from the winter village to temporary fishing camps along creeks where salmon returned to spawn. Other species of fish, most notably halibut, were added to the diet. In general, men caught the fish and women smoked and dried them for winter consumption. Consequently it was only through the joint, but separate, efforts of the men and women of a family that the abundant resources of the North Pacific enabled them to live free from concerns of subsistence for several months of the year. At slack times in late summer, women collected and preserved berries, as they did seaweed in the spring. These provided welcome variety in their midwinter diet. The oil that was a major ingredient in food preservation came from olachen fish in the south and seals in the north. Seals and land animals, notably deer, were hunted in the fall, and their meat was also smoked and dried.

In a normal summer and early fall a diligent family could collect and prepare enough food for the entire year, with enough surplus for trade and/or feasting. All this would only be true if the Tlingit were at certain places at definite times and were in groups of suitable size for the available supply. This dictated a food-collecting season from May through November and a craft- and ceremony-oriented season during the remainder of the year.

There was no agriculture of any importance in this area. Gathering wild plants was largely women's work, but plants formed a relatively minor part of the overall diet. However, while women were not of central importance in collecting activities, they were very important in the production of finished salmon.

While the subsistence pursuits were essential as a base for Tlingit wealth, the subsistence goods themselves did not constitute wealth. Owning more salmon than your neighbor in a normal year meant little. Rare items made by artists and craftsmen or obtained from long distances by trade were indicators of wealth. Crafts, arts, and other manufacturing tasks were gender linked. In the arts best known on the coast, wood carving was the realm of male artists and basket weaving and blanket making was the realm of female artists. Likewise, men were responsible for making and repairing fishing and hunting tools while women made most of their own tools and clothing.

The most important part of the economy in regard to the improvement of rank was trade. Long before European contact the Tlingit were active participants in intercultural trade routes that extended up and down the Pacific Coast and inland to those nations east of the Coast Mountains. It was through this trade system that everyday resources could be transformed into items of luxury. The furs and copper of the Subarctic peoples of present-day Yukon and British Columbia, for example, entered the coast trade as rare items of high value. Likewise, the slaves and characteristic craft items of the southern part of the coast arrived in the north as luxuries and symbols of wealth. Such possessions, subsequently, could be exhibited and dispersed in potlatches that affirmed or raised social status. It was never the possession of goods that affected rank and importance. It was the giving of this wealth in public feasts that conferred high status on individuals.

In the economic realm of trade the division of labor by sex was far more complex than it was in subsistence. While more men than women went on the long-distance trading journeys, some women did routinely go along and act as negotiators. As noted above, this role was unexpected by early European traders, missionaries (Jones 1914), and anthropologists (Krause 1956) alike, and many commented on it, often emphasizing a seeming "stubbornness." Jones (1914:51) reported that "no person is more stubborn than the average Thlinget women," while Krause (1956:136) noted that "frequently the women carry on the trading and they are even more inclined to be stubborn than the men." Many likewise were surprised that often women were given their husbands' money to handle for them (Anonymous 1924:257–58; Condit 1926:257; Jones 1914:50–51; Knapp and Childe 1896:61). Jones put it most bluntly: "The husband's earning are wholly turned over to his wife. She is, therefore, the banker of the household. If he desires to make a purchase he must appeal to her and get her consent" (1914:15). In a more poetic turn of phrase, James H. Condit (1926:257) complained that a particularly bothersome Tlingit woman "evidently believed that the hand that pulls the purse string rules the world as well as the hand that rocks the cradle." Modern informants contend that this tradition was a practical response to the fact that "men are foolish with money" and a good woman's role includes the protection of her family's wealth. One contemporary elder complained to me that her daughter-in-law had "allowed" her son to buy a luxury boat rather than a solid, plain fishing boat with his earnings from working on the Alaska oil pipeline. It was in a man's nature to go for something "flashy," but it was a woman's duty to limit him to a practical moneymaking vessel. Both Frederica de Laguna (1965:15) and Ronald L. Olson (1956:680) agreed that Tlingit men and women were expected to be of good character and able to increase their wealth. Olson contends that girls, more frequently than boys, were disciplined "to teach them that they must work, save, get wealth and goods" (1956:680).

In many aspects of the culture the role of gender identity was either a nonissue or a secondary one. Political leadership, as it was, was embedded in the realms of kinship and rank. In general the highest-ranking member of any unit of a matriclan was considered the head of that unit. While those specifically recognized as "chiefs" by European reporters were generally men, there were exceptions (Emmons 1907:345; de Laguna 1972:463; Kastengren 1920:422). De Laguna writes that "the [head of sib] title might be held by a woman, if she were the person of highest rank. Thus, the mother of one of our informants became 'head of the tribe' and so received custody of all the sib heirlooms. . . . The chief of the sib and his immediate family were the real aristocrats, called by some informants 'royalty.'" The title *anyeti* described by my informants as "upper-class person" was not gender linked, while the title *aankaawoo*, influential house leader or rich person, was generally, but not solely, used by men (Klein 1975:109–12). These titles and roles are largely determined by wealth and kinship. While the influence and limited authority held by these "important" people is clear, none seem to hold positions of major political power. The right to order others, outside of the use of clan lands and rights, was severely limited, but influence and respect were accorded by rank and personality. De Laguna (1972:465) notes of the sib or clan chief that "his word alone could command respect, not only because of the actual political power he wielded and because of his own high rank, but also because he was known to be well educated and therefore wise."

One position of recognized power was that of "Indian doctor" (*ikt*) or shaman. Through the use of personal spirit helpers, shamans could cure the sick and combat the evil brought by witches. They could become wealthy by their craft and wield considerable influence over individuals. Both men and women became shamans and witches: neither position was gender linked. Contemporary informants insist that there were no differences in the abilities of the male and female shamans and witches of the past. Tlingit myths record the tales of heroic women doctors (de Laguna 1960:140–41; Olson 1967:115; Swanton 1909:182–86), and ethnographies reflect these women as secular facts (Klein 1975:85; Olson 1967:112).

The role of Indian doctor went beyond its importance as a socio-religious position to become one of the few routes to circumventing, at least in part, the overwhelming monopoly of the kinship-wealth-rank system. The possibility for those who were born of low rank to increase their social standing and power well beyond their mothers' was possible in theory but was not likely to occur in fact. [1] The Indian doctor's skills were based on his or her special relationship with the supernatural beings and knowledge of the natural curing arts. The ability to obtain these skills appears to be largely unrelated to one's rank or kinship category. Furthermore, the benefits of successfully holding this position were similar to those granted people highly placed in the ranking system: power and wealth. Power, here, unlike the secular power of the highly ranked, was supernaturally based. The successful shaman was feared to some extent. The spirits connected to him or her were inherently powerful and could be harmful to others. The same power that could be used to heal patients could also do harm, if needed, to protect the shaman. After death, shamans' bodies were considered especially dangerous since the now uncontrolled spirits remained with them. [2] So while a shaman might have no authority within the kinship hierarchy, he or she would possess inherent power in interpersonal relationships. Wealth was also an advantage of a successful career. Shamans were paid for their cures, the amount of payment reflecting on the status of the patient. Prices were based more on status of the patient than on the nature of the disease. In other words, a family would publicly announce how much they valued the sick individual. Since the status of any family member reflected on the status of all, it was to the benefit of the family to give the doctor as much as they could afford. Doctors with good reputations for curing were called on by rich families and were paid accordingly. It was through doctoring, then, that a low-status individual could become wealthy and be treated in a manner usually restricted to higher-ranked individuals. Since kinship was so critical to ranking, however, the doctors did not normally have the ability to pass this prestige on to others.

---

1. In the United States the fact that any child, including the little girl born into a homeless family, can grow up to be president is a common cliché taught our children. In fact, it does not happen.

2. Today when some development projects in villages threaten the graves of Indian doctors, this combination of fear and respect quickly comes to the fore.

A widely known mythic story celebrates this method of advancement in heroic terms. Djiyin, as recorded by John R. Swanton (1909:182–86)[3] and Ronald L. Olson (1967:115), describes a poor orphan girl who is aided only by her caring but poor paternal aunt. She goes into the wilderness, where she is possessed by a series of bird spirits who make her a great shaman. She discovers vast stores of food and wealth while her home village starves. Members of the village finally find her and are invited to share in her wealth but with her aunt and two mistreated orphans being treated more grandly than the more highly ranked guests. She rebuilds her clan house and claims a high status. In her subsequent healing she introduces the concept of witchcraft to her people.

In the public structure of Tlingit society, or better, the aspects of Tlingit society that would be considered public in the Euro-American system, Tlingit women, just like Tlingit men, were central actors who prospered and worked according to their rank and accomplishments. The subsistence economy required a partnership of men and women for success. The rank system, furthermore, applied the same way to both men and women. As noted above, both were trained to increase their wealth while defending their character. In the luxury trade women played crucial roles as mediators and traders. Titles of high rank, such as anyeti, were used for women as often as for men. In fact, a strong tradition mandated that the correct marriage was between a man and woman of equal status. This emphasizes the recognition of individual non-gender-linked ranks. Tlingit women had the training and access to resources to raise their ranks beyond their rank at birth just as men had similar opportunities. The only other route to societal high status, as an Indian doctor, was open to both men and women. In this highly rank-conscious society, then, both men and women had access to all the ranks and were by the definition of the ranking system itself equal as categories.

---

3. Myths, like many stories and symbols, are owned by particular kinship groups and cannot be casually used by others. I have been instructed by Tlingit that the stories in Swanton (1909) can be used as if in the "public domain."

THE MATRILINEAL SYSTEM

Just as the public domain is not fully public, the private domain of kinship and family is not fully private. The central factor that ties all aspects of Tlingit society together is the matrilineal kinship system. Newborn Tlingit children automatically belong to all the kinship groups of their mothers and are classed as in-laws to all of their fathers' groups. This initial classification forms the basis of their life prospects; for many, parents' rank, which they inherit at birth, will remain theirs throughout their lives.

The structure of the system is based on moieties, clans, subclans, and houses. The largest group is a moiety, which largely directs marriage patterns. Moiety exogamy mandates that Eagles must marry Ravens and Ravens, Eagles.[4] The two moieties, Eagle and Raven, are also the only two units within Tlingit society that are considered unequivocally and permanently to be socially equal. Children today are often taught this with the phrase "The eagle flies higher, but the raven flies faster." The adults instructed me that Eagle people speak long and beautifully in a public meeting while Ravens come to the point. In other words, the Eagles and Ravens have different skills, but both are equally valuable.

Within each moiety there were several named matriclans that are associated with specific emblems and are differentially ranked. Unlike the moieties, the relative ranking of these units could change with the behavior of the individuals who belonged to them. These clans were not geographically defined or necessarily isolated in any region. Larger clans had houses in several villages (Krause 1956:77). Ceremonial rights and privileges and the resolution of disputes were largely centered in this level of the system.

Local clans and house groups, however, were the most important kinship units in terms of an individual's daily life in Tlingit society. The local clans consisted of clansmates who lived within one village and those who had left the community but traced their birth to this group. If the local clan had only one house in any town, then the clan

---

4. In some areas, Eagle is alternately called Wolf.

and house groups were the same. These local units gave individuals rights over ceremonial crests, activities, and items as well as residential rights and usufructuary rights over hunting, gathering, and fishing areas. These were the people with whom clansmen lived and clanswomen were identified.

The avunculocal residence pattern of the area mandated that young men moved to their mothers' brothers' houses at a young age to learn the skills and knowledge needed by men of their group. As they grew older they remained there and at marriage brought in their wives. Men then spent their early years in the house of the opposite moiety but lived their adult lives in their own clan house. Young women, in contrast, stayed in the house of their fathers, which was of the opposite moiety, until their marriage. Highly ranked women were isolated from the general household for an extended period of puberty seclusion that lasted from the onset of puberty until shortly before marriage. They then moved to the house of their husbands and continued to reside in a house of the opposite moiety. A woman, then, while she had rights in her clan house, would expect to never live there. This did not dilute her jural rights, or her loyalty to this house.[5] In this residence system the men of the clan who fished and hunted together would also be co-resident. The women would be scattered and live in a variety of other houses. In fact, a preferential cross-cousin marriage pattern modified the latter. Today, marriage with one's father's clan is occasionally referred to as a "royal marriage," and this seems to have been the traditional preference (Durlach 1928:65). De Laguna (1960:186) likewise states that a woman of one's father's local clan was a preferred mate. Olson (1967:22) writes, "There was a very strong feeling that all women of a household should be of the same clan." De Laguna (1960:192) agrees that this was clearly a preference among high-ranking families. The combination of residence pattern and preferential marriage pattern resulted in an interesting residence pattern for females. Although normally women never lived in their own clan

---

5. In times of war between houses or clans, the women who belong to one but are married to the other will "return" with their children to their matrilineal clan house.

house, some women never had to move from their childhood home since their potential spouses had moved into their parents' house at puberty. As George P. Murdock (1949:35) and Margaret Blackman (1982:30) noted among the Haida, to the south, two lines of relationships were built up: the first was the normal mother's brother-sister's son link of the avunculocal pattern; the second was a parent-daughter link. When this system was strictly followed, one house would contain men who belonged to one matriclan and women who belonged to another of the opposite moiety.

Almost every factor of an individual's life was at least in part determined by his or her position within the kinship and residence systems. Whom do you marry? Where do you live? With whom do you do your work? What heroes do you revere? To whom do you look for leadership? These are largely kinship questions. While the nuclear family, like in virtually all societies, is a crucial unit for enculturation and emotional support for an individual, the larger kinship and residence units are extremely strong influences.

It should be clear that the often-used dichotomy between public and private domain or familial and jural relations (Rosaldo 1974:23–35) does not apply to this society in any natural or fluid fashion. While it is true that those few issues that go beyond the kinship lines of the actors are treated as the most serious of all, it is also true that they are resolved by negotiations based on kinship membership and rules. This is the same if the two parties are in-laws residing in the same house or distant strangers. For example, a crime committed by one person against a member of a diferent clan called for a solution and agreement by high-ranking members of both clans. A satisfactory resolution can only be accomplished if both clans believe that their loss was fully compensated and that their effort to compensate the loss fit the original problem. As Kalvero Oberg (1934:146) has noted, "Theoretically, crime against an individual did not exist."[6] Thus problems go over kin

---

6. Rank is clearly involved in this as well. The death of a member of one group cannot immediately be compensated by the death of the person who caused it in the other group even if everyone agrees on the details of the case. If the rank of the two individuals involved was not essentially the same, one life will not be equated with the other. (see Oberg 1934).

lines and still must be solved by kinship groups. Structuring the differences between public and private matters or public and private property into analytical categories is not a sensible course within this context.

MOTHER AS CLANSWOMAN

In much of the literature on traditional culture and in the words of the contemporary elders, the role of mother in the past seems strikingly different from the role of mother in Euro-American culture today. Mother as nurturer is not the strong theme. Grandmother often appears in that role. Care of young children was often in the hands of grandmother, who received help from others in the family. De Laguna (1972:507), quoting informants, writes, "'The grandchild loved the grandmother more than their own mother and father, because their grandmother is always there' commented a second woman. 'We love our grandchildren better than our own children,' said a third." In other words, the day-to-day child care that has become defined as the primary responsibility of mother in Euro-American culture was not an all-encompassing role in traditional culture but one shared by many, especially grandmothers and grandfathers.

Against this background the structural importance of the role of mother becomes evident. She is not only a crucial member of a child's nuclear family; she is the most immediate senior member of this group whose past history and future accomplishments most directly affect the standing of the child. Her social standing is the starting point of her children's rankings. An unwise or improper marriage or union on her part leaves her children unsupported and despised. A proper marriage with her rank equal entitles them to the respect of that rank. She is also the first clan teacher for her children. Given the avunculocal residence pattern, Tlingit children, until they leave their childhood residence, may have their mother and her other children as the only clansmates they see and know in an on-going, daily fashion. As we have seen, in high-ranking houses where preferential marriage patterns are strictly followed, there will be female relatives of their mothers as well. Even here, however, it will be the adult women of their clan who nurture and teach the children the correct clan lessons. As a boy comes of age and a girl marries, they move into houses where neither their father nor mother reside. The boy is in his clan house, and his mother's brothers teach him his future role. The girl is in her husband's house and must continue her childhood role of nonclansmate in another clan's house. [7] She continues, of course, to be a member with full rights and responsibilities, if not a resident, of her own clan house.

A successful mother could affect the ranking of her children after their births in two ways. First, she can train them to be successful in the skills and manners that she has mastered. During a young woman's puberty seclusion, she is expected to learn the most important skills of being a successful adult woman. While a girl's father's sister was important in this training, her mother and grandmother were important figures as well. Reports indicate that training in the manipulation of wealth as well as correct demeanor and moral living were important lessons. Today Tlingit elders often look back on these earlier customs, ultimately destroyed by mission teachings, fondly. One high-ranked elder spoke of seclusion as "like finishing school or college." Even after the children are adults, close relationships between mothers and children are expected to continue. Jane Fishburne Collier, writing of patrilocal societies in which women have no access to prestige and authority, described a common road to success for women in such societies—through the sons.

> The most available male for the role of political front man is a woman's son. Although she must wait years for him to mature, her patient labor in his behalf will pay off in the end: she can use the period of his immaturity to bind him to her by teaching him that he owes life, security, and position to her efforts. (1974:92)

Among the Tlingit, a matrilineal society in which women do have access to power, a similar relationship can be, and is, read in another light. While a successful son would reflect well on the standing of his mother, the successful mother reflects more on her son. She does not

7. Under preferential marriage patterns this may well be her father's house as well, and she will not, in fact, leave her parents.

teach him that "he owes life, security, and position to her efforts"; he recognizes this because it is true. As a son matures, his mother, now an elder or approaching this status, should have already settled into a permanent standing based on her original kinship ranking and her accomplishments as a woman.

Second, successful mothers who are able to increase their wealth and able to sponsor potlatches or aid with potlatches held by kin groups could effectively raise the status of all individuals within that group. In other words, a highly successful woman could raise her own status and those of all clanmates, including her children. Since the gathering of wealth was so clearly an important woman's role, women were often important organizers of a potlatch even if a man might sponsor the event.[8] The good mother or good sister or even good wife, then, was a strong, successful individual who could honor herself and her kin.

Since social rank was the most important identifier of an individual in terms of the richness of his or her life, the mother's role in establishing a child's rank is of foremost importance. While rank was not the same as kinship here, since individual accomplishments were important, it was deeply integrated into the kinship system. Karen Sacks (1982:110) writes that "in nonclass societies, people relate to each other as relatives, as opposed to members of a class or subclass or occupation, as in class societies." Here, in a nonclass but highly stratified society, people relate to others as both relatives and ranked individuals simultaneously. None were ever truly isolated from their kinship or social status responsibilities and honors.

In closing, Jane Fishburne Collier and Sylvia Junko Yanagisako (1987b:7) and others contend that "gender and kinship are mutually constructed." Among the Tlingit, gender, kinship, and rank seem to be mutually constructed. In the Tlingit world, certainly, none could be intelligently discussed or understood without the others. Here, too, despite a ranked social setting, the dichotomy between private and public proves false. Not only is the integration of gender, kinship, and

---

8. The role of women in potlatches has long been discussed, and there may be a regional variation in this. See Kan 1989:236 and Dauenhauer and Dauenhauer 1990:23–73 for recent discussions.

rank clear but the integration of these concepts with all aspects of the Tlingit political and economic systems are also striking. The one outstanding aspect of Tlingit culture—its focus on social rank—must also be seen as a part of the complex whole. The ranking system cannot differentially evaluate the social realities of men and women because no other part of the society does; it is necessarily part of the whole culture.

Rank or class, then, does not necessarily or directly relate to intensive gender differentiation. In societies in which an individual's gender is a differentiating factor on the issues, or ideals, on which rank is based, researchers should expect to find extreme and exaggerated gender differences. In a society like the Tlingit's, however, where the rules for rank are embedded in a system of gender integration and kinship, no new or extreme concept of gender inequality should be expected.

ACKNOWLEDGMENTS

The fieldwork and archival research for this chapter was generously supported by grants from the Ford Foundation, the Jacobs Fund (Whatcom Museum, Bellingham, Washington), the Woodrow Wilson Foundation, and the Regents at Pacific Lutheran University.

I would also like to thank the authors in this volume for their constructive critiques of my work and their help and direction in completing this volume. Lillian A. Ackerman, my co-editor, was supportive and diligent every step of the way. Additionally, I would like to acknowledge the rock-solid support of my parents and colleagues, most notably, Ruth and Stanley Freed.

I shall always read this volume with the memories of special women and friends who did not live to see it: the anthropologist Happy Leacock and the honored Tlingit elders "Tootsie" Fawcett, Katherine Mills, and Elsie Pratt who encouraged and directed me in learning about Tlingit women.

4

THE SUBARCTIC

ASYMMETRIC EQUALS
WOMEN AND MEN AMONG THE CHIPEWYAN

HENRY S. SHARP

The Chipewyan are found from the west coast of the Hudson Bay in Canada inland to the west of Lake Athabasca. Southern groups live as far south as the Churchill River in Saskatchewan; northern Chipewyan still range hundreds of miles into the tundra in the Northwest Territories. The Subarctic as a whole is geographically diverse and includes mountain ranges and foothills, but it is generally a land of low relief. Much of it is characterized by permafrost that restricts drainage of the sparse rainfall. Few places in the Subarctic escaped glaciation. Those soils that exist are poor and acidic and support only a thin and unnutritious cover of slow-growing vegetation.

The Subarctic climate is harsh. Temperatures reach above 80°F in summer and below −50°F in winter but sometimes hit 100°F and −70°F. The wealth of the Subarctic comes from the long hours of summer daylight when immense numbers of birds come to exploit the growing season's explosion of plant and insect life. Fish generally abound but are often difficult to catch as they move through the omnipresent waterways to exploit food sources or sink into deep water to escape the winter cold. Large animals tend to be migratory or to employ special techniques such as hibernation or burrowing to escape the winter cold.

Human population densities were sparse: the Chipewyan averaged about one person per one hundred square miles. By dispersing themselves into highly mobile small hunting groups, linked by affinal and bilateral kin ties into a food production and distribution network, the Chipewyan made a life that was often secure and comfortable. Above all else, they were hunters of all species of large game, but the focus of their life was the barren-ground caribou, a species that is ever in motion and whose yearly migratory cycle exceeds 1,500 miles.

ASYMMETRIC EQUALS

This chapter examines the relationship between gender and power among the Chipewyan Indians of the sparsely populated boreal forest and tundra of the central Canadian North. The Chipewyan, who call themselves Dene, are the easternmost of the great congeries of Northern Athapaskan-speaking peoples ranging in unbroken continuity from Hudson Bay to the interior of Alaska. The cultures and languages of the Dene groups that occupy this vast domain of forest, mountain, and tundra are closely related, and both the languages and their speakers are referred to as Northern Athapaskan (J. G. E. Smith 1970, 1975). The sheer scale, remoteness, and lack of development of these lands are virtually incomprehensible to people accustomed to urban life and contemporary transportation networks. The Chipewyan homeland is far north of the parts of Canada that have experienced agricultural exploitation or intensive non-Native settlement (Gillespie 1975, 1976). The Chipewyan people effectively have the free use of their traditional lands and have been able to retain a degree of autonomy in the conduct of their collective affairs and daily lives essentially unknown by Native Americans living within the continental United States.

This chapter is predicated on the proposition that the most productive approach to understanding gender, power, and the relationship between them is to focus on the complementarity of gender relations. Human culture is *human,* a product of the interaction of both/all genders. Chipewyan women are as fully involved with and as responsible for the process of generating Chipewyan culture and for the nature and content of Chipewyan culture as are Chipewyan men. My commitment to this (somewhat out of fashion) theoretical stance is equally the result of my ethnographic experience and my discontent with approaches focusing on dominance (Sharp 1981:425–27), oppression (Sharp 1982:221–22), or the contemporary buzzword, hegemony (I regard the three as interchangeable synonyms). The basis of my theoretical discontent is twofold. First, these concepts are too contingent on culturally specific—and selective—definitions of power, the meaning of categorical difference, and the meaning of hierarchy. Simply put, the concepts are too closely bound to the utopian discourse involved in the contemporary negotiation of Western political values and gender roles. In a more general sense, to utilize oppression—or dominance, a term that draws its power from its use in ethology—to explain relations between genders is to presume that a terror model rather than a consensual model (Swartz, Turner, and Tuden 1966) lies at the base of human cultural behavior. A dominance model is unsatisfactory even to explain animal social behavior not based on reciprocity. I have argued against it in interpreting wolf social organization (1982) and am not prepared to accept it as a theoretical model for the operation of human culture.

The second source of my discontent also lies in the nature of the models of social organization implied by the two approaches. To focus on dominance as the relevant factor in understanding gender relations is to assent to a minimalist model of society; a model that can be represented by the statement $A > B$. Such an approach is not without utility as a means of focusing on a limited aspect of a society, but it is nondynamic. It may provide a static picture of an aspect of power within a society, but it is not capable of dealing with power as a process and is an insufficient base from which to analyze the construction, operation, or negotiation of gender relations within a society. The model of society implied by a complementarity model is quite different and may be represented by the statement $A + B + \ldots N = 1$. This approach, aside from being better suited to handle nonbinary gender situations, is inherently dynamic. It is capable of examining gender and power both as structure and as process. It is a model far better suited to the analysis of gender as an active creation of human beings engaged in the process of living together.

Because of its complexity and because of the context of negotiation of gender and power current in our own culture, gender is a topic inherently politicized in anthropology. Its analysis and the selection of the relevant variables for analysis are unequivocally constructed for the elucidation of issues internal to our culture rather than for elucidation of issues internal to other cultures. The contrast between English-speaking values, categories, and behavior and Chipewyan categories, values, and behavior is so great that the perceptual framework provided by the social context of our culture has prevented examination of the balance and complementarity of gender roles within Chipewyan society—a problem particularly pronounced in regard to the allocation of power.

These issues are particularly appropriate in considering the Chipewyan precisely because Chipewyan culture has such an established reputation for male dominance and the abuse of women. The Chipewyan are not significant in the English-speaking North Americans' debate of gender issues, but they do play a role as exemplars of the negative side of aboriginal Native American life (e.g., George 1991; Giago 1991; Mahon 1991; Martin 1991; Valentine 1991). Within the anthropological literature they have been cited specifically for the mistreatment of women (e.g., Oswalt 1967), and, along with Northern Athapaskans in general, their cultures are often perceived in largely negative terms as marginal, weak, and vanishing. This tendency has been noted and commented on by specialists (e.g., Brody 1981:49–55; Koolage 1975; Krech 1980; Slobodin 1975b, 1975c).

This perception of Chipewyan culture, both inside and outside of anthropology, as weak and male dominated provides an interesting case for the utilization of a theoretical emphasis on complementarity. Three different types of data will be examined to do this: (1) excerpts from Samuel Hearne's famous journal, *A Journey from Hudson's Bay to the Northern Ocean*; (2) my own ethnographic observation of social relationships among contemporary Chipewyan; and (3) the representation of gender as it appears through certain Chipewyan categories.

THE CHIPEWYAN

In absolute terms, the land of the Chipewyan is harsh, as cold and insect infested as it is vast. Western conceptualizations of this area have focused on that harshness since the time of the earliest contact with the land and its people. That harshness consistently has been interpreted to mean that the hold of humanity in the area is tenuous, that the circumstances of human life here are beastly, and that the people themselves are only scarcely less beastly than their environment. In these environs of uncertainty, it is thought that the aged and infirm were routinely abandoned and that starvation was an annual scourge. It is rarely noted that these Northern Athapaskan cultures have been among the most successful of all Native North American peoples in holding onto their lands, their languages, and their way of life.

The Chipewyan are sandwiched between the Cree of the boreal forest and the Inuit of the Arctic. Both of those peoples are better known than the Chipewyan, and it is they rather than the Chipewyan that normally serve as ethnographic examples for this part of North America. The archaeology of this vast region is often problematic. That of the central Canadian Subarctic is poorly known, but it appears that a tradition of material culture, in particular a tradition of stonework, developed in unbroken sequence from 1,500 to 2,000 years ago until the abandonment of stone tool making by the historic Chipewyan. Traditionally, the people of these lands were hunters of large game and practiced no agriculture. The difficulty of gaining access to their homeland and of securing safe and predictable transportation within it combined with its lack of suitability for agriculture prevented extensive white settlement. The only large-scale incursions of whites into their homelands have been — and still are — localized and sporadic results of the exploitation of mineral resources or the administrative demands of church, mercantile, or governmental bureaucracy (Irimoto 1981; Jarvenpa 1976, 1977).

Contemporary Chipewyan are limited participants in the market economy of modern-day Canada. They are far removed from the urban centers of industrial power, and many communities are not accessible by road, including the community of "Mission" on which this chapter is based. Transportation costs are high and the influx of consumer items is limited although there has been a marked increase in commodity consumption in the last ten years. The influence of commercial communications, particularly television, became markedly stronger after 1975, and the first threatening indicators of a decline in the role of the Chipewyan language have been visible for a decade.

Subsistence is based on a combination of monetary income from wage labor, small-scale entrepreneurship, and governmental subsidy augmenting subsistence harvesting of the diminished but still substantial animal, fish, and bird resources of forest, lake, and tundra. Aboriginal Chipewyan culture made only limited use of plant resources. Estimates vary, with the actual figures probably unknowable, but the commonly accepted estimate is that 90 percent or more of the diet came from animals. Of all the food sources, the primary one in the thought and diet of the Chipewyan was the barren-ground caribou. This intensive utilization of animal tissue is expressed directly in the sexual division of labor (Sharp 1981, 1988a). Chipewyan culture splits the division of labor between male and female so that males provide raw animal tissue from the direct exploitation of animal resources through hunting while women convert raw animal tissue into food (Sharp 1988b).

The Chipewyan were caribou hunters. This was a tradition of individual and collective self-definition as a people with a culture distinct from that of other Native peoples. The division of roles in the production of food was also a major aspect of the generation of self-identity in the construction of gender role and the placement of the individual within Chipewyan society (MacNeish 1956). This tradition of construction of self and collective identity—and of gender role—continues in contemporary life and religion in spite of changes in their actual diet and economic activities. The far northern reaches of North America have experienced the growth of North American industrial society in a manner very different from areas farther south, and the peoples, their lives, and their cultures, reflect that difference of experience.

HEARNE'S CHIPEWYAN

Samuel Hearne was the first Western observer to live among the Chipewyan for any length of time. His account ([1791] 1971) of his search between 1769 and 1772 for the fabulous copper mines of the

Canadian barren grounds was published late in the eighteenth century and became a widely known and influential classic of the contact literature. It has been reprinted many times and is still widely read today. It is far from the only written source on early Chipewyan life, but its almost iconic role helped set the pattern of characterization of the Chipewyan still prevalent in our culture. It is because of its influence in our culture that I shall use it to demonstrate the conundrum posed by the Chipewyan.

Hearne's account is not directly concerned either with women or with their place in Chipewyan culture. Their voices are essentially absent from his writings and their concerns only incidentally voiced. His primary representation is of the harshness of Chipewyan life. What he has reported about women has been generally received as a picture of male domination within the context of a continuous and dramatic struggle against the incredible harshness of the physical environment. In fact, Hearne seems to provide a prima facie case against gender equality. Speaking of his aborted first attempt to locate the copper mines, he reports the opinion of Matonabbee, his chief guide and informant, that

> not taking any women with us on this journey, was the principal thing that occasioned all our wants; for, said he, when all the men are heavy laden, they can neither hunt nor travel to any considerable distance; and in case they meet with success in hunting, who is to carry the produce of their labour? Women, added he, were made for labour; one of them can carry, or haul, as much as two men can do. They also pitch our tents, make and mend our clothing, keep us warm at night; and, in fact, there is no such thing as travelling any considerable distance, or for any length of time, in this country, without their assistance. Women, said he again, though they do every thing, are maintained at a trifling expense; for as they always stand cook, the very licking of their fingers in scarce times, is sufficient for their subsistence. (Hearne 1971:55)

Hearne himself says, "We could not do without their assistance, both for hauling our baggage, as well as dressing skins for clothing, pitching our tent, getting firing, &c." (12).

The image Hearne presents is of Chipewyan women as beasts of burden, a view not at odds with Chipewyan perspectives on their history. Viewed from a perspective that focuses on domination as the means of interaction between genders, his image is powerful. But the very material that brings forth that image equally demonstrates both men's need for women's labor and their dependence on it. That dependence among the contemporary and no longer polygnous Chipewyan can place the control of a man's reputation on the willingness of his wife to engage in the skilled labor defined as female (Sharp 1988a: 66–67). Hearne did not see—or indicate that Chipewyan men saw—the need for women's labor as leading to the empowerment of women—economically, politically, or otherwise. This interpretation has, in large, been followed by an English-speaking world more interested in domination than complementarity.

> The men are in general very jealous of their wives, and I make no doubt but the same spirit reigns among the women; but they are kept so much in awe of their husbands, that the liberty of thinking is the greatest privilege they enjoy. The presence of a Northern Indian man strikes a peculiar awe into his wives, as he always assumes the same authority over them that the master of a family in Europe usually does over his domestic servants. (Hearne [1791] 1971:76)

This view of marriage as based on exploitation and "awe," with its implied dynamics of jealousy and infidelity, is antithetical to a view of marriage as an alliance between groups of equal social or economic status. When I first began fieldwork in the late 1960s, there was still in practice a conventional pattern of public respect—perhaps even deference—by a wife toward her husband. This public and conventional pattern was often at dramatic odds with the relations between husband and wife outside a public arena and was part of a series of conventions about the public expression of relations between men and women. The relationship between politeness and power is a tenuous one. If public deference, or the appearance of it, is an expression of power between the genders, it is a most uncertain and imperfect measure of power relations. Polite behavior can be most misleading precisely because of its conspicuousness.

Their marriages are not attended with any ceremony; all matches are made by the parents, or next of kin. On those occasions the women seem to have no choice, but implicitly obey the will of their parents, who always endeavor to marry their daughters to those that seem most likely to be capable of maintaining them, let their age, person, or disposition be ever so despicable. (Hearne 1971:310)

The reason for Hearne's interpretation of women as dependents, if not outright chattel, is clarified by his understanding of Chipewyan betrothal practices: "The girls are always betrothed when children, but never to those of equal age, which is doubtless sound policy with people in their situation, where the existence of a family depends entirely on the abilities and industry of a single man" (310–11). Chipewyan marriage is an alliance between independent residential congeries of bilateral kin (Sharp 1977b, 1979). The search for alliance, which includes a specific concern for the material well-being of the future bride, is an exercise in domination only in contrast to Western culture's elevation of the ideology of individual freedom and choice to the level of sanctity.

Chipewyan marriages, particularly before the missionizing period, were alliances whose continuation reflected the concerns of all who were party to the alliance.

Divorces are pretty common among the northern Indians; sometimes for incontinency, but more frequently for want of what they deem necessary accomplishments, or for bad behaviour. This ceremony, in either case, consists of neither more nor less than a good drubbing, and turning the woman out of doors; telling her to go to her paramour, or relations, according to the nature of her crime. (Hearne [1791] 1971:312)

The assumption of male dominance and male control interprets as male prerogative what can equally be seen as the continuing process of negotiation between the spouses and the social groups allied by the marriage.

The conundrum that the Chipewyan pose lies in the bleakness of Hearne's representation of them—a bleakness that darkens to include as routine behavior the outright purchase of wives, wife capture, rape, beatings, murder, starvation, and abandonment. The point here is neither to castigate Hearne nor to accept his work blindly but to recognize, even though it is possible to provide alternate interpretations far more compatible with twentieth-century understandings of how societies work and how gender is constructed, that it is possible the image he presents of Chipewyan life might be accurate. That would make Chipewyan and Northern Athapaskan life and culture a real fly in the ointment of existing understandings of how small-scale societies operate as well as being a major reason that anthropology has so often chosen to treat them as an exception easier to ignore than explain.

Hearne's journal is an invaluable work by a remarkably skilled observer who published late in his life on the experiences of his youth. He provides a window into the past of Chipewyan culture that cannot be ignored. The interpretive patterns in Hearne's journal have become iconic both as data and as interpretive pattern. The most obvious way to approach the iconic status of Hearne's work is through simple discounting, through a demonstration that his biases have led him into significant misunderstandings of his experiences, but textual reinterpretation is not without its own risks. Demonstrating that Hearne misinterpreted what he saw is not the problem. The problem is the interpretation of the discounting. If we can show that his representation of the eighteenth-century Chipewyan is suspect, then the implication is that the "true picture" of gender relations among the eighteenth-century Chipewyan—what Hearne did not write about—must be closer to understandings of gender held by the contemporary society clever enough to produce the discounting. This is an implication of questionable methodological validity.

It is obvious that there are differences between the values and style of an eighteenth-century Englishman and the values and style of contemporary readers. Reinterpreting the text to correct for those differences of style and values is a task of merit in and of itself but not really of relevance here, save that it would provide sufficient reason to question Hearne's interpretation of what he saw. It would not provide sufficient reason either to deny Hearne's ability to report what he saw or to discard his reporting of what male Chipewyan told him about women and the nature of social relationships. We have the means to correct for Hearne's interpretive bias and to reinterpret his text, but we are without the means to judge the truth and value of what he did not report.

There are other factors that may be more reliable than reinterpretation of the effects of Hearne's cultural baggage and biases. One example is the special circumstances under which Hearne observed the Chipewyan. During his time among them, extensive and intensive as it was, his experience was largely restricted to the company of trading parties. The ordinary conduct of Chipewyan life, the routine pursuit of a subsistence lifestyle, was largely removed from his view. Most of the travail and hardship of life in the Subarctic results from the attempt to impose a human order on the rhythms and patterns of the animate and inanimate response of the environment to climate. The imposition of order on nature is a hallmark value of all Western civilization and excessively pronounced within the economic sphere. I think that almost all of the non-disease-generated hardship reported in early accounts of the Chipewyan is the direct result of the particular demands that trade with Western man places on movement. The imposition of patterns of movement responding to the demands and logic of eighteenth-century English economic thought, practice, and shipping schedules, rather than to the responses of the animal, fish, and bird populations to the seasonal and climatic cycles of the Subarctic, was a sure way to intensify the uncertainty of life in the North. If the Natives were going to trade with the Europeans, they had to move at times and by routes that bore no relation to the demands of subsistence and were out of synchronization with the timing and movements of the seasonal round of subsistence activities (Helm 1993; Sharp 1977a).

The Chipewyan most likely to suffer the consequences of not following the annual round of subsistence activities and the most likely to be removed from the constraints and protections of ordinary social life were the trading and raiding parties engaged in commerce with the Hudson's Bay Company. The lack of emphasis on subsistence and the storage of food, particularly dried caribou meat, is reinforced by Hearne's own judgment of the lesser "happiness" of the lives of the traders compared to those that did not abandon a subsistence lifestyle (Sharp 1988a:1–5, on Hearne 1971:82–83). Presumably, the women Hearne was most familiar with, those women in or subject to the company of bands of traders roaming over thousands of miles, would be the women most removed from the normal protections of ordinary social life and the ones most vulnerable to abuse, domination, and low valuation.

If this line of argument resolves some of the difficulties of Hearne's account by implying that its image of women was drawn from lives that were atypical, it does not do so so completely as to eliminate the issue of gender inequality. Even if the women Hearne observed were atypical, they were Chipewyan and the trading parties were an aspect of Chipewyan culture.

Hearne's sociological insight is another issue that can be challenged, as a few examples will illustrate. He summarizes his experience of polygyny, child betrothal, and the influence of successful hunters by stating, "The existence of a family depends entirely on the abilities and industry of a single man" (310–11). It is as if each man were locked in a struggle of rampant individualism in which all other Chipewyan would allow his dependents to starve if he failed to provide food for them, or as if all Chipewyan live as single families divorced from all contact with other Chipewyan. The marriage as alliance issue is relevant here. Hearne takes "family" to mean an isolated unit formed around a conjugal pair, a Western idea of family that is of limited utility. Conjugal pairs—or polygynous sets—do not exist in social isolation. Indeed, the whole strategy of Chipewyan social organization is to link "families" into alliances of reciprocity that counteract the uncertainty of subsistence activities through the sharing of the (almost necessary) imbalances in that production (Sharp 1977b, 1988a).

In the subsistence economy characteristic of northern hunters, obtaining raw materials is rarely the choke point in the production process (Sharp 1988a, 1988b). Chipewyan groups, specialized in predation on migratory resources, operate on the basis of periodic kills of large quantities of game rather than on the sustained yield pattern (ibid.) more commonly known to anthropologists from hunter-gatherer cultures in Africa and the tropics. A single hunter can often provide in a day or two enough raw meat to keep several women busy working for several weeks processing it into storable dried form. The same holds true with other raw products (fish yields, hides, etc.) that require intensive skilled labor to convert into usable form (decorative work, hide preparation, clothing, tents, bedding, etc.). As Westerners (using my students as a database), we find the actual activity of locating and killing wild game under hostile climatic conditions the origin point in a causal chain and the aspect of that subsistence chain that is most likely to fail. Reading the Chipewyan production process in terms of our own values translates into a perception that status and power among the Chipewyan derive from the primary production of the resource. The intensive labor involved in processing that raw resource—the labor that buffers the sporadic nature and inevitable failures of primary production—is seen as secondary and not as a source of power.

Without the labor of the women to process the raw material into usable form, the production efforts of the men accomplish little. I have already mentioned that contemporary women are able to influence and manipulate substantive aspects of their husbands' reputations by manipulating the rate and skill with which they process raw resources. Indeed, in a polygynous society with an unbalanced sex ratio (J. G. E. Smith pers. comm.), where the production of the finished necessities of life is female labor intensive, it is access to female labor that may be the most crucial means of differentiation between men. The finished product is what leads to status, influence, and reputation. Rotting flesh, poorly dried meat, or raw hides gain a man little. His ability to produce means little if the women attached to him are unwilling or unable to process what he produces. Hearne was undoubtedly correct in his observation of polygyny; he was undoubtedly correct that a single hunter could provide for numerous women; he was undoubtedly correct that those women were dependent on the efforts of that hunter. There may be no way, now, to determine eighteenth-century Chipewyan values, but it is undoubtedly just as correct that that "single man" was as dependent on the women attached to him as they were on him.

One of the more dramatic events in Hearne's journal was the encounter between his party and a young woman living alone deep in the forest (Hearne 1971: 262–67). This "Dog-ribbed" (modern Dog-rib) woman had been taken captive, along with "three other young women," by the "Athapuscow Indians" (Cree). Her infant had been murdered by the Cree, and she determined to escape from them in spite of otherwise favorable treatment. She had become lost in her attempt to return home and had spent seven months living alone in the forest. After encountering her, "the poor girl was actually won and lost at wrestling by near half a score different men that same evening." Hearne's account is silent as to her role in this, presuming that she was unwilling to come along and that she played no role in the decision as to whom she would go with. His account reflects rather badly on the autonomy of women—especially when Hearne's chief contact among the Chipewyan beat a wife, who objected to his participating in the wrestling, so badly that she died—but it also documents a crucial factor in any interpretation of the behavior of Northern Athapaskan women: they had the skills necessary to support themselves—by themselves—for extended periods.

It is difficult to see abuses such as this, even though the woman belonged to a foreign tribe that was often the subject of raids and warfare, and not be swayed by dominance arguments. It is also a very curious basis for the construction of a society when the logic of male dominance is the need for one man's protection from other men.

The issue of wife wrestling, one of the more notorious practices used to illustrate the male-dominated nature of Chipewyan culture, provides a final illustration of the interpretive conundrum the Chipewyan present. Women were prizes (Slobodin 1975a) and not only in wrestling contests. A Chipewyan male was apparently entitled to challenge any other married Chipewyan male to a wrestling match for possession of the challenged man's wife. The wrestling was of a special kind in which the two opponents faced each other, grasped each other's hair or ears, then pulled until one of them fell to the ground. If the married man struck the ground first, the marriage bond was sundered and his wife was transferred to the victor. The victor was not obliged to retain the woman, but, if released by the victor, she was not free to return to her husband. Hearne cites examples of these matches in which the sole purpose of the challenger is to obtain temporary labor to unload a boat. When accomplished, the woman is sent packing, unable to return to her husband (Hearne 1971:104–7).

Wife wrestling seems to provide the clearest evidence possible for the oppression of women in Chipewyan society. But as is so often the case when ethnographic material is separated from its context, the loss of that context may induce a false image. Hearne gives no indication of what—if any—customary limits were placed on the practice, but it is hard to imagine Chipewyan society surviving without some constraints on it. Politically important men like Matonabbee, "who at that time had no less than seven wives, all women grown, besides a young girl of eleven or twelve years old" (Hearne 1971: 265), had to have had some protection other than their physical strength to obtain and retain their wives. The relative age between potential contestants must have been a factor, otherwise no man would ever be able to retain a wife as he aged. That some conventions existed is indicated by Hearne's description of husbands shaving and greasing their heads to ensure their victory—and retention of their wife—against a challenger.

It is implausible that, if wife wrestling was so effective a means of terminating a marriage, the Chipewyan women of the time were incapable of arranging a challenge to their husbands. It is easy to imagine how wife wrestling could serve as a means through which women were able to escape an undesired spouse or, by the threat of a challenge, exercise control over a husband (Sharp 1979:40). What is lacking from our information is any indication of how, when, and by whom these matches were instigated, so that, by default, the assumption is that women played no role in their instigation. The exclusion of the relevant social context—women's voices—creates an illusion of a cultural context within which women have no voice.

If even this cursory discounting of Hearne's account gives reason to question the bleakness of the place women occupied in eighteenth-century Chipewyan society and inclines us toward a view more in line with our contemporary view of the role of women, that same lack of completeness precludes discounting as a means of obtaining a satisfactory resolution of the issue. The data in Hearne's journal is not sufficient to resolve the conundrum about Chipewyan gender relations that the iconic status of the journal has created. What makes the situation more aggravating, after more than twenty-five years of fieldwork, is that I have never been able to reconcile the harshness of the image of Chipewyan gender relations presented in the historical record with the nature of gender relations that I have observed among contemporary Chipewyan.

CONTEMPORARY CHIPEWYAN SOCIAL RELATIONS

Until the middle of this century, the Mission Chipewyan lived dispersed over more than 80,000 square miles of bush in pursuit of a subsistence existence. Wage labor was only engaged in during sporadic periods of residence near the points of trade. Caribou hunting was the primary source of food, and the trapping and wage labor at the trading posts at holiday periods provided the cash/credit part of their income. Bush settlements, some of considerable size, sometimes formed at locales where there were temporary concentrations of food resources, but most of the year was spent in residential aggregations of twenty persons or less. With the increase in village residence after midcentury, there was an increase in the independence of women as part of a larger process in which the interaction between the Chipewyan and the rest of Canada created an economic and social climate that encouraged the expression and development of Western ideas of individualism and the family while Chipewyan ideas of kin solidarity and economic/social cooperation were discouraged (Sharp 1975, 1979: 42–49). By the mid-1970s, the Chipewyan had been semisedentary village dwellers for nearly two decades. The move into settlements followed the collapse of the barren-ground caribou herds in the late 1940s, which made a subsistence lifestyle all but impossible. Village life is more heavily tied into the larger market economy of Canada than is the subsistence lifestyle, but their homeland remains unsettled and remote from markets and production centers. The Dene are the largest industry in the region, and administering to them provides employment to most of the resident non-Native population and a few of the Dene themselves. Chipewyan incomes were derived from trapping and casual (and seasonal) wage labor in the early part of the decade, with substantial participation in the labor force of mining operations by the end of the decade. The slow recovery of the caribou herds, a weak fur market, and the lack of opportunity for employment made fiscal support from the federal government, primarily through Indian Affairs, the most consistent source of income throughout the decade.

Most of the food the Chipewyan consumed, at least through 1977, came from hunting and fishing activities in the bush. Caribou, moose, and fish provided the bulk of the protein; lard, flour, sugar, and tea were the primary purchased staples. Housing was either self-constructed cabins or frame homes purchased at a nominal fee from the federal government. The Chipewyan had an anomalous economic situation with low per capita incomes in a region where prices were extraordinarily high. However, because housing and fuel (wood) costs were almost negligible and most food came from traditional subsistence activities, disposable income was relatively high. The diet was poorly balanced by Western nutritional precepts but was very high in protein. Chipewyan consumption of meat far exceeded that possible among even wealthy families in southern Canada. Malnutrition remained an intermittent factor in everyone's life. Gender was a relevant factor in individual cases of malnutrition, but it was so mixed with other variables in the allocation of food resources—particularly age, sentiment, demographic variation within households, and individual personality and temperamental differences—that it did not act in a uniform manner.

Concomitant to the development of village life came better health care. Loss of life to the more common infectious diseases declined, and although I have no statistical data to support this, the people feel that it resulted in lower death rates in childbirth. Sedentarization (J. G. E. Smith 1978) also meant the sustained use of a single lake as a source of drinking water without any effective methods for preventing the buildup of pollution. There was a marked increase in the incidence of hepatitis, meningitis, and endemic waterborne diseases. I observed no relation to gender in the incidence of these diseases—and never heard the people speculate on one—but one might have existed if there was a relationship between gender and malnutrition. Perhaps the major change that improved health care brought to women was the transference of the administration of parturition from midwives selected from among the expectant mothers' female kin to a professional nursing staff. There was a decline in infant deaths associated with parturition and a concomitant rise in the population. Among the major effects of the acquisition of parturition by Western medicine was the loss of influence of the midwife and the hospitalization of the expectant mother. Beginning in the 1950s, it became the practice to leave pregnant women in the village during the hunting and trapping seasons rather than having them accompany their kin into the bush. This was instrumental in establishing the idea that the primary location of the household was at its village residence rather than at its bush dwellings.

Sedentarization helped induce a number of changes that affected the role and position of women in the local economy. Sustained residence in villages reduced the need for the traditional products of women's labor, including hand-sewed garments, the tanning of hides (primarily moose) to produce the leather for those garments, and dried meat and fish, at the same time that it helped provide a limited cash market for handicrafts. A community freezer compensated somewhat for food storage, but dried meat remained a highly valued item whose production was decreased more by lack of supply than any loss of skill or motivation. Certain handicrafts, particularly moose-hide moccasins and mitts, were not replaceable by commercial products. Their production was highly valued and still led to considerable status. Sewing remained a valued skill and a significant part of female gender identity (Sharp 1975, 1986), but few of the younger generation of women were becoming proficient at tanning leather.

If women's traditional skills were declining in economic importance and the skills themselves were no longer part of every woman's skill kit, there was no discernible male perception of that decline. By the late 1950s, the now-established practice of sustained residence within the village had disrupted the historical pattern of seasonal dispersion that had scattered women over 180,000 square miles for most of their lives. As, for symbolic reasons (Sharp 1975, 1979, 1988a), women's opportunity to travel in the bush is highly restricted, village life brought large numbers of unrelated women together for periods of sustained residence for the first time in Chipewyan history. The potential for time away from the routine of their extended households greatly increased the opportunity for women, particularly in their youth, to socialize in nonkinship contexts. It is too soon to know the full impact of these changes, but the development of ties of friendship and contact between neighbors helped create an identity among women of themselves as a social category and opened new opportunities for mutual support between women that could be translated into political and economic activities.

The major economic changes were derived from sustained co-residence and the economic intrusion of the Canadian government into Chipewyan lives. Since the bulk of the food depended on the bush activities of men, the time women spent managing their households was much more likely to be in the company of men and women who were not close kin. The hierarchical lines of authority within domestic units were in a state of flux as women, even fairly mature women, began to escape the control of senior relatives. The Canadian government assumed that its role in providing income for families should operate as it did elsewhere in Canada. This, in effect, meant the institutional imposition of the ideology of the nuclear family on the Chipewyan, however un-self-aware that imposition was. Following customary practice, the focus is more on the needs of dependent children than on adults and it is presumed that the mother of those children is the adult charged with their care and safekeeping. Payments are directed to the mother for her use in raising the children. Instead of a credit system with the local store, with the father's reputation as a trapper and worker being the basis for determining purchasing power, it became the perception of family needs in accordance with criteria established by the government that determined the purchasing power of most domestic units. Canadian belief in the nuclear family and the delivery of services with the expectation that their management would be carried out by women was leading to greater economic autonomy for women.

The assumption of routine purchasing and budgeting by women was not restricted to credit. Many government checks, particularly Family Allowance checks, were payable to whatever woman the government determined to be responsible for the children. By the mid-1970s, the government had established job training programs that provided periodic paid opportunities for participation by women. The job market in the community, although very limited, was beginning to provide opportunities for women as the local federal and provincial bureaucratic infrastructure came increasingly under Native control. With the assumption of their own administration came the need for what Canada stereotypically regards as female positions, largely those of a clerical nature. These training programs and jobs provided women with their first opportunity for a separate income independent of the sale of handicrafts, items for which there was never much of a local market and which had often been produced at an economic loss to obtain cash.

The increasing independence of the younger and generally better-educated women was a major factor in the breakdown of the practice of arranged marriages. Chipewyan culture is strongly egalitarian (Sharp 1979, 1988a). Chipewyan egalitarianism can often override gender distinctions. The exercise of egalitarianism is not something given; it is something that has to be asserted by each individual (Sharp 1977, 1979, 1988a:121–24). As younger women began to achieve greater social and economic autonomy, they were able to utilize the egalitarian ethos to resist parental pressure to marry a designated spouse. "Romantic love" became a major ideological presence in the 1960s and fit well with the increasing autonomy of young women.

Effective birth control became increasingly available throughout the 1970s as the medical profession slowly overwhelmed the opposition of the Roman Catholic church. During the same period that marriages were beginning to be delayed and women were becoming better able to exercise choice in marriage, the power of the Church's opposition to divorce began to weaken. Divorce and remarriage have always been frequent occurrences in Chipewyan lives. In a small population facing high mortality rates from accident and childbirth and where both adult males and females need to be allied with an adult of the opposite gender to participate fully in the economic/subsistence system, the reallocation of adults after the disruption of a marriage is crucial. The more Westernized economic climate in the village gave women greater options in making the decision to disrupt a marriage; it made it easier for them to leave the community or to establish an independent identity and/or residence.

Westernization of the economic system, with its increased ideological stress on individualism and its strong pressure to deemphasize kinship ties beyond the nuclear family, had not had a marked effect in altering the political system of the village in terms of the way gender was expressed. The primary reason for this lies in Chipewyan culture's formulation of the life cycle, a formulation in which aging tends to reduce the influence of men and increase the influence of women (Sharp 1979, 1981, 1988a). The Chipewyan, not unlike many other American Indian cultures, do not hold to the separation of physical causality from supernatural causality (Levy-Bruhl 1967, 1979). The collective knowledge of supernatural causality, Inkoze (Sharp 1986, 1987, 1988b; D. M. Smith 1973, 1982), defines a mode of causality independent of the assumptions of material/physical causality in contemporary Western culture (Sharp 1991). In marked contrast to Chipewyan elsewhere (D. M. Smith 1973, 1982, 1985), this knowledge is restricted to males. The effect of this system of knowledge is to set all males, save those standing in certain kin or residential affiliation, in competition to display the behavior that indicates their possession of this knowledge. Women's abilities are not perceived in terms of Inkoze as are men's. Demonstration of Inkoze requires performance, something that tends to fall off as the body weakens with the aging process. For men, this means a decline in status as their Inkoze should prevent physical weakening with age. Because women's abilities are not perceived in these terms, their declining abilities do not result in a loss of status. The things women do are perceived as skills that are not dependent on the "supernatural." They can be taught, and their teaching brings respect. The activities of man are not perceived as skills and cannot be taught. For men, respect can come only from performance. Elder women did form a recognized political bloc with a substantial influence, but gender solidarity among younger women had not begun to express itself in political form in any coherent manner by 1983.

As I indicated at the outset, discussion of the economic or political status of women does not really provide a satisfying answer to the issues involved in the relationship between gender and power. It does make for a marked contrast with the traditional view of Chipewyan society. The historical representation of gender in Chipewyan society, even in Hearne, is based at least as much on the attitude of the recorder as it is on events recorded. To show that the "position of women" is improving does not really address that issue, since what is meant by improving is only that the Chipewyans are coming to more closely resemble whatever our culture currently considers socially and ideologically desirable.

If Chipewyan women have for centuries endured and created cultural circumstances that perplex us, we are perplexed because we have shunted aside the issue of Chipewyan values. To approach that perplexity—and to be able to begin to deal with the issue of power—requires a different approach than is to be found in the examination of Chipewyan economic or political circumstances or discounting the historical record for Western bias. It requires an excursion into Chipewyan symbolism.

Symbols and Metaphors of Gender

The purpose and nature of explanation within Chipewyan culture is often quite different from its purpose and nature in our own culture (Sharp 1986, 1987, 1988a). Explanation in our culture tends to deal with the meaning of events by fixing them in history, locating them within a progressive flow of time and space while excluding competing explanations to determine the "true" causal relationships. Chipewyan culture tends to explain events by linking alternate explanations; the process combines alternate explanations into a context of explanatory factors without reducing them to a single sequence of causality. These differences make for real difficulties in understanding the Chipewyan treatment of hierarchy and the implications of categorical differences.

One legacy of the history of the development of our language and the role of binary thought in our philosophy is the assumption that categories are monothetic (Needham 1975), that they are discrete bounded entities. A and not-A cannot be the same. Chipewyan categories are, to a far greater extent than is the case in our culture, polythetic (Needham 1972, 1975). Chipewyan symbolic logic is not binary. A and not-A can be the same, or, since neither A or not-A have discrete boundaries, they can overlap. It is the case of "fuzzy logic" in which the degree of resemblance between categories can be zero. In Western thought about the relationships between monothetic categories, it is extraordinarily difficult to think about different categories without imposing a hierarchical ranking on them; hierarchy exists between every linked A and not-A. Even when a rational effort is made to avoid the implication of hierarchy, the emotional reasoning that parallels rational thought projects hierarchy onto categorical differences (Hobart 1985; Parkin 1985). This assumption of hierarchy due to categorical differentiation does not operate nearly as often in Chipewyan culture. If A and not-A are different, and they may or may not be, they are merely different. There is no implicit assumption of hierarchy or ranking of the categories just because they are different.

Even to speak of gender in the customary usage of our culture is to accede to the implication of hierarchical ranking in binary classification. Gender is a cultural construct that, among other things, is imposed on the phenotypical expression of the chromosomal diversity present in human beings. The nature of the variation in the genetic construction of human beings is such that the biology of sex is not binary. Since the biology of sex is not binary, the existence of binary cultural categories of gender in any particular culture is something that needs to be demonstrated rather than assumed. Gender in Chipewyan culture is a pervasive mode of classification, but it is not a universally applicable classification. At minimum, gender is a triadic system involving male, female, and a third category/context in which male/female is not relevant. This third category is not precisely defined; rather, it acts like certain mythical beings that are only ambiguously human or animal and characteristic of the period before contemporary categorizations became fixed. It is not correct to see this category of beings in terms of transformations between categories of beings; rather, who and what the being is is not knowable from what it is but only from what it later became. From this category of Chipewyan thought emerges Male and Female, but this emergence is of a particular character. In some contexts, particularly those relating to the system of supernatural knowledge, Male is an achieved status marked by the presence of Inkoze. In those contexts, Female is an ascribed rather than an achieved status. If the minimal case is the classification of humans when gender is not relevant and no gender assumption is made or implied, a more frequent occurrence is categorization into adult: child as an equivalent to gender categorization. The point is that Male and Female cannot be presumed. They are context-specific classifications that may be either monothetic (i.e., bounded) or polythetic (i.e., bounded only by association) as well as relevant to or not relevant to any "event."

There is buried deep in Chipewyan grammar (Carter 1974) a distinction between beings (human and animal) who obtain their own food and those who scavenge or are dependent on others to provide their food. Chipewyan men provide food. Chipewyan women are dependent on men to provide food. At the broadest level, this distinction provides a basic encoding of a Chipewyan model of culture as an asymmetrical system of food exchange. Culture is the province of females, determined and defined by the presence of women (and, less clearly, children). Food production (hunting) is Nature and the province of males (Sharp 1976, 1981). Traditional Chipewyan female self-definition centers on processing raw meat into food, in particular, the preparation of dried caribou meat Sharp 1988b). By the time these distinctions have worked themselves through to the level of speech acts and social behavior, they are most commonly expressed in animal metaphors. The most frequent and significant of these metaphors express a complex series of relationships between women and dogs, reflecting their shared dependency on others for their food.

69

The countermetaphor equates males with wolves as producers of food (hunters), but animal metaphors linking men and wolves are almost never heard. These metaphors are expressed through Chipewyan belief and commentary on the nature and behavior of wolves. Dog metaphors about both males and females exist, largely in relation to what Westerners call sexuality (Foucault 1980:23–24), although the linkage between dogs and women is much broader, stronger, and more frequently heard.

Dog metaphors carry a negative symbolic load, one most explicitly related to the dog's role as scavenger and consumer of human feces. Dogs also serve as metaphors for human sexual behavior as exemplars of uncontrolled and unregulated sexuality. At surface levels this may be as simple as a woman's linking the amorous pursuits of "them boys" (the unmarried men of the community) to the packing of male dogs in pursuit of a bitch in heat. At subtler levels they serve as metaphors for the use of sexuality as a means of expressing dissension in marital relationships, the difficulty of regulating the sexual behavior of women, and that sociobiologist's delight, the uncertainty of paternity with its consequent ambiguity and hostility about parental obligations toward a child of uncertain paternity.

The identification of women and dogs is negative in value, and its rhetorical form is often harshly negative. Perhaps the best example is the implicit grammatical pun in which the kinship term for "my daughter" is what the word for "my dog" would be if a human possessive form were used in reference to the animal (Sharp 1976). However, these equations are essentially ambiguous in their implications. Dog and Woman are strong symbols of culture, and both imply male dependency on them. (Dogs are used for transport as well as for protection from both natural and supernatural threats in the bush. In earlier times they served as pack animals and played a role in human hunting.) Vituperation of a female through a dog metaphor always carries the counterimplication of the male speaker's dependency on the dog for his own survival. The analog with women is obvious; the worse the insult delivered, the stronger the implicit message about the weakness of the speaker because of his dependence on women for standing as a cultural being.

The differential valuation of any symbol, whether negative or positive, is not separable from the context of the entire symbol set, including the inverted messages implied by that symbol. Precisely because the symbols, their meanings, and their context are shared, devaluation binds the devaluer to the devalued as strongly as it binds the devalued to the devaluer. The negative symbolic treatment of women only serves to emphasize the bond between women and men and to emphasize the dependency of men upon women. As the negative symbolic treatment serves to emphasize the bond between men and women, the negative symbolic treatment of women provides a basis for women to exercise power over men.

This point is broader than the Lévi-Straussian position that every symbolic relationship implies its inversion. It is both an indicator of how and why women have and continue to participate in the generation of Chipewyan culture and a parallel of the means by which women exercise power in the face of apparent male domination. There is a complex set of conventions about responsibility for others that operates in Chipewyan and other Northern Athapaskan cultures (Sharp 1994). One effect of these conventions is that the burden of responsibility for harm that comes to an incompetent person may fall on others in their company who are more competent. To assert the incompetence of another person is often to assume responsibility for the results of that other person's incompetence. Once responsibility is assumed, the Chipewyan will go to considerable lengths to prevent incompetent persons from coming to harm as a result of their own incompetence. Asserting that a woman is unable to perform a task is both a statement about women and an indicator that the speaker may in some way be responsible if the woman comes to harm (or fails) in attempting a task. If the speaker asserting greater competence does not intervene to prevent harm from befalling the less competent, the blame is in part his or hers. The negative value placed on symbols of female gender is a classic venue for the operation of this dynamic. To assert female inferiority is to assume responsibility for the consequences of that inferiority. The greater the negative symbolic load placed on Female symbols in a Male:Female opposition, the greater the implicit obligation on real males to real females.

What makes the dynamic so crucial to understanding the operation of Chipewyan symbols of gender is that the negative symbolic load in a gender symbol can be actively asserted as well as passively received. Real female individuals can assert their own inferiority, thus binding those to whom they are speaking into assuming responsibility for the consequences of that inferiority. "Weakness" becomes a form of power, and the creative expression of weakness is an effective means of manipulation and control in interpersonal relations (Sharp 1994).

The difficulty of understanding the symbolic valuation of women is further complicated by the Chipewyan perception of the life cycle and by the role of "supernatural" causality in human life. Reincarnation into human form exists — and there is no reason the return to the living must involve a person of the same gender. The possibility of transformation into animal form also exists without reference to gender. Reincarnation is, at least in some circumstances, optative. The recently dead may choose to seek out, through dreams, pregnant women and ask to be reincarnated in the child she carries. That gender is not necessarily fixed beyond a particular life cycle must be a mitigating factor in the perception of Chipewyan gender symbolism. The nonlinearity of the life cycle combines with the exclusion of women from the possession of Inkoze to define the lives of men and women in very different terms. Females are more vulnerable to the action of Inkoze than are males, and they are inherently polluting to the implements used to practice Inkoze. Inkoze always has the potential of rebounding on its user. One potential consequence is a fatal gender reversal that turns a man into a caricature of a woman (Sharp 1986).

If the separation of male and female predicated by Inkoze is symbolically harsh to our eyes, it illustrates another factor for the operation of Chipewyan culture in spite of what looks to be an unpleasant male bias. Inkoze, the essence of maleness, is a mode of thought removed from most of female existence. They are aware of it, their lives are affected by it, and it is their gossip (Sharp 1979) that largely creates any man's reputation for possessing it, but they do not think or define themselves in terms of it. Women's lives are predicated on different principles than are men's, and each gender thinks in the corresponding terms in the creation of their lives. The gulf between women and men in thought and perception of the culture they share is so great that it is the sharing itself that unites them rather than the content of the culture they share.

CONCLUSION

This chapter examines a culture historically regarded as a classic case of male domination to show that that image is not correct; it has only partially succeeded. The contemporary Chipewyan are unequivocally a culture in which neither male nor female are dominant. Chipewyan culture is a product of the interaction of all the persons who are part of it. This does not mean that the manner of interaction and the symbolization of that interaction conforms to our current ideas about how the genders within a culture should interact or even that all Chipewyan like the pattern of gender interaction within their culture. This pattern often offends our sensibilities, but this does not mean that they are male dominated or that the concept of gender dominance is applicable to them. I hope I have at least shown that a focus on gender complementarity is a much more revealing analytical strategy than is a focus on dominance for understanding the operation of Chipewyan culture.

The historical situation is a bit more complex. In a certain sense, the Chipewyan remain the theoretical "fly in the ointment" on the issue of gender equality. My restriction of the data to selected aspects of Hearne's writings is an artifact, an artifact chosen because of the iconic status of his writings and to illustrate the type of data that can be marshaled to support a male dominance perspective. Many other sources of data on the early Chipewyan are available, particularly the archives of the Hudson's Bay Company. It does not now seem likely that the record contains adequate information on eighteenth-century Chipewyan values either to refute the image of male domination or to provide us with an adequate understanding of 18th-century Chipewyan women's lives. The texts can be reinterpreted, and it is easy enough to cast doubt on that image of oppression and male domination but not at all clear what should replace those images.

There is little that material taken from the lives of the contemporary Chipewyan can do to directly resolve the historical questions about the lives of their ancestors. The Chipewyan remain a viable culture whose living members, although changed by the changing circumstances of their lives, are well embedded in the context of their history. It is not reasonable to explain away either their past or their present on the basis of a presumed transformation in the nature of people themselves. Chipewyan thought and social practice about gender is truly alien in the form of its symbols and their content. Chipewyan concerns often make no intuitive sense in the light of contemporary American concerns. They are a complex and difficult people whose actions and thought do not easily translate into our frame of reference. It has been my experience that both Canadian and American undergraduate students find it particularly hard to empathize with them. What does emerge from consideration of contemporary Chipewyan lives is a richness of context and detail that mitigates the harshness of the Western historical image of them. The burden of our incomprehension of the Chipewyan rests in the nature of our attempts to understand them, not in the Chipewyan themselves.

5

The Plateau

COMPLEMENTARY BUT EQUAL
Gender Status in the Plateau

Lillian A. Ackerman

The Plateau of northwestern America was formed by extensive lava flows and cut by two great river systems, the Columbia and the Fraser. These rivers and their tributaries provided the most abundant salmon runs on the continent south of Alaska (Kroeber 1947:188, 55). The salmon constituted a key resource around which Plateau subsistence and religion revolved. It was the resource that helped form and define the Plateau Indian culture.

Geographically, the Plateau culture area consists of the territory between the Rocky Mountains on the east and the Cascade Mountains on the west; from the Great Bend of the Fraser River on the north (Ray 1939:1) to, roughly, the Blue Mountains on the south. The area includes eastern Washington, northern Idaho, portions of eastern Oregon, an extension into Montana, and southern British Columbia in Canada. Much of the country is semiarid, mountainous in parts, with pine forests in the higher elevations. There are rolling uplands and fertile valleys along many rivers. Bunch-grass steppes abound (Kroeber 1947:56), which in contact times provided the means for supporting large herds of horses. Ecological zones are varied within this large area, and these were skillfully exploited by the aboriginal people.

The first whites to enter the Plateau were the members of the Lewis and Clark expedition in 1805. They followed the Columbia River down to the Pacific Coast, meeting and writing about the Indians who lived along the river. They were soon followed into the area, first by British and then by American fur traders who vied with each other not only for furs but also for ownership of the country itself. The first fur traders in the area were members of the North West Company, based in Montreal. In 1821, this company merged with the Hudson's Bay Company (Trafzer and Scheuerman 1986:19). Their rival was an American company owned by John Jacob Astor, which was ultimately unsuccessful. Astor sold his regional assets to the North West Company in 1813 (Ruby and Brown 1970:46). These commercial activities led to tension between Great Britain and the United States over ownership of the Plateau country. The boundary was finally set at the present international line.

Missionaries soon followed the fur traders. First into the Plateau, in 1835, were Samuel Parker and Marcus Whitman followed by Henry Spalding and others the next year. Whitman settled among the Cayuse Indians, and Spalding settled among the Nez Perces (Trafzer and Scheuerman 1986:22). The Whitman Massacre in 1847 temporarily ended the Protestant presence in the Plateau. The Catholics represented by the Jesuits arrived in the Plateau in 1840. American settlers began moving into the Oregon Territory in the 1850s (Burns 1966:18).

With settlers arriving in the Northwest in large numbers, the U.S. government assigned Isaac Stevens, the first governor of Washington Territory, the task of placing the Indians on reservations. The Treaty of 1855 was thrust on them and resulted in several wars: the Yakima War of 1855–56, the Coeur d'Alene–Spokane War of 1858–59, and the Nez Perce War of 1877, with many skirmishes and murders in between instigated by both sides (Burns 1966:29).

Inexorably, however, the Indians were placed on reservations where government agents and missionaries pressured them to change their culture to the Euro-American or Euro-Canadian model. The Colville Reservation Indians, for instance, could no longer depend entirely on their traditional gathering-fishing-hunting economy since the land left to them was inadequate to support them completely. They had to turn to farming or go hungry (Ackerman 1982:65–66, 85–86). At least outwardly, they had to change their religion, and their native guardian spirit religion went underground. Village chiefs were abolished in 1938, and new political forms were required (ibid., 82). These alterations led to social changes, but a surprising amount of the traditional culture has survived on all of the Plateau reservations. Today, for instance, the guardian spirit religion is practiced openly. Further, the Indians have learned to protect themselves and their culture politically and through the courts.

Some of the early fur traders, settlers, and missionaries commented on women's activities, giving us a glimpse of the gender system before much cultural change took place. Father Joseph Joset, a Jesuit missionary, declared, "The women are haughty and independent," and attributed this behavior to the women's ownership of the foods they gathered. It was easy to obtain a surplus of wild foods and other resources for trade, and with it, they "bought all they needed, even horses" (Joset n.d.). Joset complained that women did not learn "Christian subordination" and were independent to the point of driving their husbands away if they were displeased with them. Women also appeared to have a great deal of informal political influence (ibid.).

Polygyny was deplored by the missionaries because they believed the institution debased women. One, Mary Richardson Walker, even compared the role of Plateau women to that of southern slaves (McKee n.d.:408), not realizing that women controlled the fruits of their labor and profited by them. Henry H. Spalding (Drury 1936:34) noted that women, as well as men, were shamans. Some women participated in war as helpers and even as warriors (Point 1967:192, 158). These and other early observations suggest the presence of autonomous women in several Plateau societies.

It has been stated that complementary gender roles automatically lead to gender stratification, and no society with a "complementary but equal" social system is possible (Lamphere 1977:616). The sexual division of labor itself is said to create sexual asymmetry and female subordination (ibid., 619–20). A differing view is that the sexual division of labor may be fundamental to the genesis of sexual stratification, but it does not automatically lead to female subordination (Schlegel 1977c:25). The data presented here support the latter view, that sexual asymmetry is not automatic in a hunting and gathering society with a complementary sexual division of labor. The gender roles in the traditional[1] culture of the Plateau Indians of Northwest America, though complementary, with little overlap existing in the work of men and women, failed to lead to a condition of male superiority. On the contrary, the genders were socially and economically equal within Plateau societies. Even though differential access of men and women to certain public roles existed, nevertheless, that access was balanced, facilitating gender equality in traditional Plateau culture.

HISTORICAL CONTEXT

Plateau Indian territory was occupied by white settlers only a little over a century ago. Many of the eleven Plateau Indian groups who now live on the Colville Reservation (Sanpoil-Nespelem, Colville, Lakes, Southern Okanogan, Methow, Palus, Chelan, Entiat, Wenatchi, Moses Columbia, and the Chief Joseph band of the Nez Perces), where most of the following data were collected, were displaced from their native lands and placed on the reservation in 1872 (Gidley 1979:30). The Indians continued their traditional economic and political way of life despite difficulties until 1938, when their system of chiefs and independent villages were displaced by a reservationwide political system, and 1939, when Grand Coulee Dam was started, eventually destroying the salmon runs and many of the gathering grounds. Thereafter, the Indians were forced to participate fully in a cash economy.

No class structure existed in traditional Plateau societies: egalitarianism was a moral principle articulated by Plateau peoples themselves in

---

1. I date the aboriginal culture as occurring before 1855, at which time the Plateau Indians were forced onto reservations, thus diverting the evolution of their culture into an alien path. I define the traditional culture as being made up of those cultural elements derived from the aboriginal culture. Some of these elements did not last long; others remain to this day or evolved in the Plateau tradition instead of accommodating to Euro-American models. An example of Plateau-type evolution is the extension of the incest taboo to include all known relatives. A cultural loss is the office of the village chief, which gradually disappeared after allotments were made and which finally disappeared in 1938 through the substitution of Euro-American political forms. A traditional cultural element that remains is the somewhat attenuated extended family. The subject of this chapter, gender equality, is a traditional element of Plateau culture that has survived and accommodated to the new conditions. Thus, traditional culture, as I see it, is an inheritance from the past with those additions that are characteristic of the indigenous culture.

the past (Ray 1932:25–26, 1939:24–25) and in the present. Wealth was accumulated by any vigorous and ambitious individual of either gender, and the means of obtaining wealth were unrestricted and open to all — a key feature of egalitarianism. Though wealth was desired for the comfort it provided, it led to no political or social advantage. The choice of a chief was not made on the basis of wealth but on the basis of a combination of leadership qualities and heredity. Verne F. Ray (1932:110–11) notes that chiefs were often poor as they gave away what they had to less fortunate members of the village. Perhaps they were only characterized as poor, since L. V. W. Walters (1938:94–95) records that chiefs received gifts of food and materials for redistribution as needed, though they were expected to use some of the goods to support themselves. Further, chiefs traditionally had multiple wives who produced a surplus of foods and goods that was used for redistribution and for hosting guests during meetings, funerals, and other formal occasions. Nevertheless, because of their obligations, chiefs were rarely the wealthiest people in the group. Wealth was not conceived as owning subsistence goods: everyone had access to these. Instead, it was defined as having surplus horses, access to trade goods such as food and materials from the Northwest Coast cultures (whale meat, mussels, dentalium shells), handicrafts from other Plateau tribes, and goods from outside the Plateau, such as Plains buffalo hides and Northwest Coast canoes. Having a variety of such goods made life convenient, more interesting, and even luxurious.

The data on gender roles have been gleaned from missionary sources, fur trader accounts, and earlier ethnographies, as well as from fieldwork. Data presented below without references are derived from informant testimony and participant observation. To organize the discussion of gender roles, the narrative is divided into four cultural spheres: economic, domestic, political, and religious (Schlegel 1977c:8).

THE ECONOMIC SPHERE

In order of importance, the major economic activities of the aboriginal Plateau people were gathering, fishing, and hunting. Roots, berries, and other plants made up fully half of the diet according to the estimates of informants (Ackerman 1971:598; Anastasio 1972:119); and they constituted nearly 70 percent of the calories in the diet in parts of the Plateau (Hunn 1981:132). The equally important salmon runs provided about one-third to one-half of the food; hunting provided the rest (Anastasio 1972:122, 123). A division of labor by gender existed in which men fished or hunted at appropriate times of the year, while women gathered plants in all seasons except winter and processed both plant and animal foods for storage and winter use (Post 1938). The Plateau arrangement of economic responsibilities is common in societies with complementary gender roles.

Married couples were separated from each other during many parts of the annual cycle, and each partner was in complete charge of his or her economic activities. Each individual decided when, where, and how their economic responsibilities were to be met.

The winter village dissolved into its constituent families and individuals around April to pursue economic activities (Ray 1932:97–98). The women left the village to camp near the gathering ground to collect roots and other plants, which were particularly welcome after a winter of dried foods. Before general collecting began, however, a group of designated women led by a "gathering leader" dug the first roots for the First Foods ceremony at the camp which ensured the crop for the season (ibid., 27). After the ceremony, gathering became general. In the Sanpoil-Nespelem area, thirty to forty days were needed to collect enough roots to sustain a family through the winter (ibid., 98). If a woman was ambitious, she collected additional roots for trade and ceremonial occasions. Women continued to gather plants throughout the growing season (early spring to late fall) in between other tasks.

In the meantime, the men were building a salmon weir under the direction of a Salmon Chief, or leader (not necessarily the political chief but a shaman with Salmon Power). While this was primarily a male task, a woman with Salmon Power occasionally directed the work (Post 1938:12). Women made a necessary contribution, as only they could obtain the material to make lashings for the weir tripods. The knowledge of what this material was and where it could be obtained was forbidden to male informants in the past. They still profess their ignorance of this material today.

In May, the salmon runs began, and those men and women at gathering camps who were not involved in building the weirs traveled to various fishing spots in the Plateau area. The Salmon Chief performed a First Foods ceremony with a few other men, which ensured the fish runs for the year (ibid., 15–17). Thereafter, fishing was open to all men. While the men fished, the women butchered and dried the salmon (Ray 1932:70) and later transported them to the winter villages.

After the salmon weirs were built, women camped some distance away and did not approach them closely, due to unspecified taboos — undoubtedly, menstrual prohibitions. Since some women might break the taboo inadvertently through the sudden advent of the menstrual period and frighten the salmon away, all women avoided the weirs as a precaution. Further, those men and women who had had a recent death in the family or a man whose wife was pregnant with her first child also avoided the weir and refrained from eating fresh salmon (Post 1938:17). These avoidances suggest that the menstrual taboo was part of a group of prohibitions, not confined to women, the breaking of which would upset the powers attracting the salmon upstream. Demonstrating further that simply being female did not automatically lead to prohibitions, informants note that a female shaman with Salmon Power could be summoned by the Salmon Chief to clear debris away from the weir if the fish run failed. By invoking her guardian spirit during this task, the shaman persuaded the salmon to return to the stream.

Walter Cline (1938:137) noted a woman who, by inference, had the same power as the one described above.

> A sex tabu, binding on women in general, was not enforced on a woman with great power. It pleased the woman in question, whose power had brought a big catch of salmon, to go swimming just above the salmon-weir, an act forbidden to women. When the people complained, she replied, "I made the salmon come. It's all right if I take a swim."

Thus, though fishing was primarily a male activity, women had important roles in it.

It is unlikely that a female shaman with Salmon Power had to wait until menopause to use that power. Female healers practiced their skills as early as their twenties, and Walters (field notes, unpaginated) noted that a woman with hunting power used it even when she was menstruating. She would "sing" (pray) to drive the deer downhill so the hunters could capture them. She then had the kill butchered in her tent and distributed it to other people there.

Large hunting parties were organized in the fall, with the express purpose of obtaining enough meat (mostly deer) to last the winter. Women had important roles in this primarily male activity also. They made up one-third of the hunting party, and their function was to dry the meat and run the camp. They also participated in driving the game in some areas (Ray 1932:78). Consequently, women had to be vigorous and in their prime to help in the hunting, although an older woman was sometimes included in the party.

After the first hunt, a First Foods ceremony was held by the hunting leader, analogous to the First Foods ceremonies noted above for the plants and salmon. Thereafter, after every hunt, the oldest man in the party, not the successful hunter, distributed the meat to one member of each family, usually a woman. If a man was unmarried, he was included in this distribution (Post 1938:22). Though a Plateau woman received the meat to feed her family, she apparently held title to it. Any surplus meat she acquired could be used for trade or in any way that she wished (Walters 1938:75). No one had the authority to countermand her decision.

The Plateau method of meat distribution does not fit into Ernestine Friedl's (1975:22) account of how hunters in other hunting and gathering societies acquire political power. She suggests that successful hunters earn political power by distributing meat to other males, thus laying obligations on them. If Friedl's theory is correct, the Plateau practice of distributing meat to women implies that women were politically important. Her theory may simply be too narrowly applied by confining it to one gender. In the Plateau, prestige, which translated into political influence, was acquired through hunting, but it was far from the only avenue to prestige and political influence; nor was it the most important. Plateau fishermen and gatherers who were skilled acquired prestige and influence equal to that of good hunters, according to the unanimous testimony of informants. They stress that individuals of all genders with superior economic skills were politically influential: influence was not restricted to hunters or males. Thus, even though economic gender roles were different, they were complementary.

The question is, did the people themselves recognize the equal importance of male and female roles. Elderly informants were asked which foods were more important in the traditional diet: meat and fish, or roots and berries. Informants of both genders unanimously stated that all four of these foods were equally important. Some commented that meat cooked without berries or roots is poor; others noted that fish is always cooked with berries. The work of both genders was judged by both genders to be equally important, indicating that complementary economic roles did not lead to gender stratification in this group.

The equal importance of complementary gender roles in the economic sphere was reinforced by the existence of a ceremony celebrating a child's first economic endeavor. When a boy killed his first deer, at age ten or twelve, or caught his first fish at about age five, or when a girl of about age six collected her first roots or berries independently to take back to her family, his or her grandmother arranged a small feast for elders during which the child's food was ceremoniously consumed along with other foods (Ray 1932:133). The purpose was to celebrate the advent of a new provider for the group. The ceremony was identical in intent for both sexes, and the economic skills being celebrated were complementary to each other.

In other aspects of the economic sphere, men and women had identical, rather than complementary, roles. Both were completely independent in owning personal property, holding nothing in common (Walters 1938:91). Informants note that men possessed only personal clothing, weapons, tools, and horses. Women owned clothing, tools, horses, the mat lodge, and all the stored food. Wealth was conceived of as having a quantity of basic goods, trade goods, and horses. Through the initiative of the individual, a surplus of goods could be accumulated for trade. Men and women both were heavily involved in trade and were independent of each other in this activity. Women dealt mainly with food, since they were the sole proprietors of it (Griswold 1954:117; Walters 1938:75). They traded processed (dried or baked) food commodities to areas where such foods were scarce. They also made baskets, cured skins, and sewed clothing for trade. Through this trade, they were able to acquire horses to carry their children and household goods. Men's major stock in trade was horses, but they also fashioned weapons, fishing implements, and other handicrafts as trade goods. Trade items belonged to the individual who acquired them, though they could of course be given as gifts. Neither husband nor wife could claim the property of the other. In case of divorce, each had substantial goods that they had acquired individually and kept. While the goods themselves could be regarded as gender typed, the trade of both kinds of goods was deemed equally important by informants.

The acquisition of goods through inheritance was not extensive. It was the custom to bury some of the goods with the deceased and distribute much of them to mourners, with the survivors getting relatively little but often the most valuable parts of it. Horses were usually taken by a brother (Ray 1932:152). Houses were destroyed, and the widow or widower did not inherit any goods from their deceased spouse. On the Nez Perce reservation around 1965, informants said that if the surviving spouse kept any of the goods, the spirit of the deceased could then return. Out of loneliness, it would "steal" the spirit of the surviving spouse, who then would die. Children receiving a deceased parent's goods were not at risk.

To illustrate the complementary aspects of the economic sphere in the traditional culture, the traits discussed above are shown in table 5.1. An entry crossing the midline of the table indicates that the statement applies to both genders equally. Other traits are arranged opposite each other, indicating the complementarity of access by men and women. When the material is evaluated qualitatively, there is no doubt that the genders had balanced access to the economic sphere in the traditional culture: they were complementary but equal.

TABLE 5.1. THE ECONOMIC SPHERE — TRADITIONAL CULTURE

Men	Women
Salmon Chief, hunting leader	Gathering leader
Weir construction by Salmon Chief	Weir construction by female shaman
	Lashings for weir
	Ensuring of fish runs by female shaman
Distribution of meat	Receipt of meat
Economic skills leading to political influence	
Male and female foods	
First economic contribution of child	
Exclusive personal property	
Equal participation in trade	

THE DOMESTIC SPHERE

Plateau groups lived in winter villages of one to two hundred people, headed by a chief. The chief was most often male, and his major function was acting as a judge in settling disputes (Ray 1932:111). In the winter villages, extended families headed by grandparents and consisting of several of their adult children with their spouses and children lived together in mat lodges. The grandmother's influence was paramount over younger family members, tending to override the grandfather's influence. Alexander Ross (1904:280), an early fur trader, noted in the early 1800s that the family was ruled by the joint authority of the husband and wife "but more particularly by the latter." Comments made by elderly informants indicate that overall authority was not institutionally assigned to either the man or the woman in any marriage; that is, no institutionalization of dominance existed. When dominance did occur, it was due to the presence of a strong personality, often belonging to the woman.

Though marriages were said to be patrilocal by one observer (Ray 1932:140), another (Mandelbaum 1938:117–18) noted that a young couple could take up residence at either of their villages. My own research has confirmed ambilocality in traditional Plateau culture, with a probable patrilocal preference.

First marriages were ideally arranged by parents, but second and subsequent marriage partners were always chosen by the individual. Marriage consisted of a couple taking up common residence, and divorce was simply accomplished by leaving the area with one's goods. Both men and women had an equal right to divorce, and many individuals went through several spouses in a lifetime.

Divorce did not result in economic deprivation for either party. Both had the choice of moving in with their consanguineal kin or living independently. A woman was well able to support herself and her children with the food she gathered, some of which could be traded for meat and fish (Ray 1932:143). It was likely that a man might have been somewhat less independent, for while he also could trade meat and fish for plant foods, he probably could not set up a household without a woman's labor. These services could be provided by a female consanguine, but unmarried men preferred mobility so they could find a new wife.

Polygyny occasionally ocurred in the traditional culture (ibid., 142), while polyandry did not. Some would argue that this asymmetry implies the existence of male dominance, but Remi Clignet and Joyce A. Sween (1981) have shown that the presence of polygyny within a particular culture does not automatically imply male dominance within such marriages. The participation of Plateau women in polygynous marriages did not place them in a subservient position. Co-wives were often sisters or cousins who remained friends and allies. Nonrelated co-wives were often rivals, but since women were economically independent, they had the option of divorce when displeased and used this option more often than not.

Domestic violence, specifically, violence used by men against their wives, occurred in the past and was common enough to be noted in the literature (Ray 1932:145). According to both male and female informants, the practice was considered shameful. Members of the extended family tried to stop the violence if real harm might ensue, and older family members often counseled the man to reform or to divorce his wife if they could not get along. Thus a woman was neither publicly nor privately forced to accept domestic violence. Further, women had the option of leaving their husbands when violence occurred, and many did. Parents of a young woman in this situation often "took their daughter back," thus dissolving the marriage.

Informants note that a few women sometimes used violence on their husbands. This is no more condoned than the reverse and is often a cause of divorce. There is no cultural pressure on an abused spouse to endure a violent marriage.

Rape occurred in traditional Plateau societies (Ray 1932:146; Turney-High 1937:83-84), though informants insisted that it was an unusual crime and was not condoned. Two naratives of the punishment of rapists were collected in the field. Both involved turning the man over to a group of women who physically molested him and publicly humiliated him. He was then ejected from the village.

The exercise of authority within the domestic sphere was a mixture of identical and complementary elements. Both parents had equal authority in the discipline of children and equal authority in arranging first marriages for their children. While only fathers exchanged gifts (horses) to cement a marriage agreement, it was the women of both families who, several months later, exchanged the gifts that formalized the affinal relationship. Thus men and women had different but equally important roles to play in the creation of a new marriage.

In case of adultery, a man had the right to kill his wife's lover without fear of reprisal. Supposedly, he could also kill his wife (Mandelbaum 1938:116), though contemporary informants indicated that this was unusual, even in the past. Several less violent outcomes were possible. The affair could be and often was ignored; the couple might quarrel over the affair and then make up; or they could divorce. Part of the counseling a young man received from an elder in his family just before his first marriage involved this situation. He was told that if his wife committed adultery, he should refrain from violence. The best solution was to ignore his wife's affairs, and if he could not, he should leave her.

The wife did not have the right to kill her husband's lover. However, she too had an institutionalized recourse. With the help of a group of female friends, she beat her rival, thus driving her away. The man was often so flattered that his wife fought for him publicly that he returned to her.

The berdache institution—in which men wore women's clothes and performed female economic tasks, while women wore men's clothes and engaged in male tasks—existed in Plateau culture; both men and women were able to change their gender roles. Their relative numbers were never estimated by early observers, but several cases of gender reversal by both men and women are mentioned in the literature (Schaeffer 1965; Teit 1906:267; Turney-High 1937:85).

In summary, the domestic sphere consists of a mixture of complementary and identical roles for men and women in traditional Plateau culture (see table 5.2).

THE POLITICAL SPHERE

Access to political influence or power was identical for both genders through the exercise of superior economic, religious, and other skills. "Good providers," male or female, had more influence with their peers than those who were less successful economically. They were credited with superior intelligence and were heeded when they offered opinions. Their opinions were often solicited when not offered spontaneously.

Despite men and women having equal access to political influence or power, gender access to political authority was more unbalanced. The political structure was simple. A chief, most often male, presided entirely independently over the village. He was elected to this office by the assembly, which consisted of all adults in the community. It was often during assembly meetings that opinions were solicited from the most respected members of the community. The assembly was consulted by the chief in all important matters. In addition, the chief managed access to economic resources, which required sound judgment. His major talent was arbitration, and with this skill he tried to keep peace within the village (Ray 1932:109-10).

Though the political chief's office was almost always occupied by a male, Ray (1939:24) reports that women were eligible to be political

TABLE 5.2. THE DOMESTIC SPHERE — TRADITIONAL CULTURE

Men	Women
No institutionalization of dominance in couple's relationship	
Ambilocality	
Right to select second and subsequent marriage partners	
Right to divorce; no economic deprivation	
Polygyny	No polyandry; easy divorce
Domestic violence	Easy divorce
Rape	Public humiliation and banishment of rapist
Discipline of children	
Arranging first marriages for children	
Exchange of gifts to cement marriage agreement	Exchange of gifts to formalize marriage
Right to kill wife's lover	No comparable right, but institutionalized right to beat rival and drive her off; right to divorce
Berdaches	

chief among the Lakes and the Southern Okanogans, but he has published no details. I collected an oral history describing the career of a Chelan female political chief five generations ago, but the oral history does not provide detailed information. The subject of the history was the widow of a Chelan chief who presided over the group while her son was still a minor. Before he could be confirmed in the succession, he died in a snowslide, and his mother continued to be chief of this group until she died. Her grandson succeeded her.

Walters (1939:95-96) also reports elected female "chiefs" in three groups, but these are somewhat different from the office of political chief. The *sku'malt*, or woman of great authority, was formally elected by the group and was always a relative of the political chief. Informants note that she was supposed to have spirit power "of a certain kind" and to show intelligence and wisdom. She carried out the same judicial and advisory functions as the chief. Since the judicial role of the male chief was his most important function (Ray 1939:22), the sku'malt must have been equal to him in importance in those groups that had the office. Thus the possibility of women serving as chiefs in at least four Plateau groups (Lakes, Southern Okanogan, Chelan, Methow) in the same way as males cannot be dismissed easily, despite incomplete confirmation in the field (ibid., 24). The sku'malt office, where it existed, was obviously complementary to that of the chief.

The role of a chief's wife was also complementary to a chief's role in many Plateau groups. The wife's character was always considered when a candidate for chief was being considered. His wife advised him on important decisions, and she served as chief when her husband was away. After his death, she nominated his successor, usually the chief's son, and in some groups acted as chief for a year during the mourning period. In other aspects of the political sphere, access was identical for both men and women. Both spoke and voted in the assembly, and a married couple's votes did not need to coincide.

A Wenatchi informant commented that the assembly consisted only of men when war was being discussed, since war was their province, but this was not necessarily so in other groups. Only the Nez Perces definitely excluded women from councils, but they also excluded most men, as councils were made up of prominent warriors only. However, a Nez Perce informant noted that everyone lobbied the council members as a matter of course, and consequently, all opinions were heard.

In early historic times, a few Plateau women participated in warfare on a voluntary basis. They did not give up their female status to do this and were not assigned an unusual social status because of it. Informants note that the only difference between the warrior women and other women was their courage. Age made no difference: a young woman with children was as likely to participate as an older woman. Early missionaries (Chittenden 1905:578; Point 1967:158, 192) and oral traditions on the Colville and Nez Perce reservations note women who rode out with raiding parties.

Most warrior women saw their function as helping the wounded and rescuing their male relatives during the fighting as needed. However, they did not miss an opportunity to kill opposing warriors, and they were at similar risk. A few women participated as full warriors (Gidley 1979:90; Point 1967:158), indicating the extent of the personal autonomy that Plateau women enjoyed.

The roles of men and women in the political sphere in Plateau traditional culture are shown in table 5.3.

THE RELIGIOUS SPHERE

The religious sphere is unique in traditional Plateau culture, for access to it was almost identical for both men and women. Both male and female children searched for and acquired guardian spirits in equal numbers. In some groups, male shamans outnumbered female shamans, though they were equal in ability (Ray 1939:93). In other groups, informants said that male and female shamans were equal in number and ability.

Though Ray (1932:182) reports that only 20 to 30 percent of Sanpoil and Nespelem girls went on quests for guardian spirits, my informants from those groups insisted that all girls as well as all boys participated. The discrepancy may arise from the pressure brought by the Catholic church in Ray's time and earlier to change the status of women, to "establish Christian subordination" (Joset n.d.). One contemporary young woman related how the Church had succeeded in teaching subordination to her grandmother, which led to her ineffectuality in economic and other matters. In contrast, she and her mother followed the traditional egalitarian pattern of Indian female behavior and engaged in the effective and powerful roles of Plateau women. It is generally true on the Colville Reservation today that the middle-aged and young generations are far more defiant of Euro-American institutions, including the religious ones, than some members of the very oldest living generation. In Ray's time, therefore, it would not be surprising that only 20 to 30 percent of the girls sought guardian spirits, while today all girls raised in traditional families seek them. One woman commented on the necessity of the guardian spirit quest: "Girls had to have the chance to get a spirit since having one provided such great benefits. Everyone knew something in the old days. One could not be a very good hunter or camas digger without spiritual power, but

TABLE 5.3. THE POLITICAL SPHERE — TRADITIONAL CULTURE

Men	Women
"Good providers" influential	
Chief in most Plateau groups	Chiefs in the past in some Plateau groups
	Sku'malt—judicial and advisory functions, "female chief" in some groups
	Wife advised chief, served as chief when husband was absent
	Wife served as temporary chief after husband's death
Assembly members	
Spoke and voted independently	
Warriors (mostly men)	

could only get by." Men and women exercised their religious gifts completely independently of their spouses. The husband of a female shaman could neither influence her use of her magical abilities nor prevent her from using them.

Being successful at gambling was a highly respected ability in Plateau culture and was a gift given by a guardian spirit. Men and women gamblers were equal in numbers and skill in traditional times, but they played only in groups of their own gender. In the stickgame, in which bones served as dice, the power of the bones could be "drawn away" by the presence of a menstruating woman. The menstrual influence, however, could be counteracted by the use of magical remedies (Commons 1938:186).

As religion is the most cherished part of Plateau culture, qualifying it as a central institution (Schlegel 1977c:19), the largely identical access of both men and women to this sphere is significant in the evaluation that gender status is egalitarian among Plateau Indians (see table 5.4).

TABLE 5.4. THE RELIGIOUS SPHERE — TRADITIONAL CULTURE

Men	Women
Acquisition of guardian spirits	
Shamans equal in number in some groups, unequal in others	
Equal in power and ability	
Independent exercise of spiritual abilities	
Gamblers	

PROHIBITIONS

Though menstrual taboos and other prohibitions imposed on women have often been cited to prove their postulated universal inferior status (Divale and Harris 1976:525), other views hold that the significance of menstrual taboos varies from one culture to another and such taboos are not necessarily associated with the inferior status of women (Buckley and Gottlieb 1988:14). The latter appears to be the case in Plateau culture. The presence of menstrual taboos does not indicate an inferior female status when all other information points to gender equality. Since the menstrual taboo disappeared at least fifty years ago on the Colville Reservation, informants were unable to provide as much detail as appears in earlier ethnographies.

Mandelbaum (1938:110-12) relates that women isolated themselves in a community menstrual hut (Southern Okanogans) during the flow, ate little, avoided the men's sweathouse, and were not allowed to cook, even for themselves. Meals were brought to them. They could not eat fresh meat or fresh salmon and did not drink from a stream; drinking tubes were used instead. They avoided looking at or talking to men so that the latter would not lose their power to hunt. After the flow was over, women bathed thoroughly and returned to their usual life.

Ray (1932:134-35) argues that the many remedies for broken taboos meant that a menstruating woman often contaminated others, and she did not therefore always go into seclusion. Informants did indeed remember that women were not supposed to step over weapons or walk around the head of a bed while menstruating. Women, menstruating or not, could not take water from a stream in which a fish trap was set, and they could not visit the trap or approach it too closely. This last taboo was applied to all women so that no menstruating woman might destroy the fish run. These dangers would not have occurred if the women always went into seclusion.

Menstrual taboos were observed by young women secluded during their first menses. Before seclusion, a young girl's hair was bound in rolls behind her ears, and she was warned not to touch her head to avoid possible baldness. She was given a head scratcher instead. She wore the same undecorated garments throughout her isolation. Southern Okanogan girls remained alone in the hut for ten days (Mandelbaum 1938:110-12).

Sanpoil girls ran around the hills after dark to increase their strength. Girls often had a guardian spirit visitation during their first seclusion. For many, it was not the first spirit visitation, but it was the last opportunity to obtain a spirit, as this never happened after puberty (Ray 1932:134).

When the menstrual flow was finished, the girl built a small sweathouse to purify herself. She used the sweathouse for a month or even a year after she rejoined the rest of the family. She swam every morning (Mandelbaum 1938:110-12). Thereafter, she observed the usual menstrual taboos described above.

Fishing was a male subsistence activity, while root digging and food processing were female subsistence activities. Prohibitions were placed on the other gender during some of these gender-linked subsistence activities. Balancing the menstrual taboo, men were prohibited until recent times from being in the vicinity of root ovens when roots were baking or drying. Drying roots in an earth oven was a long and delicate task, sometimes ending in failure and the ruin of a large amount of food. The presence of men was judged to be a danger to the success of the undertaking (Teit 1930:185). This prohibition placed on men was similar in spirit to the menstrual taboo and, in my opinion, may be interpreted as complementary to it. Informants could not give a rationale for either the male or female taboo.

Children too were involved in a system of prohibitions. Girls were taught to avoid touching men's weapons and fishing implements at all times and warned to avoid areas where men made them. If a girl failed to observe these prohibitions, it was believed not only that the men's activities would be adversely affected but also that the girl herself was doomed to become an indolent individual who would never be able to acquire the skill to find and dig roots successfully.

Boys were taught to avoid touching women's digging tools, gathering baskets, or material (probably skins in the past). If they did, it was believed that they would never acquire the ability to hunt or fish skillfully or learn to shoot straight. Boys under fifteen were not to approach root ovens at all, though adult married men were sometimes allowed to do so if the root baking had advanced to a safe stage (ibid.).

Once the children matured, these prohibitions were no longer rigidly required of either gender. If an adult woman touched a man's weapon during her menses, his hunting and fishing ability might be affected, but magical measures could be applied to undo the damage. As noted above, Ray (1932:135) pointed out that a great number of these measures existed, and he concluded that the taboos were often broken.

Hunting leaders went through a ritual cleansing of sweat bathing and sexual abstinence before every hunting expedition (ibid., 78). Sexual abstinence before hunting is a custom reported in many human cultures. In the Plateau area, however, the sexual abstinence practiced by males before an important subsistence activity corresponded to sexual abstinence practiced by females before their most important subsistence activity, root digging. Before the gathering leader and her companions dug the first roots for the First Foods ceremony in the spring, they practiced ritual sweat bathing and sexual abstinence, practices that formed a counterpart to the men's customs. Informants were all agreed on this point. Three informants added that women practiced sweat bathing and sexual abstinence when digging for roots throughout the year. Other Colville Reservation informants denied that this was a custom in the past, so it is possible that the practice was not widespread throughout the Plateau area or that it disappeared from memory. A Yakima woman married to a man on the Colville Reserva-tion said that the custom is practiced today on the Yakima Reservation. She said,

> You have to live clean to dig for the first food. You have to take a sweat bath for five days . . . for everyday digging. A woman keeps away from her husband before she goes to get roots. [There are] no woman smells before hunting on the men, and no man smells on women before digging, or the roots will go away. . . . So, all my kids were born in June. Sometimes you forgot, and had to go through sweat bathing again, get clean clothes and bedding.

Despite the fact that some female informants today do not know this custom, three Colville Reservation women described it independently in convincing detail. Though more verification is desirable, it seems likely that sexual abstinence before routine gathering was widespread in the past since intermarriage spread such customs throughout the Plateau.

Thus women and men followed similar rituals when they undertook their respective economic tasks. The existence of the corresponding rituals associated with the most important economic tasks undertaken by both genders indicates that their labor was viewed by the Plateau people as equally important, realistically and symbolically.

The system of ritual precautions, which include the avoidance of the other gender's economic tools, the role of women in the building of fish weirs and ensuring the fish run balanced by the avoidance of root ovens by males, and particularly the same ritual cleansing and sexual absti-nence undertaken by both men and women before performing their most important economic role, suggest that the menstrual taboos were not unique prohibitions in this culture. Each prohibition for one gender was balanced by a similar one for the other (see table 5.5). This complementarity seemed to have had the effect of carefully defining the characteristics of men and women and firmly hammering individu-als into their place in the gender system.

This is not to deny that gender was flexible in Plateau culture. The existence of berdaches of both sexes in these societies demonstrates

TABLE 5.5. PROHIBITIONS—TRADITIONAL CULTURE

Men	Women
Avoided root ovens	Menstrual taboos
	Avoided fish weirs
Prohibited from knowing source and nature of weir lashings	Gathered material for weir lashings
Boys avoided women's tools	Girls avoided men's tools
Ritual cleansing and sexual abstinence before hunting	Ritual cleansing and sexual abstinence before gathering
Sexual abstinence before and during hunting	Probable sexual abstinence before and during gathering

that flexibility. Walter L. Williams (1986:65) notes that where males adopt female roles, gender equality is likely to be present: "Women . . . were persons of consequence." Unfortunately, the role that berdaches took in these prohibitions and prescriptions was never recorded in the literature.

GENDER STATUS IN TRADITIONAL CULTURE

By examining the tables presented above which outline the roles of men and women (but not berdaches), an evaluation of gender status can be made. In my judgment, gender equality was undoubtedly present in traditional Plateau culture, reflecting the general egalitarianism in the culture as a whole. The only possible exceptions occur in the political sphere, where men have an edge over women, and the domestic sphere, in which women appear to have some advantage. Nevertheless, the arrangement of Plateau gender roles fits Alice Schlegel's (1977c:8-9) definition of gender equality as the equal access or different but balanced access of men and women to the economic, domestic, political, religious, and other social spheres. The judgment that gender equality exists in Plateau culture is not only an etic judgment but an emic one as well. When informants were asked toward the end of the field study if they thought that men and women were equal in their society, men and women all answered affirmatively. The

Plateau is an area where women were not important because of their relations to men. They had their own importance and had access to public roles regardless of the status of their husbands. Today, women carry their husband's name in the Euro-American manner after marriage, but their individual identity and their family of origin are always known. The conclusion to be drawn from the Plateau example is that complementary gender roles do not necessarily lead to gender stratification.

GENDER STATUS IN CONTEMPORARY CULTURE

The gender equality prevailing in Plateau culture is especially evident when contemporary culture is examined. Some investigators argue that complementary access to social spheres is not equality at all and that identical access for both genders is needed to achieve equality (Lamphere 1977:613). However, if a culture with complementary access evolves to one in which both sexes have identical access in all social spheres, then there is a strong suggestion that gender equality exists in that culture in both phases of history. That is exactly what has happened in Plateau culture. As an example, table 5.6 outlines the access of both genders to the economic sphere in contemporary Plateau culture. The items that cross the midline of the table pertain equally to both men and women. Obviously, the Indian economy today is similar to that of the larger society. The Colville Reservation tribal structure has the means to hire staff and employ tribal members to fill vacancies. It follows that Plateau cultural rules are applied in hiring policies. As a consequence, Colville women have achieved without comment that elusive goal of Euro-American women: equal pay for equal work (Ackerman 1982:114). In addition, access to high-management jobs is equally available to both genders on the Colville Reservation, work is equally valued, jobs are less gender typed, and women managers have no status problems with male employees.

The contemporary domestic sphere has about half complementary and half identical access. Most women work outside their homes today as they did in the past, but instead of performing the traditional task of gathering, they have Euro-American jobs. They continue to run their

98

TABLE 5.6. THE ECONOMIC SPHERE — CONTEMPORARY CULTURE

Men	Women
Access to high-management jobs	
Equal pay for equal work	
Work equally valued	
Jobs less gender typed than in Euro-American society	
Authority equally effective in management jobs	

households with the same authority as their female ancestors. As a rule, they are considered more economically astute than men and handle the family's resources. Financial assets and property may be held jointly but are often held separately.

Both men and women are autonomous in making a decision to seek work. If either decides not to seek employment, it is not necessary to consult with one's spouse.

Divorce is still not considered an economic handicap. Women expect to support their children by themselves after divorce. They do not generally seek child support, although that is changing somewhat. Inequalities for women are creeping in, since it is harder for one person to make a sufficient living to support children (Ackerman 1982).

The contemporary political sphere has identical access for both sexes across the board, except that men outnumber women on the tribal council and may include young men but not young women. It is generally understood by both genders that this occurs because of the need for younger women to remain at home with their children or to work in the immediate community, since a council member must travel a great deal. Both genders have served as chairperson of the Colville Business (Tribal) Council in the recent past. Women are politically active in other roles and emphatically express their opinions, which are taken seriously. Married couples vote independently of each other in tribal and Euro-American elections, neither knowing how the other spouse votes (ibid., 141).

The religious sphere, too, remains an area of identical access for both genders except where the Catholic church and the Indian Shaker church are involved. (The latter religion is a combination of Christianity and the traditional Native religion.) The Catholic church excludes women from some roles, and the Indian Shaker church on the Colville Reservation happened to have more female ministers, deacons, and elders during my first period of study (1979–82) on the Colville Reservation. The traditional guardian spirit religion continues to be practiced in many families. Male and female children in these families are groomed for the guardian spirit quests in equal numbers, and men and women both become shamans in approximately equal numbers.

The evolution from complementary access to identical access of gender roles in two phases of one culture confirms, I believe, that gender equality is possible in societies with complementary gender roles.

ACKNOWLEDGMENTS

The original fieldwork described in this paper was supported by fellowships from the Woodrow Wilson National Fellowship Foundation and the American Association of University Women and by grants from the Phillips Fund of the American Philosophical Society and Sigma Xi.

My thanks to Sue-Ellen Jacobs, Laura F. Klein, and Richard A. Sattler for comments that greatly improved this chapter. My gratitude also to the other contributors to this volume who kindly read my contribution.

My gratitude also to the Business Council of the Colville Confederated Tribes, Adeline Fredin, Tribal Historian, and to the many members of the Colville Confederated Tribes who assisted me in this project.

6

FIRST AMONG EQUALS?
THE CHANGING STATUS OF SENECA WOMEN

JOY BILHARZ

The Iroquois are the best-known American Indian group in the Northeast. The term is used most frequently to refer to the Five (now Six) Nations, a confederacy dating from precontact times which united the Mohawk, Oneida, Onondaga, Cayuga, and Seneca and, by the early eighteenth century, the Tuscarora, who moved north from the Carolinas. Iroquoia was symbolized as a longhouse stretching across much of New York State and southern Ontario, in which each tribe maintained its own fire. Although there were differences among the tribes in response to European invasion and colonization, they shared a common language family, matrilineal descent, and horticultural way of life based on maize, beans, and squash. The Confederacy was headed by fifty chiefs whose titles were passed through the matrilineages; although women could not become chiefs, they played a critical role in their selection.

In 1848, the Senecas at the Allegany and Cattaraugus reservations overthrew government by chiefs, thereby effectively withdrawing from the Confederacy, and established an elective form of government known as the Seneca Nation of Indians that continues to the present, as does the Confederacy, which is centered on the Onondaga Reservation. There are at present nine Iroquois reservations in New York, including the Oil Spring Reservation, which has no permanent residents, and seven reservations in Canada.

The status of Iroquois women has been debated from 1851, when

Lewis Henry Morgan ([1851] 1962:324) claimed they were "the inferior, the dependent, and the servant of man," to the present, when Paula Gunn Allen (1986) argues that women were fundamental in shaping the League (213) and that Iroquois society prior to the nineteenth century is most accurately described as a gynocracy (32). With the exception of George P. Murdock (1934:302), who stated that "of all the people of the earth, the Iroquois approach most closely to that hypothetical form of society known as the matriarchate," most recent students of gender take a more moderate stance (e.g., Wallace 1969:29).

Claims of relatively high status for Iroquois women are usually based on such economic and/or political roles as female ownership of land, control over horticultural production, and nomination of Confederacy chiefs (Brown 1970:164; Wallace 1969:29). Most studies, with the exception of that of Cara Richards (1957), are concerned with pre-nineteenth-century Iroquois and fail to take a dynamic view of gender roles. In addition, as Elizabeth Tooker (1984) notes, it is important to understand what terms such as "property" and "ownership" meant to Iroquois at the time and not to interpret them in terms of contemporary Western economic theory.

The Newhouse version of the Constitution of the Five Nations, recorded during the late nineteenth century by Seth Newhouse, an Onondaga-Mohawk from the Six Nations Reserve in Canada, states, "Women shall be considered the progenitors of the Nation. They shall own the land and the soil" (Fenton 1968b:42). To the Iroquois, however, ownership did not mean transferable legal title; rather, it meant usufruct (Tooker 1984:116). Because women were horticulturalists, their more intensive use of land established their rights to it. In this context, men merely cleared the land for them. The fields of corn, beans, and squash, tended by communal work parties of female matrilineage members, were abandoned every ten to twenty years as soil fertility was reduced, timber reserves were exhausted, animals were killed off, and plant reserves were depleted (Hertzberg 1966:25). This ecological shift normally meant that old villages were abandoned and new ones were established, an important life event and time marker. Therefore, ownership of land, regardless of how it was defined, was temporary.

Female control over the tools of production was not of major economic value. Hoes and digging sticks were the women's primary horticultural tools and were easily made and readily discarded. Similarly, corn pounders and baskets, although essential, were neither highly valued nor necessarily durable. Iroquois longhouses, the matrilineal residential units that were also used for both storage and cooking, were subject to rot, insect infestations, and fires. Therefore, these "tools" of production seldom lasted more than a decade or two. In contrast, men's implements, such as firearms, metal traps, knives, and axes, were obtained in trade or via cash and were both longer lasting and more highly valued. Tooker (1984:115–16) concludes that women's property lacked durability and resultant economic worth.

Reciprocity was of critical importance in Iroquois society, whether between women and men, young and elders, or the moieties (Hertzberg 1966:58; Tooker 1984:19; Wallace 1969:29). It was reflected in the perception of space, with the Iroquois world divided into the complementary realms of forest and clearing (Hertzberg 1966:23–30; Tooker 1984:118–121; Wallace 1952:24–28), the former being the domain of men, the warriors, hunters, and diplomats, and the latter the domain of women, the farmers and clan matrons. Men and women had different roles, neither dominating the other, thus providing a good example of Melford E. Spiro's (1979:7) "equivalence" meaning of equality. While women provided the bulk of the subsistence from their horticulture, men's hunting was also important to provide dietary variety in precontact times (Tooker 1984:115). By the seventeenth and eighteenth centuries, male participation in the fur trade and later timbering operations permitted access to the cash economy. This proved to be a critical contribution since the Senecas were dependent on white material culture by the late seventeenth century when European trade goods dominate the archaeological record (Rothenberg 1980:67, 70). Iroquois males required access to guns and ammunition of European manufacture in order to hunt (for subsistence or trade) and wage war. Indian women preferred metal pots for cooking and European calico for their clothing but continued their subsistence activities with little need for European technology. Thus contact probably had a less severe impact on women, as Martha Champion Randle (1951:170) has suggested, since their economic role changed little and their control of the clearing remained secure. In fact, the matrilineal-matrilocal social structure may have been strengthened (Rothenberg 1980:81) as males were absent for significant periods of time, frequently in nontraditional roles. It would seem that this was a change in degree rather than kind, since the pattern of sedentary females and mobile males was one of long duration necessitating female self-sufficiency (Wallace 1969:29). Indeed, Richards (1957:36) notes a change in status among Iroquois women prior to 1784 as they took on increased decision-making roles.

Child care was totally within the domain of women, with little differentiation of gender roles until the children reached the age of eight or nine. At that point, boys would join all-male peer groups in which they sometimes were supervised by older men, but more frequently they wandered about without adult interference. Girls would remain with their mothers while learning such domestic tasks as farming, cooking, sewing, basketmaking, and tool manufacture (Hertzberg 1966:50). The presence of their children and kin-based communal work groups made the hard lives of women socially stable and emotionally satisfying. Mary Jemison, the "White Woman of the Genesee," who was captured by the Shawnee at the age of fifteen and adopted by Senecas four years later in 1762, reported that Indian life for women compared favorably with that of contemporary white women (Seaver 1961:55). Significantly, she chose to remain with the Senecas when return to white society was possible. Diane Rothenberg (1980:79), noting the resistance of Seneca women to Quaker-inspired changes, specifically individual landownership, suggests that the women were concerned with the loss of these work groups should land no longer be held communally. Other Quaker innovations, such as weaving, introduced as individual activities, were quickly modified by Seneca women to fit their collective work pattern.

Those who seek a political explanation for the status of Iroquois women cite their power in three main circumstances: their nomination of Confederacy chiefs, their participation in village and tribal decision making, and their control over the fate of war captives. Because women were entitled to demand revenge after the death of kin, some have assumed that women possessed the authority to initiate raiding parties (Allen 1986:213; Bonvillain 1980:57). In fact, however, no Iroquois had the power to force another to undertake any such action. At most, Iroquois women could make their feelings known, apply informal pressure, and perhaps shame men into retaliation (Wallace 1969:29, 46). Beyond this, women could influence the decision to go to war by means of their control over the distribution of horticultural produce. Refusal to release food to a potential war party was normally sufficient to scuttle a planned raid. Female influence over war policy was significant but certainly fell short of their having the authority to initiate armed combat.

The founding of the League of the Iroquois dates to at least the sixteenth century (Tooker 1978:420–22) and resulted from the need of the five Iroquoian-speaking nations (from east to west: Mohawk, Oneida, Onondaga, Cayuga, Seneca) to end internecine warfare (Wallace 1969:42). The two culture heroes, Deganawidah and Hia-watha (Longfellow stole his name and made him Ojibway), took the message of the Great Peace to the Five Nations, eventually securing their assent to a confederation comprised of fifty chiefs (all male), but because women were the first to accept the message of Deganawidah, the titles of the chiefs were made hereditary in the lines of females (Fenton 1968b:34). Although women could not be chiefs, they could name them, implying some control over their actions.

Section 54 of the Newhouse version of the Constitution of the Five Nations (Fenton 1968b) states that when a chiefly title becomes vacant, the women of the clan in which the title is vested choose someone to fill the office. If the choice is unanimous, the name is then submitted to the male members of the clan, who, if they disapprove, select their own candidate. If the clan members are unable to decide, the decision is referred to the clan's Confederacy chiefs who render the final decision (ibid., 44).

A more important source of control was in the women's ability to remove or "dehorn" errant chiefs, yet even these rights were not without significant limitations. In particular, section 19 states that both men and women could come to Council and upbraid a chief through the War Chief. If, after three warnings, the chief failed to comply, the matter was referred to a council of War Chiefs who could divest the chief of his title by order of the women (ibid., 34). It is not clear whether the women sanctioned the actions recommended by the War Chiefs' council or vice versa. Section 59 also concerns the Confederacy's response to erring chiefs who did not heed the third warning of their female relatives. The matter was referred to the general council of women, then the men of the Confederacy, and finally to the War Chiefs if the previous sets of three warnings were ignored. If these warnings also failed, then the men could decide to depose or execute the chief (ibid., 46). While women were the first to formally point out inappropriate actions by a chief, and in most cases their warnings were probably sufficient to correct the unacceptable behavior, there appears to have been a higher level of sanction within the domain of men.

As William N. Fenton (1949) pointed out, Newhouse's version of the founding and so-called Constitution of the Five Nations needs to be understood in the context of late nineteenth-century politics at the Six Nations Reserve in Ontario, Canada. At that time the Canadian government was attempting to impose an elective system of govern-ment on the reserve, which was led by the hereditary chiefs of the Confederacy. Newhouse, as speaker for the warriors and women, represented a traditionalist response to the forces favoring change. His manuscript, heavily edited and codified by Arthur C. Parker (Fenton 1968b:38), was intended to demonstrate the continued utility of the League, even if it meant increasing the authority of the council. Although the ambiguity of the above noted sections may represent translation difficulties, more likely it reflects Newhouse's politically motivated attempt to strengthen the voice of council at the expense of the matrons (Weaver 1984:177), perhaps to appease other factions. However, another version of the Constitution, the so-called Chiefs' Version (Scott 1911), which was approved by the chiefs at Six Nations after they had rejected Newhouse's attempt, also shows that the power of women to appoint and remove errant chiefs was not without male review (ibid., 223–32). Parker's (1968:11) view of Iroquois women with ultimate political power therefore appears unsubstantiated.

Additionally, while women were instrumental in naming the Confederacy chiefs, it is important to note that this prerogative of women in certain clans cannot be extrapolated to infer political power for *all* women. As Tooker (1984:113–14) points out, Confederacy chiefs were not properly representative of clans. Of the eight chiefly titles belonging to the Senecas, three were held by one clan, two by another, one each by two others, and three clans had no chiefly titles. Furthermore, although clan matrons were supposed to consult with other clan women, this was often not the case, and they usually chose a close relative (ibid., 114).

Iroquois society in the precontact period was most likely characterized by complementary gender roles with matrilineal descent and matrilocal residence suitable for a horicultural society where males were often absent hunting or on the warpath. As noted, Richards (1957:36) has shown that prior to 1784 there was a significant shift in the direction of increased power for women. Her study considers women's roles in determining the fate of captives, arranging marriages, and the control of children. Supporting this is a change in incest regulations that had formerly prohibited marriage with both maternal and paternal kin but that, by 1851, was limited to maternal kin (ibid., 39). This suggests the increasing importance of the matrilineage in the years following contact. The descriptions of Morgan (1962) are of a nineteenth-century Seneca society following three and one-half centuries of contact and should not be seen as typical of the aboriginal condition.

The previous discussion, with several exceptions, has concerned the Iroquois in general. In the nineteenth and twentieth centuries it is most useful to focus on women of the Seneca Nation, since the changes they encountered were more abrupt and long-lasting. These occurred in response to a particular set of historical circumstances, and it would be inaccurate to assume that conclusions about their status, especially after 1848, are applicable to other Iroquois women.

The close of the eighteenth century saw the lands of the Seneca significantly reduced. Of their original 4,000,000-acre domain, the Seneca now retained fewer than 200,000 acres in ten separate tracts, including two of forty-two square miles each along Cattaraugus Creek and the Allegheny River (Chazanof 1970:22; Abler and Tooker 1978:508). The pressures of continued contact and the presence of alcohol led to increased factionalism and anxiety, underscoring the lack of effective leadership (Wallace 1969:444). In June 1799, Handsome Lake, an Allegany Seneca, had the first of his series of visions in which he met representatives of the Creator. In the words of Anthony F. C. Wallace (1969:239), these prophetic visions "articulated the dilemmas in which the Iroquois were trapped and prescribed both religious and secular solutions." It is the latter that have the most bearing on gender. The social gospel of Handsome Lake evolved more slowly than the religious ideology and, in general, supported the assimilationist views of his half-brother, Cornplanter, and showed the influence of the Quakers and federal officials who supported the movement. Handsome Lake's social gospel, which was set forth in 1801, emphasized the nuclear family, with the husband-wife relationship taking precedence over other kin ties (sections 6–8 of the Gai'wiio', Edward Cornplanter version) (Fenton 1968a:31–32). While he stressed the traditional reciprocity of gender rules, these were recast so that the proper husband was now to be a successful farmer, building a house for his wife and family. The wife's duty was to be a good homemaker (Wallace 1969:285). There is still disagreement on the extent to which Seneca men took over the farming activities (Rothenberg 1980, n.d.; Wallace 1969), but it is clear that the Quakers were successful in prevailing on the Seneca to adopt single-family log and shingle fenced farmsteads in place of the matrilineage longhouses (Fenton 1967:2). Within a generation, the transition from matrilineal extended family household to nuclear family household was complete, with families eventually becoming patrilineal with respect to both name and inheritance (Wallace 1969:312). The effect on women's roles was great. Wallace (1969:28), who used Handsome Lake as a model for his general theory of revitalization movements, refers to his reforms as "a sentence of doom on the traditional quasi-matriarchal system." Allen (1986:32) sees them as signaling the overthrow of the gynocracy and the concomitant partriarchalization of Seneca society. While women's roles in the new religion were important (e.g., there were equal numbers of male and female Faithkeepers, only female-tended crops such as corn received ritual recognition, etc.), their economic roles were reduced.

The next significant change in gender roles occurred in 1848 with the formation of the Seneca Nation of Indians, a change that further eroded the formal political roles of Seneca women on the Allegany and Cattaraugus reservations. Factionalism continued, and there was disagreement on whether annuity payments should be given to the chiefs for distribution or to family heads. Land sales, accomplished by means of forgery, bribery, and alcohol, left the Senecas without land in New York in 1840. Aided by the Quakers, Daniel Webster, and Lewis Henry Morgan, the Senecas were able to negotiate a compromise treaty in 1842 which returned to them the Allegany and Cattaraugus reservations as well as the tiny Oil Spring Reservation. Frustration over land loss and annuity payments led to the birth of the Seneca Nation of Indians on December 4, 1848, at a general convention on the Cattaraugus Reservation. Government by chiefs at Allegany and Cattaraugus was abolished and replaced by an annually elected Council of eighteen (now sixteen) members and an Executive consisting of President, Clerk, and Treasurer. The judicial office of Peacemaker was retained. As a result of this change, relations between these reservations and the Senecas at the Tonawanda Reservation were severed and the Seneca Nation withdrew from the Confederacy based at Onondaga. Since the written constitution of the Nation, based on a text by tribal attorney Chester Howe, reflected contemporary white customs, women were disenfranchised: only males could vote, and only males could hold office.

For the next century or so, women's status changed little. By the beginning of the twentieth century, their economic roles consisted of homemaking, with few, if any, holding outside employment. Wage labor was within the domain of men, many of whom now worked for the railroads that ran through the Allegany Reservation. In a way, the old forest/clearing dichotomy continued, albeit in a modern guise, with women's roles devalued, at least by white society, because they were not income producing. Since the traditional role of women focused on the home and children, Seneca women probably did not feel the status loss that appears great to non-Indian women of the late twentieth century. At Allegany, women still collected fruits and berries, made medicines, wove baskets, and planted their gardens. Some worked as domestics for white women in nearby villages, and by midcentury a few held clerical jobs.

The next assault on Seneca land came in the 1960s with construction of Kinzua Dam in Pennsylvania. This resulted in the flooding of one-third of the 30,000-acre Allegany Reservation (another 10,000 acres were occupied by non-Indian villages). Although the Allegany Senecas fought valiantly to stop the dam, again with Quaker allies, their attempts proved futile. Women still did not have voting rights in the Seneca Nation, but they rapidly mobilized to staff committees. They became involved first in attempts to stop the dam and later in organizing the removal. Several Seneca women informed congressional committees of their lack of voice in Seneca politics, indicating that the Seneca President did not speak for them. Women were active on committees and concentrated their efforts in the areas of housing and education, again paralleling traditional roles. The franchise was finally extended to women in 1964 after dam construction was nearly complete and the first families had relocated. Surprisingly, men on the Allegany Reservation voted not to grant women voting rights; however, favorable votes at Cattaraugus resulted in the passage of the measure.

My initial hypothesis in exploring the long-term effects of forced relocation was that, once again, women's roles would be diminished, but this was not supported by my research. While women reported slightly more trauma, due more to the fact that they had to deal with the daily problems that accompanied removal than with gender, they also seemed most pleased with the improved housing. To a surprising extent, the benefits that accrued to women from the dam were greater than those for men. This is most apparent in the expansion of political and economic roles for women. Jobs created by the increasing size of the Seneca Nation of Indians (SNI) government, which only hired its first full-time employee in 1962, provided employment choices not previously available for women, at least not on the reservation. Even though many were low-paying and low-prestige jobs, they were avenues to advancement. There were also administrative jobs where women could put to use the newly developed skills that they acquired as volunteers in the fight against the dam. The success of the education program was due primarily to women, who, disenfranchised at the time, set up a separate Seneca Nation Education Foundation outside the control of the Council to administer the $1.8 million program in which they maintained female input, if not control. This program, along with other development programs, was funded through "reha- bilitation funds" awarded by Congress to the Nation in recognition of its loss of land and the disruption of the lifeways on the Allegany Reservation. The allocation of these funds was determined by the Seneca Nation itself and involved significant community input. Com- munity Action Programs of the Great Society also provided leadership and management experience for women by providing additional jobs and outlets for volunteer work. With new jobs and careers open to them, a number of women continued their education as adult learners, earning bachelor's and master's degrees, a pattern that continues. The right to vote and hold office, while perhaps more related to the tenor of the times, in particular the civil rights movement, than to Kinzua Dam, gave women the long-sought entreé into the formal political structure. The experiences of the dam fight provided them with greater insight into workings of Seneca, state, and federal government systems and probably allowed them to move more rapidly into positions of authority. It is interesting that many women seem to play instrumental roles. For example, all of the 1986 SNI presidential candidates had female campaign managers. Whether this is a holdover from the times when women's political role was primarily behind-the-scenes manipu- lation or whether it is merely coincidental is unknown.

While women were elected to the Council shortly after they were enfranchised, since 1964 no women have run for president of the

Seneca Nation and only two women have been the head of a reservation (Allegany), serving as treasurer. The elective offices of clerk and surrogate (judge) have tended to be filled by women, and women currently head the SNI Education and Health departments, the largest agencies of the Nation. In both of those departments the majority of the employees are female, and they hold administrative and professional posts as well as clerical ones.

Women of the Seneca Nation still retain complete control over the clearing, as their primacy within the home has never been challenged, and they are moving into those realms of the forest that have the most direct impact on the clearing, such as education and health care. As might be expected, this role expansion has met with some opposition from Seneca men, but it is clear that women have regained a position of, at least, equality. Although job segregation exists, it lacks the differential valuation that it has in the non-Indian world.

7

THE PLAINS

BLACKFOOT PERSONS

ALICE B. KEHOE

The Blackfoot occupied the northwestern Plains, from western Saskatchewan and eastern Montana to the Front Range of the Rockies in
Montana and Alberta. This is a region of high, rolling plains, originally covered with shortgrass prairie. Its rivers drain eastward into the
South Saskatchewan and Missouri, linking the Blackfoot to the
midcontinental trading networks. A map drawn by the Blackfoot
leader Ac-ko-mok-ki in 1801 shows the vast range from central Alberta
south into northern Wyoming and east into the Missouri River Valley
plus the Montana passes and Flathead Valley, with the Snake and
Columbia rivers giving access to the Pacific coast. Since the mountains
offered fewer resources, Blackfoot country comprised the foothills, the
outlier hills, and the prairie.

Grasses, enhanced by the Indians' practice of regularly firing the
prairie, are the dominant vegetation of Blackfoot country. Stream
valleys support cottonwoods; the slopes of the mountains, including
the outlier Sweetgrass hills, Bearpaw Mountains, and Cypress Hills,
support lodgepole pines; and on sheltered ravine slopes are chokecher-
ry and saskatoon berry bushes. Camas bulbs were cultivated and
harvested from suitably watered fields, and prairie turnips were obtained from sandy, well-drained locations. Bison was the principal
large animal on the prairie; antelope were found on the open plains;
and elk and deer were found in the mountains and ravines. Eagles,
hawks, prairie grouse, migratory ducks and geese, and songbirds were

113

the most important birds culturally. Blackfoot did not eat fish, although they were available.

HISTORY

The Blackfoot speakers of an Algonkian language have lived on the northwestern Plains at least since the seventeenth century and very probably for two or possibly more centuries earlier. When first documented by Europeans—young Henry Kelsey in 1690—the three divisions of the Blackfoot (Blood [Kainah], Piegan [Pikuni], and [North] Blackfoot [Siksika]) held the parkland and plains of southwestern Saskatchewan. They moved west and southwest during the fur trade era, fighting during the next two centuries for the high plains along the Front Range of the Rockies in southern Alberta and adjacent north-central Montana. The Blackfoot depended on bison herds, hunting them by driving and impounding.

Bison pounds are the dominant type of archaeological site in the northwestern Plains. They have been the principal method of subsistence on the northwestern Plains for two thousand years and date from as early as the Paleo-Indian period. Operating a pound was a communal endeavor requiring all the able-bodied adults of a typical Plains Indian band. In the historic period, a single young man acted as scout and lured the herd to the drive lane, where other men and women waited to startle and drive the animals along the funnel into the corral, where men with clubs and bow were ready to dispatch them. Both men and women butchered the animals, and the women processed the meat for preservation by drying. Hide tanning was also the women's job. Meat was supplemented by berries, roots, bulbs, and tubers, particularly the prairie turnip and camas. Women and children gathered these foods, and women increased the harvest of camas by cultivating camas beds. Economically, women were essential in both the production and processing of the necessities of life.

The economic role of women was clearly recognized by the Blackfoot in that women owned the products of their labor, amounting, as Clark Wissler (1911:27) put it, to "the greater part of the baggage." Because the tipi was a product of women's labor, the very roof over a man's head was not his but a woman's property. Some women specialized in certain crafts, such as tipi making, and exchanged or sold their work in the specialty to other women. Wissler recorded the renown of such craftswomen:

> In pre-reservation days a woman was judged by the number and quality of skins she had dressed, the baskets she had woven, or the pottery moulded; and her renown for such accomplishments might travel far. When by chance you met a woman who had distinguished herself, it was proper to address her in a manner to reveal your knowledge of her reputation, as "Grandmother, we are happy to look upon one whose hands were always busy curing fine skins." (Wissler 1938:290)

Wealth—ownership of horses, clothes and other objects of fine craftsmanship, medicine bundles, and in the reservation era, cattle and cash (used to support ceremonies and gift giving)—distinguish leading families from commoners among the Blackfoot. Both men and women are admired for wealth and the power it brings. Particularly noteworthy is the designation *ninauposkitzipxpe*, manly-hearted woman (Lewis 1941). About a third of elderly (sixty years or older) North Piegan women in 1939, and a few younger women, were considered manly-hearted (ibid., 176). Such women owned property, were good managers and usually effective workers, were forthright and assertive in public, in their homes, and as sexual partners, and were active in religious rituals. They were called "manly-hearted" because boldness, aggressiveness, and a drive to amass property and social power are held to be ideal traits for men. Blackfoot men claim they want women to be submissive, docile, and quiet—that is, women should be opposite in character to the ideal man—but in fact, the manly-hearted woman is admired as well as feared by both men and women.[1] Her control of

1. Ruth Benedict wrote to Oscar Lewis on April 9 and August 11, 1940, discussing the draft of his paper on manly-hearted women. Benedict had directed the 1939 Columbia University Laboratory (for ethnography) held on the four Blackfoot reserves. She commented to Lewis on his paper, "It's a very pretty point and a definite addition to our knowledge of the way a cultural over-emphasis or distortion can break a normal curve into a two-mode curve. At least that is the way I should interpret it. . . . As you describe Blackfoot ethos, it seems clear that emphasis upon self-assertiveness is so strong that to

property and her ability to control social situations are the tangible manifestations of the power with which she is perceived to be gifted (Kehoe 1976).[2]

THE ROLE OF WOMEN PRESENTED THROUGH MYTH

Women's roles in ritual and myth reflect their economic power. Women are seen as the intermediary or means through which power has been granted to humans. This crucial role appears in medicine bundle openings: only a woman should unwrap and rewrap a holy bundle. She hands the powerful objects inside to the male celebrant. It is important to note that the woman sits quietly behind the man and to European eyes seems to be a servant. The Blackfoot see the woman as more powerful than the man, who dares not handle the bundle entire and alone. The modesty of the woman's dress and her manner is a sign of her *intrinsic* power: she is so secure in it that she need not flaunt her role.

The Blackfoot Sun Dance is a more obvious manifestation of the superior spiritual power of women: the Sun Dance ceremony is led by a woman and cannot be held if no woman is willing to undertake the arduous fasting and heavy responsibility of the Holy Woman role. As with the women who open medicine bundles, the costume and positioning of the Holy Woman is modest, even retiring. She wears a very plain robe, given by the mythical Elk Woman whose husband suspected her of adultery. With his comrades, a moose and a crow (or raven), Elk pursued his wife to punish her. When he found her, they agreed to test their respective power by attempting to butt down the tree at which Elk Woman stood. Elk hooked his antlers at the tree but

---

expect women reared in such an atmosphere to all be mild and submissive is too great a demand to make—and so you get the secondary mode—manly hearted women. . . . You use the fact that many people disagreed about whether some of the young women were or were not to be classified as manly hearted as an index or proof of culture change. This seems a doubtful point. . . . I should think . . . these very young women had not yet made clear enough decisions so that everyone could agree upon their manliheartedness" (letter of August 11, 1940, in possession of Ruth Maslow Lewis).

2. I am deeply grateful to Ruth M. Lewis for her generosity in sending me copies of her and her husband's 1939 field notes on manly-hearted women and copies of Benedict's letters on the Blackfoot.

could not bring it down. Elk Woman then hooked at it, and it toppled. Elk's comrades gave her tokens—Moose his hooves and Crow his tail feathers. In the Sun Dance, the Holy Woman in her elk robe and headdress with moose hooves and crow tail feathers makes butting motions toward the cut tree that serves as center pole, *axis mundi*, of the Holy Lodge.

The headdress of the Sun Dance's Holy Woman carries a token of a second ancient woman, Woman Who Married Morning Star. This beautiful young woman gazed on the brilliant Morning Star and wished aloud that she could marry him. He appeared before her and took her to the Above World, into the tipi of his parents, Sun and Moon. There the young couple lived happily, the bride bearing a son to Morning Star, until one day she disobeyed her in-laws' warning to avoid digging up prairie turnips, a root vegetable frequently cooked in stews by the aboriginal Blackfoot. Woman Who Married Morning Star one day noticed an especially large and fine prairie turnip and impulsively dug it up with her digging stick. Then she could see, through the hole in the sky land, her people in their camp below. Homesickness filled her heart. Her parents-in-law recognized it and regretfully sent her and her baby back down. Her prairie turnip and her digging stick are now in the Sun Dance (Natoas) bundle, carried by the Holy Woman as a sign of the power of woman to move between the Holy People of the Above World and the people below. The hide ropes tying the rafters of the Holy Lodge are those along which Woman Who Married Morning Star slid from the Above World to earth (Ground 1978:20).

Myths recount, one after another, how women bring blessings to the people. The most powerful medicine bundles, the Beaver bundle that must be opened with the first thunder in spring and the Thunder pipe bundle, were both brought to the Blackfoot through the agency of human women. The Thunder pipe bundle with which I am most familiar is owned by a woman, Mollie Kicking Woman (Pikuni), and had been owned by her mother before her. Bison drives depended for their success on the enactment of the calling ritual that had been taught to a woman by a spirit power manifested in a bison-shaped object, the *iniskim*. The people had been starving, and the woman was

117

in the bush searching for food for her family when she heard the spirit's song. Pitying her, it gave her the means to obtain the abundance of meat, leather, and tool material found in bison. Iniskim are commonly fossil ammonites that can be found on the eastern part of the Blackfeet Reservation in Montana. Our late friend Mae Williamson (Pikuni) told us how one had called to her many years before, when she was young, as she rode over the prairie. She picked it up, and it brought her health and prosperity. None of the medicines originally vouchsafed to men are as important to the people as these gained through women.

Although most of the literature on Blackfoot spirituality is concerned with the medicine bundles, individuals have obtained power directly and used it as shamans. The ethnographer Claude Schaeffer obtained descriptions of a holy man named Four Bears (Nisóxkyaio), a Pikuni who died at an advanced age in about 1889. Schaeffer's informants, Adam White Man and Fish Wolf Robe, had seen Four Bears when they were children, and he is alluded to by Walter McClintock (1910:321). Four Bears had power from—was pitied by, as the Blackfoot phrase it—the Moon, a feminine aspect of the Holy (e.g., the wife of the Sun). Moon's power enabled Four Bears to give some power for prosperity to youths who solicited this aid. Adam White Man's father had Four Bears come to his lodge to give such power to his sons, Adam and Bull Shoe. Honored by the presentation of blankets and other gifts, Four Bears demonstrated his power by spitting out a small iniskim, a lead bullet, and hailstones. He gave Adam and Bull Shoe hailstones to swallow, thus incorporating some of his power into their bodies. Fish Wolf Robe had similarly been given a hailstone to swallow so that he would prosper.

Older youths came to Four Bears to obtain power to succeed in war raids. Four Bears would offer these youths a choice of horses, captured guns, or engagement in battle. Most youths are said to have chosen horses. Four Bears would describe the horses to be captured and announce he was giving it to the petitioner. The youth then had to suckle like an infant at Four Bears' nipple. This act was supposed to bind the youth to his nurturer as by a string. Whenever he performed as a holy person (but not in everyday life), Four Bears dressed as a woman to signify his power came from the Moon. When a youth he had nurtured had been gone several days on a raid, Four Bears would don his woman's dress, come into the center of the camp, request the Sun to aid the young man, and ask it to move visibly as a sign of the raider's success. Lack of movement would indicate the raider's death. Fish Wolf Robe remembered that the people would look at the sun as Four Bears directed and see it move.

Four Bears had power to cause weather changes by gesturing toward the sun with a willow branch ornamented with two magpie tail feathers. His own symbolic ornaments included bracelets with elk teeth, reminiscent of Elk Woman who sang as she proved her power by hooking at the tree, "My wristlets are elk-teeth; they are powerful" (Wissler and Duvall 1908:84). When in costume, Four Bears wore on his head a band of fisher fur. Fishers, the largest of the martens, are like otters, beavers, and the mythical water-bull (also translated water-bear), a mammal that frequents water, an anomaly that because it transcends the normal order of nature must be unusually spiritually potent. Four Bears in his costume similarly transcended the normal order of men.

Blackfoot sodalities for the most part include both men and women, usually as couples. Of the age-grade societies, only the boys' lacked women members. Adult men in societies were expected to be accompanied by their wives, who took part in the rituals and feasts and sang as the men, or men and women, danced. The Bloods, one of the three divisions of the Blackfoot confederacy, had a women's society called the Ma'toki in which men served only in auxiliary roles. The Ma'toki danced as bison and apparently were believed to be instrumental in bringing bison, and thus prosperity, to the people. With the disappearance of the bison herds, the Ma'toki went into decline. The most feared of the societies is the Horns, said to have life and death power. They require initiates to be couples, because the man obtains power only through intercourse with his wife who has just received this power by ceremonial intercourse with a "grandfather," a man who is already a member. This mode of initiation parallels the role of women as intermediary between bundle and male celebrant and the Holy Woman as initiator and creator of the Sun Dance. The Ma'toki and the Horns are said to have been founded by a couple of which the husband was human and the wife a bison cow. She (in human form) was a perfect wife, but one day the husband struck her because she failed to hurry to prepare food for his guests. The wife and their little son reverted to bison form and rejoined her herd. After a series of ordeals, the chastened husband was reunited with his wife and child, and the couple began the two powerful sodalities.

ROLES OF WOMEN AND MEN IN BLACKFOOT SOCIETY

All of this may seem to indicate that Blackfoot women are superior to men. This would be a misstatement, a failure to understand the actual statuses of men and women in Blackfoot eyes. Algonkian languages do not distinguish male and female through lexical gender. Instead, they distinguish animate from inanimate. Everything that exhibits volition through movement—humans, animals, and manifestations of power such as thunder and rocks in odd places—is marked by the animate gender. Within that gender, the various species have differing degrees of power. Bison, beavers, and otters are more powerful than humans. Some humans are more powerful than other humans. In humans, degree of power (i.e., spiritual power) is evidenced by health, strength, longevity, and success in undertakings, including skill in hunting, in crafts, or in judgment. People can attempt to add to their power by going out alone to a lonely place where they make themselves pitiable by crying out, naked and hungry, begging the Almighty to relieve them by granting power.

Women are believed to have more innate power than men, because they are born with power to reproduce both the human and the material components of the social world. Fewer women than men feel the need to go out crying to be pitied and favored with power. Some do seek more power, and women as well as men inherit and buy medicine bundles. Men formerly routinely went out crying for power (the "vision quest") in adolescence, and many men did so again as adults. Men's inability to bear children was interpreted as a sign of lesser reproductive power, carrying over to an inability to make—reproduce—tipis, clothing, or well-prepared meals (see Appendix, "The First Marriages"). Men provided raw materials, from semen to slaughtered bison, and women processed raw materials into the components of civilized society.

Men and women are necessary pairs. Society cannot survive without the sexual pairing of men and women. On painted tipis (which are a form of medicine bundles), animals are depicted in pairs, male and female. Even in the Above World, Sun and Moon are a pair, masculine and feminine. Rituals invoke both, as Old Man and Old Woman (Wissler 1912:271); in the ritual of opening the Sun Dance Natoas bundle, for example, the celebrant sings (ibid., 217),

> Old man comes in and sits down. He says, I am looking for my natoas. I have found it. It is powerful.
> Old woman has come in. She says, I am looking for my natoas. I have found it. It is powerful.

Sun, Natos, is Old Man here in reference to his long existence.

The Blackfoot tell many stories about another Old Man, Napi, a character similar to Coyote in the tales of Indian peoples west of the Rockies. Napi, like the Sun, is "old" only in the sense of having existed in the beginning of time. Impulsive, naive, lustful, scheming, Napi is primordial Man. The Blackfeet Heritage Program dedicated a volume of Napi stories "to those that understand Napi, who lives in us all" (Rides At The Door 1979:6). Napi is always a man and in only a few stories is accompanied by a woman. He personifies the foolishness in human nature, and it is significant that this quality is shown as especially dominant in a man. There is no comparable corpus of stories about a foolish woman. Thus although men and women are normally paired, engaged in the complementary tasks of procuring and processing, men must strive harder to become respected adults. In contemporary powwows, men dance as individuals, using the whole body and wearing elaborate flamboyant costumes, calling attention to themselves. Women dance in company, keeping the body upright, wearing modest dresses with tasteful bead or elk tooth ornamentation and a fine shawl. The women's apparent modesty comes from self-confidence, the knowledge that in woman's nature there is less Napi foolishness, more innate power. Men display themselves more conspicuously, counteracting the insecurity accompanying the Napi in them.

What really matters to a Blackfoot is autonomy, personal autonomy. Blackfoot respect each person's competence, even the competence of very small children, and avoid bossing others. People seek power to support the autonomy they so highly value. Competence is the outward justification of the exercise of autonomy. If a person competently engages in work or behavior ordinarily the domain of people of the other sex, or of another species, onlookers assume the person has been blessed, either uninvited or through seeking, by spiritual power to behave in this unusual manner. A woman who wanted to go to war, and there were many such, was judged as a man would be by her success in counting coup or seizing enemy weapons. A nineteenth-century Blackfoot woman led war parties for years and lived celibate most of those years, not because she had to be asexual but because the role of war leader (as opposed to member of the war party), with its ritual obligations, left no time for the homemaking tasks a man would need from the woman he lived with.

A child's biological sex, for the Blackfoot, is a sign of innate capacities and probable task preferences. Men are more flamboyant, more visible because in order to live, they must strive to gain the pity of spiritual powers and the attention of women who provide them with homes and sustenance. Women keep quietly busy exercising their innate powers of homemaking and child care. Prestige and influence are earned by Blackfoot through the demonstration of vigor, competence, wisdom, and dignity. These qualities cluster around the central value, autonomy, the mark of animate gender. As Krystyna Sieciechowicz (1990:169) remarked for the Northern Ojibwa-Cree, "Status is largely achieved and should not be confused with the question of equality or egalitarian relations." Peter M. Gardner (1991) claims that individual autonomy is a dominant, usually realized, value characteristic of small nonagricultural societies (his "foragers," not really an appropriate label for the efficient animal-products economy of the prereservation Blackfoot [Kehoe 1993]). He highlights a set of societal attributes that seem, from the ethnographic literature, to co-occur in such societies and suggests that the "syndrome" reflects similar determining factors. Gardner's comparative study supports the identification of autonomy as a major value among the Blackfoot.

In the Ojibwa-Cree communities in which Sieciechowicz worked, most women commanded the same productive skills as men did and used them: deeply respected women, like men, regularly demonstrated high competence in bringing in the resources of the land. Like Blackfoot women, Ojibwa-Cree women seemed not to boast as men did, or seek overt approval, a reticence that has led, Sieciechowicz (1990:173) believes, to neglect of women's productivity. Julie Cruikshank (1990), collaborating with Dene women, found them emphasizing heroines' resourcefulness in escaping predicaments. Male central characters usually had transgressed against powerful beings and needed a shaman's aid to return to ordinary life. Female characters usually had been seized by intruders. Although male relatives often appeared to rescue the damsel, it was her ingenuity that guided them to success. These eastern and western Subarctic societies, respectively, have been similar to prereservation Blackfoot in an economic pattern that visualized men as operating distant from camp and women remaining around camp. Sieciechowicz and Cruikshank, as also Richard Nelson (1983:6) and Adrian Tanner (1979:91) on other Dene and Cree, show that this idealization fits anthropological stereotypes but not reality. H. I. S. Sharp (n.d.), pressing beyond the simplistic question of who produces most to an engagement with the issue of power, dissects the standard picture of Chipewyan women oppressed by brutal men—the darker side of Cruikshank's ingenious, resourceful Dene women. These several contemporary studies can assist a critical reading of the century-old Blackfoot ethnographies by drawing out the quotidian demands of life in northern hunting societies, which the Blackfoot border.

All our ethnographic sources on the Blackfoot and my own experience living on the Blackfeet Reservation concur on the independence and respect given to Blackfoot women. That women are intermediary between men and Power, and that Blackfoot men are impelled to strive much harder to gain power has not generally been remarked. Such observances run counter to our conventions (Kehoe 1983). The question that stimulated this volume—what have been the relative statuses of men and women, as categories, in North American Indian societies—fits our conventions but would be of little moment for Blackfoot. The fact that gender, in Blackfoot, distinguishes animate from inanimate subordinates "gender roles" to the basic prerogative of living beings, the exercise of autonomy. Rather than static categories, Blackfoot understanding posits a world of manifestations rooted in an Almighty, animating Power. Any being might be imbued to a surprising degree with power. That females are gifted with more power than males is seen in their innately greater reproductive capacity, but anyone can aspire to becoming more powerful. Talking about Indo-European gender categories misses the point.

APPENDIX

The First Marriage

The popular narrative of men's and women's original social condition eloquently conveys Blackfoot attitudes—men's pitiable natural state, women's innate gifts and the respect due their vocation. Ol' Napi blunders, as he usually does, put off by clothes soiled by hard work instead of valuing the productive industry of the woman inside the dress. This version of the narrative was told by Joseph Tatsey to the Dutch linguist C. C. Uhlenbeck in 1911. I have inserted a couple of passages, from Clark Wissler and D. C. Duvall's version, that Tatsey omitted.

> The women . . . made buffalo-corrals. Their lodges were fine. . . . They tanned the buffalo-hides, those were their robes. They would cut meat in slices. . . . [T]heir lodges all fine inside. And their things were just as fine. . . . Now, the men . . . were very poor. They made corrals. They had no lodges, they wore raw-hides . . . for robes. They wore the gamble-joint of the buffalo for moccasins. They did not know, how they should make lodges. They did not know, how they should tan the buffalo-hides. They did not know, too, how they should cut dried meat, how they should

sew their clothes. The women's chief told them: Over there near the corral are the men sitting in sight. All these women were cutting meat. Their chief did not take off the clothes, she was cutting the meat with. They were told by her: I shall go up there first. I shall take my choice. When I come back, you will go up one by one. Now we will take husbands. Then she started up. Then she went up to all those men. She asked them: Which is your chief? The men said: This one here, Wolf-robe [Napi]. She told him: Now we will take you for husbands. And then she walked to that Wolf-robe. She caught him. Then she started to pull him up. Then he pulled back. Then she let him loose. He did not like her clothes. (While the other women were picking out their husbands, the chief of the women put on her best costume. When she came out, she looked very fine, and, as soon as Old Man saw her, he thought, "Oh! there is the chief of the women. I wish to be her husband. [Wissler and Duvall 1908:221])

Wolf-robe was standing up alone. He was told by that chief-woman: Turn into a pine-tree, right there where you stand. He got angry. He commenced to knock down that buffalo-corral. And then he turned into a pine-tree. (Uhlenbeck 1912:167–69)

And he is mad yet, because he is always caving down the bank. (Wissler and Duvall 1908:22)

8

California

EVOLVING GENDER ROLES IN POMO SOCIETY

Victoria D. Patterson

The Pomo still live in the lands they have always inhabited, known today as Sonoma, Mendocino, and Lake counties, California. A varied topography ranging from the Pacific coast in the west through riverine valleys, high ridges, and deep canyons to the lacustrine marshes of Clear Lake in the east offered abundant and easily obtainable food. Acorns were the staple of a diet supplemented by a wide variety of fish, game, and seasonal greens, roots, bulbs, and seeds.

The people, called Pomos by anthropologists and linguists on the basis of language family similarities, actually spoke seven mutually unintelligible languages and lived in small bands or tribelets, separated from each other by the mountainous ridges and steep canyons of the region. All of the Pomo linguistic groups, Northern Pomo, Central Pomo, Southern Pomo, Southwestern (Kashaya) Pomo, Eastern Pomo, Northeastern Pomo, and Southeastern Pomo, shared generally similar lifeways, although the resources available to them for food and tools varied with their particular surroundings and some variety in cultural beliefs and practices developed as a result of geographic isolation and local custom. The bands were based on consanguineous relationships and maintained independent but allied political and economic exis-tences. The family was central, and the relationship between the sexes was complementary. Each had necessary and equally valued roles in the maintenance of society.

The social organization of these kin-related bands emphasized cooperation along with a respect for a certain type of individuality. The individual in a band based on kinship saw himself or herself as an integral part of the family-based community, and thus the individual's contributions and participation sustained and enriched the respect and welfare of both group and self. It is an ideal of such a community that every member will make group survival the supreme rule of common behavior. This is in opposition to the notion of "individualism" in which the individual acts on his or her own, apart from the group, to control and exploit it for personal ends, in which survival itself is an isolated right of the individual alone (Kearney 1984; Illich 1982).

The idea of responsibility toward the kin group is expressed clearly in the turn-of-the-century remarks of Tom Johnson, an Eastern Pomo from Lake County:

> What is man? A man is nothing. Without his family he is of less importance than that bug crossing the trail, of less importance than spit or dung. At least they can be used to help poison a man. A man must be with his family to amount to anything with us . . . If a man has a large family and a profession and upbringing by a family that is known to produce good children, then he is somebody, and every family is willing to have him marry a woman of their group. . . . Without the family we are nothing, and in the old days before the white people came, the family was given the first consideration by anyone who was about to do anything at all. That is why we got along. . . . The family was everything and no man ever forgot that. Each person was nothing; but as a group joined by blood, the individual knew that he would get the support of all his relatives if anything happened. (Levene 1976)

The family, essential for Pomo survival, was possible only between gendered people conceived of as men and women. Kinship, for them, presupposed two genders that it related and organized: Pomo family means a male father, a female mother, their children, their adopted children, the mother's and father's parents and siblings, their spouses and children. These formed the society.

Gender is distinct from sex role. As Ivan Illich (1982:83) has written, "Gender not only tells who is who, but it also defines who is when, where and with which tools and words; it divides space, time and technique. It is a fundamental 'vernacular' as opposed to the learned and taught behavior of sex role whose 'carrier' is assumed a 'plastic' individual having a genderless existence that is more or less shaped by 'sex.'" In a reciprocal relationship with kinship, "gender sets limits to the social structure it forms, a structure expressed in every aspect of life-style but first of all in kinship" (ibid., 82).

The opposition implied in notions of gender equality or inequality, in the sense of either a parallel equivalence or an imbalance, would be a foreign and incomprehensible concept in aboriginal Pomo society. The cooperativism that characterized their relationships engendered a web of associations that linked its participants both with each other and with the natural and spiritual worlds, which included the presence of both visible and invisible forms of energy. In this kind of system, it is contrary to think of people or things in isolation; "they exist only as aspects of relationships, linked together by this pervasive power" (Kearney 1984:75).

This perspective predisposes the individuals in such a society to a kind of altruism that can be called generalized rather than balanced reciprocity. Generalized reciprocity means giving something without expecting an equivalent return and is a nearly universal trait among gatherer-hunter peoples, which the Pomos were (Sahlins 1971).

The relationships between the genders in Pomo society conformed to and re-created the altruism and generalized reciprocity of the individual's relationship to others and the universe at large. It was less a parallel exchange and more of what Illich terms an "asymmetrical and ambiguous complementarity," where asymmetry indicates relativity and implies a disproportion and where ambiguity produces incongruity. The ambiguity that characterizes gender, in this sense, is two-sided: "Men symbolize the mutual relationship differently than do women" (Illich 1982:75). Men behaved differently than women: they were expected to be lustful while women were to be chaste; they were aggressive while women were compliant. They engaged in high-risk, low-return, uniquely male subsistence activities like hunting, while women pursued low-risk, high-return activities like gathering. These distinctions were viewed as fundamental characteristics of gender and were not ranked as part of a status or power hierarchy.

The altruism was reflected in what Illich terms "probity," the notion of uprightness, sincerity, honesty, and integrity that permeated appropriate behavior and resulted in each gender's domain being guarded by its sense of honor. This is illustrated by men's and women's careful observance of Pomo menstrual taboos, which will be discussed fully below.

GENDER IN MYTH

The major published work on Pomo myth is S. A. Barrett's collection, *Pomo Myths* (1933). This work is rendered in English and was recorded as free translations from the informants directly or through an interpreter if the informants did not speak English. The myths were told by both men and women from Eastern, Northern, or Central Pomo-speaking backgrounds. The myths were also revised "to a considerable extent" for publication, although Barrett (1933:8) notes that the sense of the stories was not altered. Therefore, the myths need to be approached with some caution as there is no way of evaluating their direct authenticity. Bearing this in mind, however, the myths offer a reiteration of the Pomo views on the relationship of gender and family.

Sally McLendon, a linguist working with Eastern Pomo, has noted that the events and activities in Eastern Pomo myths always take place in real, named geographic locations that are known to living people. She sees this fact as proof that the myths are believed to describe events that once really took place. "That is, the assertion of locational and directional detail involves the presupposition that the myths are true" (McLendon 1977:162). The same attention to locational detail is also true of myths in other Pomo languages. Furthermore, McLendon (ibid., 163) offers the words of an Eastern Pomo informant who said, "They used to say these *ma run* were true, really happened long ago, and I guess that must be true." In Central Pomo, the word *ma tu* is used to describe these stories. It is equivalent in meaning to the Eastern Pomo word *ma run* and is translated as "history" (Frances Jack pers. comm. 1984). Robert Oswalt (n.d.), a linguist working with Southern

Pomo as well as other Pomo languages, has collected some stories that were described by informants as "'instruction,' the teaching of proper behavior by illustrating the consequences of acting improperly."

In a composite myth developed by Barrett from similar versions in several Pomo languages (all collected in *Pomo Myths*), both elements — real events and instruction — establish the "vernacular" for the gendered behavior that informs Pomo society. In this composite myth, the essential elements of a general Pomo mythology are established: Coyote as trickster; miraculous birth of his children; destruction of the world by fire; creation of Clear Lake; creation of human beings; theft of the sun; and the transformation of people into animals. The myth begins with a description of the Wood-duck sisters "who always kept apart from the rest of the inhabitants of the village" and who, although greatly admired by many men, "persistently refused to have anything to do with them." Coyote was among their admirers and, at first, "tried various means to induce one of them to become his wife." When his tactics proved unsuccessful, he "determined to resort to trickery." As it was the food-gathering season, Coyote proposed that all the women go out into the mountains to gather buckeyes while the men hunted and fished and made "implements" at the village. Coyote disguised himself as the Wood-duck sisters' grandmother, and when they took her out to camp, Coyote seduced them. The sisters immediately discovered the deception and joined by other women in the camp, furiously attacked Coyote. Four children were miraculously born. Coyote rescued two by placing them in his sack. The other two were killed by the enraged women. Coyote lived in the village after that with the two children, but "he had no one to care for them" while he was away hunting and fishing and the people of the village treated them badly. "They threw rocks and sticks at the children, called them bad names, and even threw coals of fire on them." When the children got older, Coyote determined "to revenge himself and his children" for the abuse they had suffered. Everything that transpires from this point in the myth on — the burning of the world, various creations, including humans, and the punishment of humans by transforming them back into animals — comes as a result of Coyote's revenge.

After Coyote created people from various feathers, he left them to organize village life for themselves. Certain individuals were designated by Eagle to be hunting and fishing captains, drummers, singers, and fire tenders. Wood-duck was made the female captain of the entire village. The hunters and fishermen were asked to tell everyone how to get along, but they professed ignorance and asked Wood-duck what she would have them do. She replied, "I do not think we are living now as we should. We should have one head captain to govern us all, and Hawk is the proper one for that office. Coyote created us all, and I think we should make Hawk head captain, as his grandfather Coyote was before him." And this was done (Barrett 1933:95–109).

This myth illustrates the dangers of ignoring socially sanctioned gender roles and the rewards of behaving appropriately and with probity. It demonstrates the importance of belonging to properly constituted families and the perils of operating in social isolation. It emphasizes the interrelationship of gender and kinship and depicts typical gender-based economic activities. Pomo myths take place in a world fully formed. Gender roles are not created here; they are taken for granted. In the sense of Illich's "vernacular," they are not learned but fundamental. It is the transgression of this fundamental essence that causes upheaval and conflict.

The Wood-duck sisters refuse to marry, and they have no male relatives to protect them. They are vulnerable to Coyote's licentiousness and are punished by his trickery. Coyote disregards proper behavior and is himself punished by the loss of two children and the abuse of the others. Without families constituted by marriage and kinship relationships, both the Wood-duck sisters and Coyote are defenseless and assailable. Their breach of appropriate gender behavior — marrying and raising children — causes violence and chaos, a disruption of order. But after the order changes and they are made human by Coyote, Wood-duck has another chance. She is made the female captain and the hunters and fishermen look to her for advice as to how to live. They say, "We can only hunt and fish and must follow the instructions of our captains." Wood-duck chooses a male captain in Hawk, whose grandfather, Coyote, was captain before him. By implication, Wood-duck,

Coyote's unwilling consort, is possibly Hawk's grandmother. Wood-duck gains prestige and honor, as do Hawk and Coyote, through their publicly acknowledged kinship.

In the other Pomo myths reported by Barrett, the female characters are all described in terms of terms of their kinship ties—as mothers, sisters, wives, daughters, and in-laws—and their interactions with male characters take place within the bounds of kinship. The only females who are not described this way are crones—old women who are alone. Female characters help men, but they also act against men when they are not treated as their kinship position requires. For example, there is a series of stories in which a son favored his wife over his mother and the mother, furious over this breach of respect, kills both the son and the daughter-in-law. Her grandchildren, in turn, take their revenge.

Gender and kinship are further intertwined by another series of stories in which a wife, to help an ailing husband, transgresses her traditional role by going out to hunt. She is only successful because she uses magic to seduce deer. The husband, though growing strong on the magical meat, recognizes the taste is wrong and on discovering his wife's deception, leaves her. She is only able to induce him to return by offering him great quantities of gifts traditionally made or owned by women—baskets and clamshell beads.

The myths reaffirm the necessity for both genders to behave appropriately to ensure the survival of the group—the extended family. Women need to live in relationship to a family with male kin and to pursue women's work. Men need to fulfill their obligations to their female relatives or be destroyed by them. The genders, in these myths, are not in a parallel equivalence. They perform different duties and roles, but they are necessary to each other and must cooperate to maintain order in the world.

Aboriginal Economic, Social, Political, and Religious Gender Roles

In aboriginal Pomo economic life, that is, life as reported prior to the intrusion of settlers (Russians in 1811 in Southwestern Pomo Kashaya territory; Mexicans in the 1830s in Southern, Southeastern, and Eastern Pomo territory; and Euro-Americans in the 1850s in Central and Northern Pomo lands), there was a clear division of labor that encouraged specialization and enhanced group productivity. Men and women worked as members of their own genders rather than as individual constituents of a single household. All men fished, hunted, built houses, and manufactured fish and animal traps. All women wove baskets, collected acorns and other vegetal foods, and cared for children. Traditional wedding gifts emphasize this occupational identification with gender. The man's family contributed meat and clamshell beads; the woman's family gave baskets, acorn bread, and acorn soup (Edna Guerrero pers. comm. 1981).

However, there were tasks that were the province of recognized professional specialists. Professionals produced excess products for sale or had specialized skills that were bought with clamshell-bead money or traded for baskets or other goods. Both men and women made clamshell beads; some women were recognized as exceptionally skilled basket makers, and their work was sought for purchase. Men specialized in fishnet or duck net making, arrow making, and magnesite bead making.

Doctoring was a professional specialization. The aboriginal Pomos recognized two types of doctors, the outfit doctor and the sucking doctor. The two were often called in on the same case. The sucking doctor diagnosed the illness, while the outfit doctor treated the patient with ritual medicine and song. Although sucking doctors gave no medicine, they were able to cure. Men could be sucking or outfit doctors. There are no recorded instances of women outfit doctors, although women were allowed to learn the doctoring songs from their parents. Frequently, however, women were practicing sucking doctors (Loeb 1926:326).

Occupational and specialized knowledge was transmitted in families from father to son and from maternal uncle to sororal nephew as well as from mother to daughter and nieces. In fact, in all professions and for all skills, patrilineal and matrilineal transmission coexisted (Gifford 1926:328). In a few recorded cases, specialized ritual knowledge was transmitted from an older woman to a nonrelated, younger man (Barrett 1917:453).

Specialization extended into ceremonial life and included both men and women. Individuals were recognized and recompensed by the community for their knowledge and ability in dancing and in singing. Both men and women danced and sang; in singing, the high voices of women were preferred. It is said, "The women's voices get the best of the men" (Mitchell Jack pers. comm. 1985).

The learning of specialized skills and access to individuals who would transmit them was dependent on residence. For the Pomos, both matrilocal and patrilocal residence after marriage were practiced, with the married couple often moving from one parent's village to the other year by year until they chose a more permanent settlement that, for the Eastern Pomo at least, was more often the village of the mother (Gifford 1926:323). This common pattern of alternating residence gave the new couple enlarged possibilities of receiving specialized training and a wider kin network.

Within the village, families shared living quarters with extended kin under the same roof, although each nuclear group had its own fire. The living house, however, was generally occupied by women and their young male and female children, older women, and infirm men. The men and initiated boys lived in the sweat house and went home only to eat and, occasionally, to sleep. Postmenopausal women were occasionally allowed to frequent the sweat house.

The families' wealth, measured in baskets, beads, and blankets woven of tree squirrel or rabbit skins, was kept in the living house and distributed by the oldest female, who often owned the house. She was also usually an expert on genealogy and family, village, and band history.

Gender separation in living was required by the numerous taboos surrounding the behavior of a menstruating female and her spouse. A menstrual dwelling separate from the main living space was exclusively and cyclically occupied by a family's women.

Village communities were led by a captain or headmen (*ja'yadul*, Central Pomo) whose office was hereditary but whose leadership was accepted only by popular acclamation. The role was passed either from father to son or from a headman to his eldest sister's son. A woman relative, but never the captain's wife, acted "like a queen" (*maatha qhalech'*, big shot woman, Central Pomo). The captain's duties included lecturing the people daily about their behavior, arranging group activities, scheduling ceremonials, and entertaining guests. The woman chief's role was to assist as an official hostess and organize women's activities (Frances Jack pers. comm. 1983).

There were two major religious ceremonials recorded for the Pomos. The ancient Ghost Ceremony (distinct from the practices of the 1870 Ghost Dance among the Pomo) and the so-called Kuksu rituals. Both ceremonies were held separately in the springtime. Observances associated with each particular ceremony were exchanged in Eastern and Northern Pomo custom, and there was a considerable interchange of ritual function of the two traditions among different Pomo groups (Loeb 1926:342), although A. L. Kroeber (1953:261) indicates that the Kuksu rites formed the "kernel" of the Pomo religious system. Women were excluded from Ghost Ceremony activities but not from the Kuksu cult (Loeb 1926:338).

The main features of the Ghost Ceremony involved the return of the dead and the initiation of novices; the Kuksu rites involved shamanistic healing and spirit impersonations as well as boys' initiations. Women were traditionally excluded from the Ghost Ceremonies held in the underground dance house, although, according to Kroeber (1953:263), the "Pomo affirm that old women were nevertheless among the spectators. There is some discussion in the literature about whether the essential purpose of the Ghost Ceremony was to deliberately frighten women into submission, but I agree with Kroeber that to intepret these religious rites on such a level is basically an "interpretation foreign to native psychology" (ibid.)

The Kuksu initiation involved the symbolic killing and resurrection of the male and female children by first shooting them with arrows or stabbing them with spears, resurrecting them, carrying them out to the hills where they remained for four days while continuous dancing took place in the village, and their return as Kuksu society members. The purpose of the ceremony was to provide the children and therefore the society in general with "luck" (Loeb 1926:354–84). A second ritual including both girls and boys, who were treated identically during the ceremony, involved cutting the children across the back with a sharp-edged shell. The purpose of this treatment was to ensure the children's "speedy growth and vigor" (Kroeber 1953:262). There is some disagreement in the literature as to whether girls were included by all groups and what effect the initiation was to have for them (See Loeb 1926; Kroeber 1953; Heizer 1978).

Kuksu-initiated women served as *yomtas*—secret society members and shamans—in both coast and inland Pomo groups. The women who had leadership positions were either a sister or the mother's sister of the head of the society. These women could, and did, become head *yomta* if there was no male successor.

POWER AND AUTHORITY

The published literature on the Pomo, on which I have relied for the most part so far, is very sparse when it comes to issues of power and authority in relation to gender. Ideas need to be gleaned from ethnohistorical and contemporary sources and worked backward.

Among the Pomo, there were two sorts of power—secular and spiritual. Secular power stemmed from prestige, wealth, and skill and was expressed as authority. Authority, for the Pomos, meant the ability to convince others to follow. Authority could be an attribute that surrounded an individual all the time, such as that of a captain or shaman, or it could be specific to a particular activity or skill, such as fishing or basket making or singing.

Individuals gained prestige from their family's lineage and reputation, which was linked to wealth and the ability to create or obtain more wealth. Political and religious offices were connected to particular families through inheritance and selection. Individuals also gained prestige from the community's recognition of their skills. Because men had more occupational specializations open to them, they had greater access to achieving prestige and, therefore, secular authority and power.

Spiritual power (*weya*, supernatural power, Central Pomo), in contrast, is an often unbidden force that comes to individuals from "not
ordinary" sources. Its power is profound, and those who try to avoid its
call are punished by death. It is a power that is very rarely sought
because its presence requires a structured life filled with difficult
taboos and restrictions. There are numerous stories of people who were
visited by supernatural power and ignored it or hid it or tried, in other
ways, to escape the consequences, always with tragic results. The
authority that comes with spiritual power worked differently than that
of secular power. The shaman or dream doctor, while relied on by the
community for healing and recompensed with items of wealth, was also
feared and avoided in general society. This kind of power was available
to both men and women and came to both.

Underlying the whole structure of gender relationships in aboriginal
Pomo society was the potent effect of menstruating women. Menstrual
blood had the power to cause sickness in both men and women. In fact,
to menstruate was to be "moon sick" or "month sick" (Aginsky and
Aginsky 1941). Many doctoring songs mention contact with menstrual
blood as the origin of illness (Patterson 1988). In this sense, menstrual
blood has the effect of a "poison," a bad medicine, a powerful intrusion
on well-being and personal capability.

Studies of other societies have demonstrated that pollution beliefs,
in general, prevent threatened disturbances of the social order by
helping people to regulate the universe by enforcing conformity. "By
controlling their own actions, people give themselves a sense of
evening uncertain odds" (Douglas 1970). Illich's sense of probity,
described earlier, infuses the Pomo attention to menstrual taboos that
were dependent on individual actions but had consequences beyond
the individual.

The taboos surrounding menstruation involved personal and social
restrictions for women and restrictions for their husbands and for men
in general. A menstruating woman stayed in a special small addition to
the house. She could not eat meat or fish because these foods contained
blood, the substance that the menstruating female was trying to rid
herself of. She could not prepare acorns, cook, eat grease, skin or cut

up game, weave baskets, make beads, scratch herself, or drink cold water. She should not comb her hair or wash her face by herself. Menstruating women would put themselves in great danger if they went near water in lakes or swampy places or stepped on holes in the ground. "A woman when month sick should avoid springs or any kind of water, especially an old spring. They always say you might find something there that would frighten you; something you don't expect to see, a snake or something. A big snake they say." She might see something under the water like an "Indian doctoring stick, or fish woman." These sightings were powerful and caused sickness: headaches, back pains, or fainting spells—"just like they would get scared of ghosts." Two adjacent lakes called Blue Lakes near the present Lake/Mendocino County lines held an extremely dangerous serpent: "That's a bad water, awful bad and that's why there was no Indian villages around there ever" (Aginsky and Aginsky 1941).

With regard for others, a menstruating woman could not enter the dance house, could not handle dance outfits, visit the sick, be present while someone was being doctored, or leave things she had touched or used around where men might come into contact with them. As recently as the 1940s, her plates and tableware were hidden so that no one could use them. Sometimes she tied a string around her cup so that her husband would not inadvertently drink from it. In the old days when a woman was having the "monthlies," she was never to come near any of the men as it could make them sick or destroy their power or luck. "Never let a man touch 'em when moon sick." These restrictions had to be followed for five or six days, after which she could bathe, burn up the "stuff" she had used during the period, and wash her dirty clothes. After that, she could eat meat (Aginsky and Aginsky 1939).

The husbands, but not the male or female children or siblings, of menstruating women were also subject to restrictions. They were not supposed to hunt, fish, gamble, make "money" (beads), smoke, or make nets for five days. These same restrictions adhered when their wives were pregnant but extended to months of inactivity. If a man was a singer, "when their wives have the month-sick, it changes their voices" (Aginsky and Aginsky 1934). If a man started out on a war party and his wife began to menstruate, a messenger was sent after him and the raid was called off. When a man's wife was menstruating, he had to be extremely cautious. If another man touched him or even talked to him, it could bring bad luck (Loeb 1926:272–73). Mary Douglas (1975) has observed that in cultures where men adhere to the same menstrual taboos as women, the custom serves to define a married couple publicly. In Pomo society, where kinship was ever-present, it would publicly affirm those essential kin ties.

The effect of a menstruating woman was felt by the society in general. "Anything a menstruating woman was using, people didn't use. Anything she do, people don't do. Might get poisoned by bad blood." Hunters customarily presented their game to the community already cleaned and cut to avoid an accidental cutting of the bones by menstruants. If menstruating women entered the dance house or went to a place where people were dancing, "awful thing if they do." Such a woman would get faint. "The place is 'fixed' in there. She may go in thinking that nobody will know what she has, but you don't have to tell them. They always find out. The dancers can't dance right. They and the singers get mixed up; they can't keep the rules. And the dancers' legs get cramped; the singers lose their voices. Then they say someone is in there who shouldn't be." "They say that they used to wear eagle feathers on them to combat her influence. They want her to get sick so she will go away. Eagle feathers do that, make her sick" (Aginsky and Aginsky 1934).

The consequences of not following the "rules" were serious, resulting in loss of "luck," illness, or even death for both men and women. Every breach of the menstrual taboos was "punished." Although the punishment usually occurred soon after the infraction, sometimes it was not felt until middle age. Rheumatism, cramps, consumption, deafness, and blindness were illnesses caused by breaking menstrual taboos. ("The reason so many White people are blind today is that they were poisoned by menstrual blood; from touching things a menstruating woman touched.") People used to say, "If they comb their hair, when they're in that shape, the hair falls out and gets gray." Women who became prematurely gray covered their heads with kerchiefs so people would not see their hair and think they had broken the taboo. Wrinkles appeared on women who had washed their faces while menstruating in their youth. A man who touched anything a menstruating woman touched was "just out of luck. Can't kill nothing, can't shoot, can't do nothing." Women who obeyed the rules "never got sick." They felt good, they never got cramps, and it "never hurt" (Aginsky and Aginsky 1934).

For women who had been frightened by snakes or water monsters, special doctoring was required to prevent death. Certain songs were sung by either male or female doctors to treat these cases. The songs could also be sung by a male or a female to prevent menstrual sickness. For example, a woman who began to menstruate while camped near water or a man walking with a menstruating woman could sing the right kind of songs and prevent danger to themselves (Aginsky and Aginsky 1939).

Studies that indicate the synchronous menstruation of women in the same household or small group make its occurrence in aboriginal Pomo life probable (Bailey 1950; McClintock 1971:244–45). The fact of this form of extraordinary power gave women a certain secular power in the sense of controlling the group's activities. If a number of women were menstruating simultaneously, there could be literally no hunting, fishing, ceremonial dancing, gambling, or war. The captain and other professional men such as hunt or fishing leaders had to design their tasks around their women's periods. However, the key to this system was the mutual acceptance of responsibility for each other's well-being, the notion of group survival and altruistic behavior, which encouraged men and women to respect the taboos to ensure each other's health and luck. The serious consequences of ignoring the "rules" acted as a check and balance for each gender.

The restriction of access to food resources caused by menstrual taboos affecting both men and women provide an ecological equilibrium that ensured the group's survival in a relatively small geographic area. The taboos effectively controlled the use of fish and game and therefore contributed to their conservation. Despite traditional gender-linked food acquisition patterns, the taboos prevented each gender from total control of the major food resources and created a dependence on the kinship group beyond the nuclear family. If a man's menstruating wife could not prepare acorns or cook for him, he had to depend on other female relatives. And as he could not obtain meat or fish for himself or his wife during her periods or pregnancies, he had to rely on others to feed his children. (Remember Coyote's poor children!)

Sexual abstinence during menstruation extended to any activity in which a man needed to conserve power or luck. Men avoided women before any hunting, fishing, or gambling and slept in the sweat house. This habitually temperate sexual behavior had the effect of limiting the births in a family, which additionally contributed to the long-term survival of the group.

GENDER ROLE CHANGES AFTER CONTACT

At the time of contact, Pomo women were totally immersed in the time-consuming domestic chores of food gathering, food preparation, and child care. Although traditionally important as family historians and keepers of wealth, Pomo women did not have as many opportunities to achieve personal prestige as did men. While some achieved status as women of power, their major value was reflected in their lineage or family—the quality and wealth of their relatives and their reputation regarding their domestic skills. Their modesty and their adherence to appropriate behavior were what gave them esteem. Because family life was so important in Pomo society, it was extremely rare for a woman to live alone as the head of a household.

As a result of both the onslaught of epidemic disease and the genocidal policies brought by the continuing influx of settlers into the Pomo territories from 1850 on, the population of Pomo men was severely reduced and traditional culture and family life violently uprooted. The Pomo band and village were eradicated. Pomo men lost all their traditional avenues to power and authority. Their occupational specializations and traditional ceremonial and political offices were destroyed. Pomo women, in contrast, were forced by circumstances to take on new roles, behaviors, and tasks. They became the heads of increasingly male-absent households and were able to maintain their families successfully in the newly imposed economy because of their ability to earn money or goods as domestic workers. Around the turn of the century, they were hired in the Ukiah area to wash clothes and occasionally cook for pioneer families. Their power within their own communities increased as their knowledge of English and Euro-American behavior grew as a result of their intimacy with white households, goods, and habits. Their belief in Pomo menstrual taboos was shaken by their observations of white women's lives.

Pomo women had a separate relationship with white men. Although often the victims of rape, sexual exploitation, and abuse, they also received favors and money from the white men who often fathered their children (see Colson n.d.; Hurtado 1988). The intercultural sexual tension caused by this situation resulted in much anger and hostility between Indian and white women. The relegation of Indian women's labor to the most demeaning and back-breaking tasks such as laundering and the subsequent freeing of white women from such work may have had a relationship to the repressed anger of sexual competition (Colson n.d.:34).

The necessity of dealing with mixed children caused much confusion and alienation as their numbers and visibility increased. Among Pomo women, these children, at first, were links to survival when acknowledged by their white fathers, but some became burdens and painful reminders of exploitative relationships. They were often destroyed at birth. But as Pomo life adapted to changing circumstances and populations, traditional loyalty to family won out and mixed children became commonplace, acceptable, and identified as Indian (See Colson 1974, n.d.).

As the real hardships of frontier life diminished and places such as Mendocino County approached the "civilized" sameness of the Midwest, more white women emigrated. Resident women could replace Indian labor with newly arrived girls looking for work and isolate Indian women from daily contact with their men. The segregation of Pomo women from white households was so complete in the Ukiah area, for example, that as late as 1940, only one Indian women (who worked as a laundress in the local convent) worked in town despite the fact that many Pomo girls, trained in domestic science at Indian boarding schools, were sought after as domestics in the Bay area. No local hairdressers would serve Indian women, and to try on dresses before buying, Indian women had to travel to Santa Rosa, sixty-five miles to the south (see Kuhns 1947; Lombard 1942; Robin 1943).

During the 1920s, 1930s, and 1940s, some Pomo people found employment on outlying ranches: men sheared sheep, chopped wood, and rode with mule pack trains, and men and women trained and picked hops and other fruit. In the winter, before the time to train the hops vines, Pomo men from Ukiah and Hopland chopped wood for ranchers for $2 a tier (8' × 4' × 12'). They sheared sheep for 6 cents apiece in the spring and 7 cents a sheep in the fall. A good worker could shear ninety-seven sheep in a day (Aginsky and Aginsky 1946).

During the harvest seasons, men and women picked grapes, prunes, and hops. A typical day was ten to fourteen hours of work, starting at 6:00 A.M. and stopping at 7:00 P.M. with a lunch break from 11:00 A.M. to 2:00 P.M., although older people often worked straight through. A woman could pick three hundred pounds of hops a day, making $16 clear for an entire season. Although women trained hops by tying them with twine onto stakes, men generally set the stakes. No women bailed the hops or worked in the hop kilns, as this was work considered "too heavy" for them. Families camped out along the river during the hops season, bringing along their cast-iron cookstoves, beds, tables, and chairs. It was thought of as a festive time despite the work, and many social dances, gambling games, and trysts occurred during the hops season. Young women, who had been earning good wages as domestics in the Bay area, always returned home for the "hops" (Lombard 1942).

With the more or less stable establishment of two separate societies, Indian and white, white women could safely admire the arts and crafts of traditional Pomo culture far removed from any real interaction with its artisans. The new styles set by the Craftsman movement, among others, around the turn of the century, caused women to redecorate and demand Indian arts. Pomo women, as a result of this market, could return to the traditional women's art of basket making and use it to their economic advantage.

Their involvement with subsistence tasks became less as they acquired money or credit to obtain food. Domestic tasks decreased in the amount of time required to complete them as well as in difficulty. It is far easier to open a sack of flour then to prepare acorns. Pomo women began to make baskets on commission, and, as a result, they professionalized basket making. They were able to secure their new roles as principal providers and also acquire personal prestige in both white and Indian circles. At the same time, they were actively involved in preserving and transmitting at least part of their cultural heritage through the practice of marketable crafts.

With the new authority that accrued from their economic advantage, Pomo women became powerful religious leaders through the 1870 Ghost Dance movement. Although men initially led the movement, by 1908 women began to replace them as leaders and by the 1930s were the strongest religious innovators among some Pomo groups. Through the medium of the Bole Maru, the spiritual revival that followed the Ghost Dance, women gained tremendous personal and political power that survives to the present day. Through the agency of dreaming, they constructed religious events and beliefs that had ethical and political importance in redefining Indian values, goals, and relationships to whites. They became the primary healers and, through their doctoring, maintained critical links to the past while shaping the future (Oswalt 1964:218, 318–31).

The gender roles of Pomo people continue to evolve. Many rancherias, set up initially by the government in 1906 as part of the Homeless California Indian Appropriations Act and then terminated during the 1960s, have regained federal status through legal action. They have reorganized as bands of extended families, returning to a traditional governing format. Women were very active in initiating lawsuits and in organizing the earlier tribal governments in Mendocino County, but as the tribal governments grow in strength and financial stability, men are beginning to take over positions that have been held by women since the tribes' return to sovereignty. Tribal government and other local Indian organizations and programs have provided Pomo men with employment and leadership opportunities unavailable to them in mainstream society. They have taken up public ceremonial positions as singers and dancers.

As young women move from their homes to attend college or receive other training, the traditional art of basket making, however, is being passed on less and less. Women, although still active in tribal government and local education programs, have returned to more traditional roles as homemakers. But gender occupational specialization is nowhere as pronounced as it was in traditional Pomo society, and cooperation between genders varies from one individual household and nuclear family to another. Gender roles in contemporary Pomo life have become more like those of non-Indian society than a reflection of ancient Pomo tradition, although the importance of familial relationships and connections still prevails (see Kaplan 1984).

9

THE DYNAMICS OF SOUTHERN PAIUTE WOMEN'S ROLES

Martha C. Knack

The Great Basin culture area corresponds roughly with the Basin and Range physiographic province, a cold desert area of numerous fault block mountains. Few streams flow to the sea, draining rather into flat valley floors that serve as evaporation basins. Rainfall is rare, but water is available in numerous small springs. Vegetation is diverse and varies with altitude, producing the seasonal variation of ripening wild plants that was systematically exploited by the Native economy.

Language groups were few, and each controlled large land areas. Actual camp groups, however, were small, consisting of fifteen to fifty bilaterally related kinsmen who worked together on a daily basis. Throughout the Great Basin, extensive gathering and hunting of small game provided the subsistence base. Each group had a well-recognized area that it customarily utilized to gather food, generally including all possible altitudinal zones, which they harvested sequentially as the plants ripened to produce year-round subsistence in the face of technological and storage limitations. Surpluses were rare and quickly exhausted. Technology was primarily fiber work—basketry, netting, and matting, with minor buckskin work. Both housing and clothing were minimal, no more elaborate than the climate required and their mobile, pedestrian lifestyle allowed. Theirs was an unspecialized collecting culture, showing continuity with seven thousand years of regional Archaic archaeology.

Each camp group was politically independent, led by a headman with limited, situation-specific authority. Individual adults retained freedom to make their own economic decisions, including the choice to relocate to other bands where they had kin ties. Individual proficiency was recognized, but neither full-time economic specializations nor wealth distinctions existed. Among these skills were shamanistic powers, used primarily for curing and hunting. Rituals were scheduled by community need, not according to a fixed cycle. Life cycle ceremonies were generally handled by family and kinsmen, rather than religious specialists.

HISTORICAL SKETCH

The first non-Indian to enter the Great Basin was the Spanish priest Escalante in 1776. Although a few fur trappers and government explorers followed in the nineteenth century, these men found few resources to exploit and little to cause them to linger. External impact on the Great Basin was minimal before gold was discovered in California in 1848, when suddenly the Oregon Trail to San Francisco and the Old Spanish Trail to Los Angeles became highways. Ten years later, silver of the Comstock Lode was discovered on the Nevada side of the Sierras and prospectors fanned out across the basin looking for minerals.

Meanwhile, the 1850s had brought Mormons to the better-watered areas of Utah seeking refuge from religious persecution. Agriculture was possible here if very careful irrigation was practiced. Active proselytism led to a rapid rise in the non-Indian population, complete domination of all arable lands before 1880, and diversion of most streams from their natural streambeds into fields. Lands beyond the reach of irrigation ditches were used for cattle herding.

The Great Basin remained a remote and underdeveloped portion of the United States until remarkably recently, with many of what are now large urban areas, such as Las Vegas, not being even incorporated townships until after World War I. It is still an area of long roads and open spaces, with isolated metropolitan centers separated from each other by distances of typically four hundred miles or more and only tiny, agricultural hamlets between.

THE SOUTHERN PAIUTE

The Southern Paiute were Great Basin hunters and gatherers who lived in the deserts of southern Utah, northern Arizona, and southern Nevada. Their autonomy ended quickly with the arrival of Euro-American settlers in the 1850s. Yet, despite the absence of reservations for more than sixty years thereafter and later termination of some bands in the 1950s, the Southern Paiute remain a viable ethnic group today. This chapter sketches the historical changes of Southern Paiute women's roles over this period and attempts to explain the observed pattern of change.

In the traditional culture, as reconstructed through memory ethnography for circa 1850, women were the primary gatherers, harvesting dozens of different plant species for the seeds, roots, berries, and leaves that constituted the majority of the diet (Kelly 1964:132; Stewart 1942:250–54, 298–99). Protein came mostly from small game, while some limited cultivation of maize, squash, and possibly a few wild plants was practiced in small, particularly favored areas (Kelly 1964: 39–40, 151, 170, 179; Lowie 1924:200–201; Stewart 1942:254–56). Women generally processed the plant food they gathered and placed it in storage. They manufactured baskets, mats, cradles, and other objects from vegetable fiber. Rabbits were the most frequently eaten of the larger animals, and men hunted them individually or in communal drives (Kelly 1964:50–51, 156; Stewart 1942:242). They also hunted rarer mountain sheep, deer, antelope, tortoise, chuckwalla, quail, and other game. Women processed this meat, distributed surpluses to relatives and neighbors, and tanned the hides, which were a common trade item with other tribal groups (Kelly 1964:51). Women also manufactured rabbit-skin robes, the major winter clothing and another export item (Hughes and Bennyhoff 1986:241).

The division of labor was not rigid, for women also "hunted," setting traps for the small animals that lived under the grasses and bushes they were harvesting. Men helped gather the all-important piñon pine nut and mesquite harvests, to maximize the yield by engaging all available labor sources (Kelly 1964:43; Stewart 1942:250–51).

The camp group often divided during the day, with men engaging in one activity while women performed another. In such gender-segregated work groups, women determined their own economic activities in coordination with women relatives, not under the direction of male task leaders (Kelly 1964:29, 45). Among the southernmost bands, a woman was in charge of coordinating the bisexual work group during the lengthy communal agave pit-roasting process (Fowler 1989).

Paiute headmen, figures of influence rather than power, were always male. Their duties involved directing the group to food collecting areas and urging them in their efforts, although specialized leaders might actually direct game drives, hunts, or dances. Without judicial functions or legitimacy to make unilateral decisions, the headman voiced community values and consensus on disputed issues. That consensus was generated during community discussions in which adult women were active participants. Succession to the headmanship was determined by individual character as well as kinship relationship, passing often through female kin ties (Kelly 1964:26–30).

Descent was bilaterally reckoned (Kelly 1964:121–30; Lowie 1924: 287–88). Initial postmarital residence was generally matrilocal, although later movements were bilocal (Kelly 1964:99–100; Lowie 1924: 275). Brideservice was reported for most bands. Parents arranged first marriages for both sons and daughters at or before puberty, but premarital sexual experience was common and uncensured for both boys and girls. Polygyny was rare and often sororal; polyandry occurred as a tolerated although very rare marital form (Kelly and Fowler 1986:377). Both the sororate and levirate were practiced but not required. Divorce was frequent and available equally to men and women on the same grounds. Subsequent remarriages were individually arranged (Stewart 1942:296–97).

On a girl's first menstruation, women relatives built a special menstrual hut a bit away from the camp where older women discussed with her the customs surrounding menstruation and childbirth. These included taboos against eating meat, fish, eggs, or "greasy things," a category that included some types of piñon nuts; touching her face or hair except with a scratching stick; drinking cold water; coming near the sick, hunters, and gamblers; and touching a man's hunting equip-

149

ment. It was believed that her behavior at this time would influence the rest of her life, assuring her strength and good health if obeyed or premature aging if broken; only in the last two instances did her actions affect others, damaging the hunting luck of men or the health of the weakened. She was encouraged to rise early and remain active. When her flow had ceased, she bathed, her hair was trimmed and washed, and her face was decorated with red paint before she returned without further ceremony to the camp (Kelly 1964:98; Stewart 1942: 309–11). Women secluded themselves during later menstruations and observed the same food and body taboos.

Both parents were involved in behavioral restrictions after the birth of a child, which took place in a special birth house. Although women observed no prenatal food restrictions, both the father and the mother avoided meat and cold water and used a scratching stick for about a month after the birth, or until the umbilical cord separated; in some bands the husband was not expected to observe the taboos for this full period. The husband hunted actively but gave all the meat to others. At the end of the birth seclusion, mother and child bathed, the mother's hair was trimmed, and both were decorated with red paint as they reentered the camp, without further ceremonial recognition (Kelly 1964:96–99; Stewart 1942:303–7).

In all bands, women became shamans and curers and had the same prestige and status as male shamans. There were no apparent restrictions on a woman's age or nubile status. The literature does not record that women were barred from becoming any particular types of shamans, although because of the general barring of women from participation in game drives, it is doubtful that they were ever the ritual directors of these activities (Lowie 1924:291; Stewart 1942:315).

Thus in traditional Southern Paiute culture, women provided a substantial portion of the subsistence and controlled the products of their own labor by distributing it as well as the meat hunted by men. They manufactured tools for their own productive tasks and goods desired beyond the household level. They functioned in interband and intertribal trade. They were participants in the political process but not headmen; they were important in the structure of residential groups, reckoned equally in kinship tracing, and had equal determination of their marital state. Despite menstrual customs, women became shamans.

Because resources in the Great Basin were extremely localized, the American conquest proceeded very rapidly. Mormon agriculturalists arrived in Utah in the 1850s and immediately diverted the few available streams for irrigation agriculture, fenced off fields nearby, and turned domestic livestock loose on the grasslands (Arrington 1966). Prospectors arrived in Nevada about ten years later and cut timber (mostly piñon) for mine shoring and firewood (Thomas 1971). Cattlemen followed to provide the boomtowns with meat and again confiscated seed-gathering sites for stock grazing, which altered the flora of the region severely (Young and Sparks 1985). Productive resource areas came to be held privately by individuals, rather than communally by kin-based groups. Such claims to exclusive private property rights were enforced by superior technology, particularly guns and horses, and soon by superior numbers as well. Without food surpluses to support men for prolonged periods of military activity, small Paiute groups could not and did not offer extensive military resistance, although small-scale raiding was frequent. Some bands avoided contact with settlers by retreating to remote and less productive areas not coveted by them. Other bands remained in their home areas as these well-watered and relatively productive regions were appropriated by non-Indian towns and formed Native communities on their fringes. Only one reservation was set aside in the nineteenth century, at Moapa in southern Nevada in 1872. Not until after the turn of the century were other areas placed under federal protection for the use of the Paiute: at Shivwits, Kaibab, Kanosh, Koosharem, and Las Vegas.

The first Mormon entry into southwestern Utah included missionaries, charged to deal with the Indians. They intentionally hired Paiute men to serve as guides for traveling and hunting, to pull sagebrush in clearing fields, and to help build houses, irrigation ditches, and forts, ironically designed to protect the new settlers from the Indians (Cleland and Brooks 1983:I:168). From the very first year, Indian women were hired by Mormon men to help their wives with laundering

(Brooks 1972:67). Within five years of initial settlement they were also being employed for seasonal tasks, such as washing wool (Cleland and Brooks 1983:I:168). Their expertise in plant gathering was sometimes recognized, as by the settler in 1852 who wrote,

> Dug up all my Potatoes in the Garden also onions and Beets, 4 Squaws and some Indian Children and my wife assisted me. . . . I cannot help but remark, that when I am very busy, Indians come and assist me in my work, I feel to thank my Father in Heaven for putting it into the hearts of those poor fallen people to come and help me Labor. Yesterday my wife commenced husking corn and some squaws came to her assistance and soon finished what was in my garden. . . . [G]ot some squaws to husk the remainder of my corn. (Lunt n.d.)

Women were often hired specifically to harvest potatoes, turnips, and other root crops, bringing with them their own traditional digging sticks for tools (Mangum 1939). Indians, both men and women, were employed on a day-to-day basis and paid in flour and clothing.

In mining towns such as Pioche, Nevada, Paiute women began working for wages as early as the 1870s. Here, too, Euro-American employers determined for which sexually stereotyped tasks they would be hired, primarily laundry work and heavy housecleaning (Knack 1986). The Paiute soon found that asking for gifts, interpreted by whites as begging, was more successful if done by women, often accompanied by small children.

With the expansion of Euro-American towns as markets for food-stuffs and the growth of large-scale specialized farming between the two world wars, Indian women joined their men in seasonal migratory harvest labor, particularly in the Sevier and Muddy River valleys (Knack n.d.). As elsewhere, women established their own contacts with employers and were in turn paid directly by them (Knack 1987:45–46, 53, 57; Rusco 1989). Women workers determined how their income should be spent, although they, like men, were under strong ethical pressures to share with needy relatives.

All the Southern Paiute reservations were within commuting distance of Euro-American towns. From the time the reservations were founded, and in most cases before, Paiute women sought jobs in those towns. Again, the tasks for which they were hired were "women's work"—clothes washing and ironing and housecleaning. Shivwits was far enough from town that women followed a weekly commuter cycle, making the half-day walk with their children into St. George, camping there for two or three days to work for their regular clients, before returning home. "Some of the men . . . do other small chores while in St. George," commented an early female Indian agent, "or take care of the papooses [small children] while their wives are washing. The braves are excellent nurses, and very gentle and affectionate with the children, as a rule" (Work 1898:2).

There is strong evidence that Paiute women continued traditional gathering to some degree throughout the historic period. Ethnohistorical sources frequently refer to Paiute families leaving their accustomed camps in the fall to gather piñon in the mountains. Oral history records a far wider range of gathering activities until well into the twentieth century. Women manufactured basketry for their own use well after the turn of the century, by which time it had become an object of exchange to non-Indians (Fowler and Dawson 1986:729–35). But whether all women or even some women from every family gathered regularly, or how much this might have contributed to the diet, is unknown.

Evidence for women's participation in other areas of culture during this period consists mostly of fragments and inferences. Town newspapers were often scandalized by the forthright public behavior of Paiute women—drinking, arguing with men, and participating in street brawls (Knack 1986). Women were enthusiastic gamblers, much to the chagrin of the Bureau of Indian Affairs (e.g., Farrow 1917:3). Agency descriptions of community meetings on farming, housing, schooling, and other issues of community concern always mentioned women as present and often as speakers; in no case did non-Indian chroniclers acknowledge women as community leaders, however. There was at least one practicing medicine woman in the 1920s, expelled by the Moapa reservation agent for exhorting the people to follow traditional burial practices and burn the personal property of the deceased (Sandal 1921). Generally, however, data on social organization and religious beliefs, practices, and practitioners are lacking.

A field survey of Utah Paiute bands in the mid-1970s revealed that women still contributed significantly to the economy, by then nearly totally based on cash (Knack 1980). In one-third of all households, women brought income to the family, either directly through wage work or indirectly through welfare supports of various kinds. Nearly all adult women had, at one time or another, earned cash through labor or trade. In fact, young women in their twenties were more often able to find work than were their young husbands. Employed women earned only 49 percent as much as employed men, and none earned more than $5,000 per year. There was considerable evidence of sex stereotyping in employment, with women working as motel maids and short order cooks and in some clerical positions. These low-paid, low-prestige jobs tended to be short term and undependable; only 62 percent of employed women worked for nine months or more of the year, but even this was more stable than the work Paiute men could obtain (Knack 1989). Many women's jobs were part-time, and these were actively sought by young mothers who preferred to be home when their children returned from school.

Although basketry was no longer a viable craft, many older women produced beaded leather items for sale to Indians and non-Indians, establishing their own outlets and business contacts. Although skilled craftspersons, they earned less than $1,000 per year for their labor. Simultaneously they might care for the children of daughters or daughters-in-law who worked out of the home full- or part-time (Knack 1980). Women today consider their income from wages or sales to be their own. Strong ethical pressures encourage women as well as male wage earners to share with relatives and friends. Women also continue to distribute the occasional venison brought in by male relatives in a pattern of generalized reciprocity. Women are active in the networks of borrowing and lending household equipment, goods, and services, which move constantly around the community.

Women are active in political officeholding. Every Southern Paiute band has had a women chairperson at some time in the last fifteen years

(Jake, James, and Bunte 1983; Knack 1989). About one-third of Utah Paiute offices are consistently filled by women, including chair or vice-chairperson; they rarely serve as treasurer always serve as secretary. To some extent committees follow sexual patterns; men handle money matters and the federal bureaucracy (housing, economic development, and financial planning), and women deal with extensions of family matters (education, children's share of land claims monies, and cultural events). Women are often sought out for committees that interact with the local non-Indian community, for it is said by both sexes that women are "better with whites" than are men (Knack 1973–74). Powwow planning follows similar lines, with women in charge of publicity, beauty pageants, food, and traditional entertainments, while men direct money matters and competitive sports of Euro-American origin.

Women's political participation in community meetings of all kinds is at least as frequent as men's. They speak and publicly debate issues with men (including their husbands), and their suggestions, taken seriously by both male and female peers, are often adopted. Potential and actual women political leaders nearly all cite dreams and visions validating their aspirations (Kelly and Fowler 1986:380–81; Knack 1973–74).

Family histories reveal that newlyweds still reside matrilocally 24 percent of the time; patrilocally, 40 percent; and neolocally, 33 percent. Many traditional families continue to practice some of the menstrual taboos, for younger as well as older women. Although they do not physically remove themselves from the household, women avoid social contact with others, especially men, and generally abstain from meat and iced beverages. Although they deliver their babies in hospitals, nearly all Paiute mothers prefer to practice a reduced set of childbirth taboos, especially avoidance of meat and iced beverages and touching the face or hair. Many husbands avoid only meat, but even this is considered a hardship; both sexes anticipate that men will be less rigorous than women in their adherence to this custom. Traditional families save the child's umbilical cord for later ritual burial. Within the last thirty years there have been women shamans, curers, and persons thought to have spiritual power.

Thus, in the present as in traditional culture, women are major economic producers, control the products of their labor, participate in political decision making, and hold important public offices. They are central to the social organization of the community and retain high social status.

Simply observing such continuity is not enough, however, for it begs the question of why Southern Paiute women have retained their cultural position during the conquest period and into the present, when women in many parts of the world have lost theirs.

Southern Paiute ethnohistory reveals the transformation of an autonomous egalitarian hunting and gathering culture to an ethnic labor class within the rural aspect of a rigidly hierarchical, commercially based nation-state (Knack n.d.). This transition began early and was direct. Unlike the Subarctic (e.g., Van Kirk 1980) or even the Plains (e.g., Klein 1983), where Indians went through a period as producer/extractors of materials desired by the Euro-American economy, Great Basin groups rarely generated any products desired by non-Indians other than their labor. In this region, whites directly extracted the resources they wanted—minerals, agricultural and pasture lands, and water. Forced by circumstances to substitute wages for a lost resource base, Paiute labor patterns were structured and defined in sex-specific ways by the male-dominated culture of their employers. Indian women were hired only for tasks Euro-Americans defined as "women's work." Harvest labor was the exception; even though non-Indian women did not work in the fields after the first decade of settlement, Indian women were regularly hired, as the commercial desire for cheap labor apparently overrode sex preferences. Throughout the contact period, Paiute women played an important role in native subsistence production—either directly through food production or indirectly through labor for wages that could then be transformed into food and other goods. On the basis of this subsistence production, women's egalitarian position within Paiute society was maintained, reflected in their importance in political participation, social organization, and religious power.

Indian women accepted wage labor for reasons compatible with and growing out of their own culture. They were accustomed to an active role in subsistence production and probably saw the flour that was paid to Indians as not unlike the wild seed meal they had traditionally gathered and ground so laboriously. Even field harvest labor resembled gathering and was not, apparently, offensive to them.

Other characteristics of the jobs offered women were also apparently important for their ability to participate in the wage labor market. Because there were so few productive econiches, Euro-American towns grew up in the same places that Paiutes had previously utilized, so the two populations were frequently co-resident. Paiute women could work in the non-Indian part of town and still maintain their family life without interruption. Housecleaning and laundry work were part-time, involving a few days work on a weekly or monthly basis. This enabled them to continue their own activities, including active plant gathering in reduced and remote areas. Extended bilateral kinship ties and bilocal residence patterns permitted kin-related women to provide working mothers with child care. Thus maternal and family obligations, which were and are held to be of great cultural importance, could be maintained while, at the same time, allowing women to contribute to the community income.

Never producing reliable, comfortable surpluses, after loss of the most productive sites to Euro-Americans the Paiute economy could not afford the luxury of having healthy adults segregated from the productive sector. Throughout the period under discussion, Paiute families needed the income produced by both men and women, no matter how small or infrequent, to supplement their scanty income. They worked at whatever was available, which was primarily periodic wage labor. The question then becomes, why was Paiute income so small and intermittent?

The economy in which the Paiutes found wage work was not one that they in any sense controlled. Decision making rested outside Paiute society and often outside non-Indian Great Basin society as well. Very much in the manner described by Joseph G. Jorgensen's (1971) metropolis-satellite model, decisions concerning the economic well-being of the southeastern Great Basin lay with Eastern and California bank and mine owners, with railroads, and with beef and food markets in major metropolitan areas. From the earliest time of Mormon settlement, the regional economy became cash based, if cash-short. It was based on mercantile trade, exporting regional resources to a worldwide industrializing economy (Wolf 1982). When settlers displaced Paiutes for homesites, they did so, not to engage in subsistence agriculture alone, but to participate at least in part in that larger economic system. Paiutes, having lost physical control of subsistence resources and unable to regain it through private landownership or federal trust protection, could enter this economy only as laborers servicing non-Indian economic needs. To phrase it in another way, as the mode of production shifted from native subsistence production for use to Euro-American production for exchange in a capitalist market, Paiutes lost control over the means of production. Within this new system, Paiute women, as well as men, became members of the labor class.

The historical pattern of Southern Paiute women's political and economic roles corresponds remarkably well with Peggy Reeves Sanday's (1974) early model of women's status. She predicts a sequence of five factors, each a necessary but not sufficient antecedent of the next: substantial female contribution to subsistence production; female production of goods desired beyond the domestic level; female control of the distribution of the products of their labor; officeholding or significant public political participation; and female solidarity groups. From traditional culture through known history and into the present, Paiute women have continuously contributed substantially to the subsistence economy, which has in turn enabled other aspects of their roles to be maintained as well. They continued to control the products of their labor and continued to produce goods, labor, and cash, which were desired and exchanged beyond the household level. On this foundation they maintained a high level of political participation and high social status. Although no longer members of an autonomous economic system, Southern Paiute women today enjoy an active role in community life, a high status within that native community, and a striking personal self-assurance that are products of both the past and the present.

10

THE GENDER STATUS OF NAVAJO WOMEN

MARY SHEPARDSON

Navajo Indians have claims to distinction. They are the largest tribe in the United States, some two hundred thousand strong with a reservation of some 14 million acres in Arizona, New Mexico, and Utah. In historical times their economy has changed from hunting and gathering to small-scale agriculture to pastoralism. Today wage work and business enterprises and professions have been added. Unlike most pastoral societies, this tribe is matrilineal and matrilocal (preferred) with apparent high status for women.

I base my reanalysis of Navajo culture on the period after the conquest and exile to Fort Sumner. The Treaty of 1868 allowed Navajos to return to a part of their old Navajoland, set aside as a reservation.

Two points of view must be considered, the *inside* and the *outside*. What the Navajo think about high or low status is the inside view, and my opinion is the outside view. I am a white, Anglo-Saxon Protestant (WASP) woman anthropologist. I am interested in the Navajos not only as people, acquaintances, and friends but also as a society that is important in cross-cultural comparisons with other societies of the world. That is my bias. I believe that cultural attitudes and behaviors fall into three categories: those that unquestionably indicate high status, those that are rated differently by different analysts, and those that are unquestionably restricting and demeaning.

In Navajo life clan affiliation is a basic index for women's high status. The Navajo receive their clan affiliation at birth. They are "born into" their mother's clan, which then becomes their clan, and "born for" their father's clan. Mother's clan is of primary importance, and father's clan is of secondary importance. Navajo kinship furnishes the network of relations of responsibility and expectation of helpfulness. If you ask Navajos a question about kinship, you may receive the answer, "It's all in the clans."

The Navajo do not own land outright, but their right to use land is founded on kinship-based residence groups. They possess use rights to areas they have settled, cultivated, and used for grazing livestock. If the land is not in continual use, it may be preempted by other families. Preferably, the groom on marriage comes to live in the bride's residence group. Women share in the work of grazing, agriculture, and crafts, all of which makes a substantial contribution to the subsistence economy and is valued. They own their own stock and control the disposal of their own handicraft products.

Other indexes of women's status are several important social rights and symbols. Divorce is easy for both men and women in the Navajo way. The woman "puts the man's saddle outside the hogan" and he gets the message. If the man wishes a divorce, it is said, "He went out to round up his horses and never came back." A woman keeps the children within her extended family, and the man returns to his family of origin until he marries again and moves to his new wife's hogan.

Puberty rites are celebrated for girls, not for boys. A great goddess in Navajo mythology is Changing Woman, who created the Navajo and the four original clans. She was the first to be honored with Kinaaldá, the girl's puberty rite. She was the mother of the hero twins, who rid the world of monsters. She symbolizes, through changes from youth to age and return to youth, the four seasons of the year. She is the Earth Mother. All these factors mean high status for Navajo women.

Women have equal rights with men in terms of inheritance (Shepardson and Hammond 1966:90). When Blodwen Hammond and I began our study of inheritance patterns in Navajo Mountain community, we were told, "Every family does it differently." Differently, yes, but not randomly. Use rights to the family land continue with the family members living on the land at the time of death of any of the

160

members. Statements on inheritance range from "Women inherited from their mothers" and "Men inherited from their fathers" to "It's in the clans." The procedure after the death is to call a meeting of kin who are likely to inherit. An influential relative is chosen to administer the distribution. Those who do not attend may very well be cut out of the inheritance. Inheritance operates according to matrilineal principles. This means that a man's relatives in the maternal line—his own siblings, his mother, his mother's sisters and brothers, and her sisters' children—take precedence over his wife and his own children (although they may have received token gifts both before and after his death). A woman's children and other relatives in the maternal line take precedence over her spouse. Other types of potential heirs may include members of the residence group and individuals selected for special attributes: dependents and/or trustees for dependents, persons who cared for the deceased before death, those present at the distribution of the estate, those who know how to care for the objects of property, and those who are in greater need.

WORLDVIEWS AND VALUES

Let us now consider in more detail worldview and values. Navajo values are derived from myths, adventures of the Holy People, Earth people, and animals, and natural phenomena. The Holy People taught Navajos correct attitudes and behavior as well as the ritual perfection of the chantways (Halpern 1957:86–97). The main values of harmony, order, good health, long life, and beauty are expressed in Blessingway. This rite is regarded by Navajos and those who study Navajo ways as the most important religious ceremony. Leland C. Wyman (1975:xiv) calls it "the backbone of Navajo religion." John Farella (1984:32) says, "This is the main Navajo rite, the main stem from which all other ceremonies branch out. It is the main stalk . . . synonymous with the continuation of their way of life." Blessingway contains the often quoted prayer,

> In beauty we walk
> Beauty before us
> Beauty behind us
> Beauty above us

> Beauty under us
> Beauty all a round us
> In Beauty it is returned
> In Beauty it is returned.
> (Adams and Newlin 1987:10)

Emphasis is placed on sharing, on cooperation rather than competition, in the family and in the clan network. The work ethic is impressed on children, who begin to herd sheep and help with domestic chores at an early age.

There is value in talk and discussion. Words have power. A criticism of leaders that one hears often on the reservation is, "They're not talking it over with the people." This value ensures that women participate in discussions and decision making. Louise Lamphere writes,

> Among the Navajo, domestic and political spheres are relatively undifferentiated and most crucial decisions are taken within the domestic group rather than in a wider political arena. Authority within domestic groups is egalitarian, with the emphasis on individual autonomy. Under these conditions, Navajo women have a great deal of control over their lives. They do not need to wrest power from others who hold positions of authority or attempt to influence decisions that are not theirs to make. (Lamphere 1974:103)

The sweathouse has been compared by Clyde Kluckhohn and Dorothea Leighton (1948) to a men's club, a man's place of refuge from women. Jerrold Levy, in a personal communication, says that sweathouses are family affairs where some family business can be discussed. Men's discussions of wider issues can take place at the large outdoor ceremonies. Women also use the sweathouse for "women-only" family business. Traditionally, there were no continuously functioning men-only or women-only associations.

Life is highly ritualized. There are many symbols such as Mother Earth, Father Sky. Even mountains have indwelling spirits. There are male rains and female rains, male winds and female winds. Farella (1984:133) quotes Washington Matthews who wrote, "Of two things that are nearly alike, it is common among Navajos to speak of or symbolize the one which is the coarser, rougher, or more violent as the male, and that which is finer, weaker or more gentle as the female."

In some of the great chants, there are male and female branches based on differences in the ritual. The difference between the male and female branches of Shooting Way, Wind Way, or Mountaintop Way elicits different explanations. Either branch can be sung over both men or women. Father Berard Haile (1938) suggests that the difference lies in whether the protagonist of the basic myth is a hero or heroine. Gladys Reichard (Newcomb and Reichard 1975:v) says that the main distinction is that in one branch the emphasis is on driving out evil (male branch) and in the other branch the emphasis is on the bringing of good (female branch).

The Navajo value system is filled with taboos, most of them shared by both men and women. The breaking of some taboos results in illness. For example, marrying into a clan that is too closely related is regarded as incest, just like intermarriage within the nuclear family. Both threaten the couple with epilepsy.

Navajo women are greatly restricted by a menstrual taboo that is based on the belief that menstrual blood can harm others. Charlotte Johnson Frisbie (1967:7) says, "Menstruating women may not see sand paintings, enter a ceremonial hogan, be a patient, attend or lead a Sing or join in the dancing which occurs at certain ceremonies. In secular activities, they should not go into the field, carry water, or use the sweathouse. Any contact with livestock . . . is forbidden." Irene Stewart, in a personal communication, confirms this taboo. She says, "Navajo women during menstruation are advised to be separated from others, men, women, and children. Because of the uncleanness of the blood, it is considered dangerous. I heard it said that 'hunchbacks' result from the contagion." Flora L. Bailey (1950:10) states, "Great care is taken to avoid any contact with it lest illness result. . . . [A]rthritis deformans . . . makes you 'humpbacked.'"

Anne Wright (1982) studied attitudes toward menstruation among traditional Navajo and educated, modernizing women. Of twenty-eight traditional women, she found that an equal number had a negative and a positive reaction toward menstruation. "One woman recalled the anxiety menstruation brought with its potential of hurting others." Many traditional women felt that menstruation "eliminated old used blood which otherwise would be stored up in the body to the detriment of one's health" (ibid., 57). Similarly, Wright says of menopause,

> For Navajo women who observe the taboos, this commonly represents the end of a great burden. For a few women this change is especially important because it presents the opportunity to become a medicine woman, or hataalii. With the end of menstruation, a woman is freed from the ceremonial taboos which would normally interrupt her pursuit of the elaborate ritual/medical knowledge. (Ibid., 62).

The view that menstrual blood is dangerous gives rise to some questions. If it is so dangerous, why is the girl's first menses celebrated? Kinaaldá is a true rite of passage, the change of a child into a woman. In this ceremony, she is instructed in her future role. Her body is molded for strength and beauty. She blesses the children. Fertility is honored. Changing Woman was the first to menstruate, the first to have Kinaaldá, and the first to teach the Navajo the value of the ceremony. One cannot overestimate the importance of this rite in creating a positive self-image in a young girl. Hammond and I were often told with pride of the location of "my coming-out party," as our interpreter called the event. But what of the danger of menstrual blood? One suggestion is that it is nullified by Blessingway songs; another is that the danger is less with youth and increases with advancing age.

If menstrual blood is polluting, are men who have been at war, who have killed enemies and seen enemy blood, also considered polluted and/or polluting? Irene Stewart (1980) writes,

> I never heard of a man coming back from war as dangerous to others. Enemy Way is an old rite for men, women and young people who have been war prisoners and who have returned to their people to be given this ceremony for cleansing and peace of mind. It's like a devil-chasing ceremony with bathing, songs and prayers performed followed by the Blessingway. (n.p.)

In short, the participants in war need to be protected from enemy ghosts but are not in themselves dangerous to others. This is by no means the same thing facing menstruating women, who are excluded from ceremonial participation for several days every month of the year until menopause.

DAILY LIFE

Let us look at daily life. Traditional Navajo live in extended family groups. Typically, these groups consist of father, mother, unmarried children, and married daughters and their husbands and children. Each nuclear family has a hogan in which to eat and sleep. Ownership is individual, but the animals are herded in family flocks. Small farm plots of corn and melons and little orchards of peach trees are cultivated. Crops are shared within the family.

In the past, hunting was an important source of food. Today it is mostly indulged in as recreation. Some hunting was ritualized. A leader who knew the prayers and songs would assemble a group, usually composed of men. The ritualized hunt of large animals began with a meeting in the sweathouse and the chanting of prayers. Karl W. Luckert (1975:62) says, "Women are permitted to accompany the hunting party. But they must stay in a separate shelter, built especially for women. They will tend the venison, cut and sun-dry the meat, so that there will be less weight to carry home." Women were free to join the communal hunts of small animals such as rabbits. In the myths, women were not excluded from hunting. Father Berard (1938) recorded a myth entitled "Concerning the One Who Was Changed into a Deer." A girl who had turned into a deer was hunted down by her brothers and turned back into human form. Before the sister departed to be forever with the divine deer, she taught her four brothers the proper ways to hunt; presumably, she had obtained this information from her friends, the deer. The older brother was taught the Game Way; the second, the Corral Way; the third, the Wolf Way; and the youngest, the Hunting Way of Talking-god (Luckert 1975:183).

There is some sexual division of labor. In building houses, men prepare the wooden framework and women apply the outer layer of mud. Women cook, but men also know how to cook. Women take part in grazing, lambing, shearing, and hide tanning. They share in planting, weeding, and harvesting and accompany their men to gather piñon nuts. Women's chief crafts are weaving, pottery, and basketry. Men's crafts are making bows and arrows and working with wood, iron, leather, and silver (Kluckhohn, Hill, and Kluckhohn 1971:425–29; Parezo 1982:431–34).

However, there are crossovers. Men can follow women's crafts and vice versa. If a man does too much "women's work," he risks being labeled a transvestite, or *nádlee*. This is a "risk," of course, only if the man is not a real transvestite but wants to be a weaver. Nádlee is a mixed status. Begochidi is the hermaphrodite of the myths. He is a trickster and at the same time a creator. According to Farella (1984:140–41), "*Nádlee* is both male and female, a person who used to be respected, not one who is made fun of. This is still a very important teaching. . . . I think the term refers less to external genitalia than to the potentials one exhibits in behavior." Hasteen Klah was a highly respected medicine man, sand painter, and weaver who worked with Franc Johnson, Gladys Reichard, and Mary Cabot Wheelwright in their studies of Navajo ceremonies. He was also a nádlee. When Hammond and I were collecting genealogies in Oljato, on several occasions our informants would volunteer the information that a relative of theirs was a nádlee. When asked how nádlees were treated by the people, we were assured that they were treated like anyone else.

KINSHIP

As stated above, there are restrictions against marrying into one's own clan, one's father's clan, or with a person "born for" one's "born for" clan. Clan relations create a network for hospitality and aid through which Navajo culture has spread widely.

Traditional marriages are arranged between two families by father, mother, mother's brother, and other relatives. The prospective bride and groom may never have seen each other. Although they have the right to refuse the marriage, many young people are grateful to their parents for providing them with a mate. In Navajo Mountain, Hammond and I found that arranged marriages lasted as long, sometimes longer, than marriages by choice of the participants. At marriage a contract is formulated regarding the work the in-marrying groom must do in his bride's family group and how much livestock and jewelry will constitute the bride-price as a family gift. While the bride-price can be viewed either as enhancing or as demeaning to one's status, in comparison with the European custom of dowry paid by the bride's family to the groom's family, I find the Navajo custom enhancing. In no sense is the Navajo bride regarded or treated as a purchased chattel.

The wedding takes place at the bride's home. The young couple is treated to much advice from both families. In a symbol of sharing, they eat cornmeal mush out of a wedding basket. At this time the mother-in-law/son-in-law taboo must be activated. They cannot look at each other for fear of going blind. The rationale is that there should be no sexual relations between the two. Another explanation for this custom is that it relieves the tensions in the familiar, perhaps worldwide, mother-in-law/son-in-law syndrome. This is a difficult custom to practice. If, usually under Christian influence, the taboo is ignored and no eye trouble has resulted, both parties appear to be greatly relieved.

When the wife becomes pregnant, she and her husband both observe certain taboos to ensure that the child will be healthy and well formed. A female child is as welcome as a male child. Sometimes a woman will prefer a daughter or a man will prefer a son to help them with the work. There are herbs that can be used to ensure the gender of the child: *Phlox stansburyi* for a girl and *Chrysothamus depressus* (rabbitbrush), which is a "male" plant, for a boy (Vestal 1952:40, 49).

Women nurse their babies for as long as possible to delay the next pregnancy. Stewart says that Navajos understand a physical connection. There are other traditional methods of birth control through the use of herbs. Vestal (ibid., 35, 40, 49) lists them as follows: *Rhus trilobata* (squaw bush, skunk bush), used as a contraceptive and to induce impotency; *Phlox stansburyi* (plumeway plant), used as a contraceptive; and *Bahia dissecta*, for menstrual pain, arthritis, and contraception. If these herbs effectively act as contraceptives, this greatly widens a woman's area of choice through planned parenthood.

An infant is kept close to the mother day and night and can suckle on demand. Use of the cradleboard enables the mother to watch after the child and still continue her work. James S. Chisholm (1983) describes the effects of the use of the cradleboard on both infant and mother.

The mother teaches the small children and growing girls. For this she must know some of the ceremonial songs and stories and the patterned taboos as well as skills in household, agricultural, and grazing tasks. Older boys are taught skills, values, and good behavior by their fathers.

Excessive sexual activity by a man or a woman is deplored. The words for loose woman or prostitute are 'aljilnii and kiyaah sizíní. The word for a sexually promiscuous man is ta'disho. Excessive sexual activity with promiscuous partners for whom one takes no responsibility is labeled "just like dogs." Since men should pay for sexual favors according to the teachings of the myths, it may be possible to label women who are regularly promiscuous as prostitutes. There is no institutionalized pandering or brothel keeping. One curing ceremony has been labeled "Prostitution Way" by Kluckhohn and Father Berard, but Reichard strongly objects to this title as misleading. She says, "'Excess', 'Recklessness' or 'Rashness' Chant would more accurately suggest its meaning" (1950:140).

Virginity is preferred, even demanded, in certain ceremonial roles. Reichard (1950:174) points out that "the person in charge of the rattlestick, the master symbol of the War Ceremony (Enemyway) should be a reliable female virgin; sometimes only a very small girl can fulfill the requirements." I have heard it said that a virgin girl brings a higher bride-price, but I know of no specific instance of this. However, women who have indulged in premarital sexual activity do not seem to have difficulty finding husbands. There is no stigma of illegitimacy on the child of an unwed mother. The child is readily acceptable to the new husband and to the mother's extended family.

There are no heavy sanctions against a woman who commits adultery, no stoning to death as in the Bible, no cutting off of noses. Frank Mitchell (1970:889) speaks of adultery in the recent past:

In those days, the elders in the family talked about such things and said, "If your wife does this, do not abuse her or get jealous of her. She has this privilege; she is a human being. You have your choice of leaving her or staying with her regardless of what she does."

The custom of plural wives (but not plural husbands) was acceptable. Frequently, a man married sisters in sororal polygyny, and often a man, married or unmarried, would wed the wife or wives of his dead brother. A man would marry a woman with a female child whom he could marry when she grew up. These patterns were not always welcomed by the women involved.

We knew of a family in which the only child, a girl, was kept out of school to herd sheep. Then suddenly when she was in her teens, she was whisked off to a program of accelerated study for children who were too old to enroll in the beginning grades. She was taken well out of the reach of her stepfather.

As to polygyny, there were ambivalent reactions. We knew of cases in which the first wife drove off the interloper and others in which the first wife herself was chased out of her hogan. A woman in Narrow Canyon told us how she had run away from home to avoid marrying an old man, rich in sheep, but had been persuaded by her favorite brother to accept the marriage for the good of the family. Later she bitterly resented her husband's desire to marry her sister. Once again she was persuaded to accept the situation. "It's not a bad way of life if you can stand it," she told us.

A joking relationship that is the antithesis of avoidance is familiar to the Navajo. Obscene teasing is permitted between both maternal and paternal cross-cousins who are not potential mates (Reichard 1928: 72). It is called "joking in the clans" and involves clan relations of exogamy. Whenever we got on this subject our informants were convulsed with laughter. [1]

Both Navajo men and women may be referred to by nicknames that are not always flattering, such as "The Gambler," "The Gossiper," "The

1. There is a word for wife, *ba'aad*, derived from animals, somewhat comparable to our use of "bitch." There is a similar word for wife, *shi'chooni*, which is translated "my companion."

Limper," and "The One Who Shouts." Nicknames are not used in direct address (Young and Morgan 1951:443).

Girls are given war names ending in -baa, which is glossed as "warrior woman." This custom seems odd to the outsider because women rarely go to war. However, there is power in the name, which can protect the owner. It is given in early childhood and may be kept secret. According to W. W. Hill (1936:8), Navajo women did sometimes go to war.

> A woman, if she wished, might join a war party. There were never more than two women in a party. They fought just as did the men but were forbidden to take scalps and must not have sexual intercourse with any members of the party. None of the informants had ever heard of a woman leading a war party.

Hill describes a kind of Navajo Joan of Arc who took part in an attack on the Hopi village of Oraibi. "There was a young woman among the Navaho. She was on a very fast horse and rode right into the center of the Oraibi. She called to the Navajo to come on and give all they had. The Navaho encircled the Oraibi and started to slaughter them (ibid., 5)."

COSMOLOGY

Witchcraft is another source of power, the power to harm. Women, as well as men, can be witches. They can perform a ritual over bits of cloth containing sweat, nail parings, or strands of hair to hurt a specific person. Hammond and I (Shepardson and Hammond 1970:146) found more accusations of witchcraft leveled against men than against women. We concluded that the Navajo have greater confidence in the goodness of Navajo women than in the goodness of Navajo men.

Judge Zhealy Tso showed me the report of a witchcraft case that was brought to his Navajo Tribal Court. A woman was accused of witching another woman. The evidence was brought in by the Navajo policeman — strands of hair and bits of cloth. The woman admitted her guilt. The judge said to her, "I don't believe you have this power. I believe it all died out in 1906, but if you have, can't you use it to do good, not harm?" She said she would try. Judge Tso's problem was that the Navajo Tribal Court, under the watchful eye of the Bureau of Indian Affairs, had removed the offense of witchcraft from its Code of Indian Offenses. The decision he made was satisfactory to all parties concerned, since they all believed in the existence of witches and witchcraft.

There are many female figures among the Holy People—Spider Woman, who taught weaving, Earth Woman, Salt Woman, White Shell Woman, and Water Woman. There are male/female cooperating pairs such as Dawn Boy/Dawn Girl, Holy Boy/Holy Girl, and Rock Crystal Boy/Rock Crystal Girl. They emphasize the principle of sharing or complementarity. Many symbolic figures of women supernaturals are drawn in the sand paintings. Medicine men dominate the ritual Sings. However, women also can learn to be Singers and lead in ceremonies, regularly after menopause. They play important roles in the whole curing process. Diviners such as Hand Tremblers, mostly women, diagnose a disease and suggest the proper ceremony to be performed: they have been affected by unusual trembling of the hand and arm, with their fingers pointing at something; after being blessed with pollen and learning from a Singer man how to interpret the motions, they can perform. Some women are herbalists who collect medicinal plants.

Women also help in the Sings by organizing the feeding of some hundreds of people at night chants. They furnish baskets and yarn to decorate prayer sticks. In Enemy Way, they chant to exorcise alien ghosts, and they may ritually kill the centrally important scalp symbol but only through a surrogate. Reichard (1950:175) says, concerning the inclusion and exclusion of women from parts of rituals.

> Navaho ritual, true to the dogma that opposites must be included, prescribes honors in one activity and represses them in another. Women are barred from holding aggressive offices in the War Ceremony [Enemy Way]; that is, they may not conduct it; the stick receiver and the ashes strewer must be a man.

There is also, as previously mentioned, the female virgin who is in charge of the rattle stick. In the evening "squaw dances," a woman chooses a man and holds onto him until he has paid her a forfeit. In ceremonies requiring sand paintings, a woman can assist if she has been sung over in the ritual for which that particular sand painting is being made. Women share the responsibility of protecting the Earth Bundle, a bundle containing soil from four or six sacred mountains, and its renewal. Originally a gift from Changing Woman, who showed how it was composed, the Earth Bundle is essential for use in the most important Navajo rite, the Blessingway.

There is an important story called Separation of the Sexes in the Origin Myth. One version is that when First Man and First Woman were living in the Lower World, First Man discovered that First Woman was committing adultery. In the ensuing argument, her mother, Woman Chief, said that women could get along without men. Outraged, the men crossed the river, leaving the women on the bank. Among the men was a hermaphrodite who knew the work of both sexes. This enabled the men to live in comfort. The women, however, failed at subsistence agriculture. They masturbated with stones, thereby creating monsters (all male). Finally they begged the men to take them back. They were received on the promise that they would never again try to assume leadership.

A prominent contemporary Navajo woman, Ruth Roessel, finds this pledge still acceptable (1981:132). Even today, Navajo women do not often take political leadership, although traditionally they were consulted. I, as the outsider, see in this a negative factor in the rights of women. I am too sharply reminded of another myth about a man, a rib, a woman, a serpent, a tree, and an apple. Events are different, but the message is the same: women brought evil into the world. Navajo women created monsters; First Man created witchcraft. So even here the sexes share in the creation of evil. This myth still has modern consequences. When I asked a judge why so few women were elected to the Navajo Tribal Council, he referred to this myth. That, he said, was why Navajo women could not be trusted in politics. I contend that neither of these sacred stories can do anything but lower the status of Navajo and Christian women.

In other parts of the mythology, Navajo women's high status is confirmed. Wyman (1970:10) quotes Father Berard on the Navajo hogan: "This place home is to be the center of every blessing in life: happy births, the home of one's children, the center of weddings, the center where good health, property, increase in crops and livestock originate where old age, the goal in life, will visit regularly. In a word, the hogan spells a long life of happiness." According to Wyman,

> The home of First Man became the pattern for the interlocked forked pole hogan of today. . . . The south pole was called the pole of Mountain Woman, the west pole was called the pole of Water Woman and that of the north the pole of Corn Woman. . . . Blessingway ceremonials should be performed in it. Blessingway insists that its center is the place home from which its blessings will radiate. (Ibid., 11)

And Gary Witherspoon (1975:125–26) says,

> The solidarity of mother and child symbolized in patterns of giving life and sharing items which sustain life, is projected in Navajo culture as the ideal relationship between and among all people. All one's kinsmen are simply differentiated kinds of mothers . . . and since everyone is treated and addressed as a kinsman, all people are bound together by the bond of *k'e* [kinship]. . . . [T]he *k'e* that exists between mother and child provides the foundational concepts and forms for all relationships in Navajo social life. Moreover, this foundational bond of kinship is not limited to people, for the earth is called mother, the sheep herd is called mother, corn is called mother, and the sacred mountain soil bundle is called mother. The symbols of motherhood and the *k'e* solidarity which they symbolize pervade Navajo culture and provide the patterns and sentiments which order Navajo social life.

Culture is not solely a set of symbols embodied in words. A culture provides patterns of belief and behavior that enable a group of people to reproduce, to function together, and to continue through generations as a society.

WOMEN AND STATUS

My reanalysis of the status of Navajo women does not overturn the stereotype of their high position. I did not, however, find a "matriarchy" as some have loosely labeled Navajo society. One has only to read Ruth Roessel's *Women in Navajo Society* (1981) and Irene Stewart's *A Voice in Her Tribe* (1980) or, better still, live for some time in Navajo country to realize how important and how valued are men's roles. "Sharing," not "dominating," is the theme of Navajo life. Men and women share in the work of the subsistence economy and in the teaching of values, proper behavior, and skills to the children. In the healing arts and religion, men dominate but by no means completely. Grandfathers, fathers, uncles, husbands, brothers, and sons contribute to the positive emotional ambience and smooth running of the Navajo extended family. I prefer to take a phrase from Diane Eisler's *Chalice and the Blade* (1987:xvii) and call this a "partnership" society.

After the Treaty of 1868, the new federal authority did not support the high position of Navajo women. Clan relationships based on the matrilineal principle were ignored completely in the census records. Males were listed as head of household by the Bureau of Indian Affairs. When surveys made in the 1930s showed that the range was dangerously overgrazed, the bureau divided the reservation into eighteen districts, estimated the carrying count of livestock that could be grazed in each district, and surveyed the present ownership of sheep, goats, and horses. The bureau then ordered the reduction of the herds. Permits were issued showing ownership and numbers.

> In fact, sheep at least were tallied under the name of the person who brought them in for dipping although they might be the property of several kinsmen and not of a single individual. . . . [Records] I have seen are particularly surprising in listing almost no women as owners, although it is well known that Navaho women own livestock in their own right. (Aberle 1966:66)

Hammond and I had noticed this discrepancy when we examined the permits for Navajo Mountain (District 12). The federal work program offered in compensation for the enforced stock reduction involved jobs mostly for men. Those jobs that were available for women were fewer and less highly paid.

Women were not allowed to vote in the newly established Navajo

Tribal Council elections from 1923 to 1925 when their sisters in the larger society had attained the franchise (Shepardson 1963:78).

Only in the last two or three decades has the status of women been raised through education. Training for skilled labor and professional positions has become available. Scholarships for higher education in a number of colleges in the United States are offered to Navajo and other Indians. Nearly twice as many Navajo women as compared to Navajo men held tribal scholarships as of 1979 (Shepardson 1982:156). Affirmative action in employment in the U.S. Public Health Service and the Bureau of Indian Affairs has opened new administrative positions. Women have taken advantage of these opportunities.

Rural women face different challenges. In a study of Shonto, Scott Russell and Mark McDonald (1982) found that rural women who work in agriculture and stock raising spend more hours and earn less per hour than do wage workers. Rural women's income has declined. However, "there is only a slight erosion of their status. They have high status for their work in arts and crafts" (263). It is interesting to see that in another study (Levy, Henderson, and Adams 1989) it was found that instead of changes anticipated because of the increase in wage work and unearned income (welfare), elements of localized matrilineages and large extended matrilocal families have been persistent.

In conclusion, I wish to quote from two Navajos, one a prominent, Western-educated woman and the other a traditional man with no formal education. Roessel (1981:106) writes,

> In a traditional society there never was a feeling of dependency upon the man or the husband in which the woman was considered unequal and did what she was told by her husband.

Son of Old Man Hat said,

> I've thought about men and women, and I always thought a man was bigger and stronger. A man is sensible, and knows more, and he's smarter than a woman. . . . A man can do all the hard work. . . . I was that way for a long time until I got gray hair, then I found that a man is way behind and a woman is way ahead, because a woman can do all kinds of hard work too. I found out they have many sufferings and they can stand them. . . .

175

A woman is stronger than a man. A man will beget children, he makes children all right, but he doesn't suffer, he only makes a woman suffer. So that's why now, today, I think a woman is stronger than a man. (Dyk 1938:48)

11

CONTINUITY AND CHANGE IN GENDER ROLES AT SAN JUAN PUEBLO

SUE-ELLEN JACOBS

During the past eighty years or so, women's roles at San Juan Pueblo have changed at an increasingly rapid rate, corresponding to the rate at which the Tewa have participated in the changes brought about in their village by their contact with other peoples. This chapter focuses on continuity and change in women's roles within one large extended family (consisting of about 400 individuals out of an approximate total community population of 2,000; 1980 figures). The information presented is based on the published ethnographic record for this period (1900–83) and oral histories, observations, experiences, and impressions I have recorded during fifteen field seasons of varying lengths

Author's Note: This chapter is abstracted from the draft manuscript of the monograph I am writing entitled, "As if in a Dream: Images of Change at San Juan Pueblo, New Mexico," based on ethnohistorical research begun in 1970, formal interviewing, and participant observation (begun in 1972). The chapter is dedicated to "RCB" and her husband, "SM," both of whom have urged that I tell these (and other) Tewa stories in print. SM died in early 1989 at the age of 101; RCB died in 1990, sixty days before her ninetieth birthday.

An earlier version of this chapter was prepared for a 1980 American School of Research seminar and subsequently was to be published in a collected work on the Tewa and Hopi. The collection never materialized. Approval for publication was granted by individuals who participated in the research and tribal officers who asked that their identity not be revealed. I am grateful to the following persons who made substantial comments on the first several drafts of this chapter: over a dozen individuals at San Juan Pueblo and anthropology colleagues Marianne Gullestad, Steven Harrell, Richard Ford, Alfonso Ortiz, Judi Heerwagen, and Wendy Hill.

(ranging from 5 weeks to 14 months) at San Juan Pueblo. My aim in presenting this material is twofold: (1) to contribute to the ethnographic record of life at San Juan Pueblo and (2) to contribute to the recent debate on women's status and position relative to that of men. Therefore, before providing an overview of continuity and change in women's roles in this Tewa pueblo, I first give an overview of that debate.

The Position of Women: Theoretical Overview

Early theoretical and empirical research in feminist anthropology has led some researchers to conclude that universally "men and women compose two differentially valued terms of a value set, men, being as *men*, higher" (Ortner and Whitehead 1981:1–16). The arguments concerning asymmetry in cultural-specific valuations of gender were cast in hightly defended etic terms (see, e.g., Whitehead 1981:109). Using an etic model for analysis of cultural behaviors and beliefs allows systematic cross-cultural studies of human behavior by imposing an analytical model into which all human societies may be subjected for purposes of qualitative and quantitative comparison. This procedure has resulted in many treatises concerned with demonstrating commonalities found in human cultures. However, it is my contention that to understand diversity and commonality within and across human cultures, one must examine cultures within their ethnohistorical and contemporary contexts. Furthermore, understanding specific cultures is best accomplished by obtaining both emic and etic descriptions and explanations for the way things are.

My concern with these matters is based on a desire to reach a cultural understanding of how people manage their *everyday* lives and why they use the specific management strategies in diverse political, economic, environmental, and other situations. I am also interested in the ways people strive to meet specific biophysiological and psychosocial needs on a daily basis.

Everywhere the following three basic human needs must be satisfied: (1) acquisition, preparation, and consumption of food; (2) maintenance of shelter and other forms of bodily protection; and (3) nurturance and socialization of dependent offspring. People carry out their roles in meeting these needs in the context of specific rules for social organization that are, in turn, governed by specific ideological requirements of the society in which they live. These aspects of human behavior constitute researchable cultural imperatives.

During fieldwork, anthropologists attempt to deduce the rules for role performance by collecting information about religious, economic, political, and/or kinship institutions. Typically, analyses of collected information divide roles according to their place of performance, for example, the *domestic* (also referred to as familial, self-interest, inside, or private) and the *public* (also referred to as communal, social good, or outside) domains or spheres (see Hartsock 1983:267–301 and Ortner and Whitehead 1981:7–8 on the use of these terms as *contrastive* sets).

The expectation of some social science researchers has been that women will perform roles related directly to maintenance of the domestic sphere while men will perform roles related to the public or nondomestic sphere. For the most part these two spheres are treated as separate, rather than overlapping and mutually dependent—or at least contiguous—spheres of human endeavor. Likewise, the domestic and public domains (the arenas where people perform their roles) are often treated as separate, rather than mutually dependent and overlapping places of social interaction. Furthermore, in examining the performance of roles in either domain, most social science research on gender roles is concerned with determining the locus of power and authority to demonstrate the relative power (or powerlessness) of women and men. Sherry B. Ortner and Harriet Whitehead (1981) and others have pushed these issues further to consider social value, social honor, or "prestige structure" in an attempt to define the status and authority of women and men cross-culturally. Such research emphasizes role performance and cultural symbols used to mark the value of role performance. The research appears to be specifically designed to "discover" the seeming universality of (1) the sex or gender basis for the division of labor by sex; (2) the domination of women by men or, put another way, "the fact that, in every human culture, women are in some way subordinate to men" (Rosaldo 1974:17); and (3) the alleged "universal

179

devaluation of women" (Ortner 1974:69; Ortner and Whitehead 1981:1–16). This approach tends to obscure the interactive and mutually dependent relationships that women and men have in any society.

The theoretical models used for studies of the above questions invariably place a greater value on the roles and work of men and a greater value on activities carried out in the public as opposed to the domestic and private spheres. When Ortner and Whitehead say that "men, being as *men*" are valued more highly, we must ask by whom? the men? both women and men within the culture being studied? or by both women and men who are studying the culture? In other words, who is assigning the value to roles and work of women and men, and who is placing the value on domestic and public spheres or domains? Admittedly, it may be true that in some societies, a higher valuation for men's work and for work performed in the public domain is assigned emically (i.e., by the individuals living therein) and this according to the ideological requirements of those societies. However, one must wonder if such reported values are not assigned etically by outside researchers who come from Western traditions where this valuation is a norm based on ideological requirements of many Western societies, and these therefore do not reflect the "on-the-ground" or emic perspective. This question has been raised and the premise tested in recent years and found to be the case (e.g., Briggs 1970; Schlegel 1977c; Weiner 1976; and more recently, Cesara 1982; Etienne and Leacock 1980; Gewertz 1981; Nash 1981).

In societies where the focus is on communal rather than individualistic success,[1] whether this is in the production of crops, propitiation of deities or forces of the "natural" world, or other activities needed to sustain the society, questions concerning the value of individuals and their contributions to society must consider the *sum of relationships* in the whole society. "Rules" regarding inheritance, lineal relationships, endogamy and exogamy, participation in religious functions, the

---

1. If one follows Ortner, Strathern, Rosaldo, and Rubin, who all follow Lévi-Strauss, the dualistic, hierarchically ordered, contrastive sèts (with the second term in each pair being of "greatest value") are as follows: individual/communal (or individualistic/communalistic) = nature/culture = self-interest/social good = domestic/public = women/men.

holding of political office or other authoritative positions, and responsibilities for economic production and community reproduction may be deduced by asking and observing how individuals behave on everyday and special occasions. Queries and observations can lead to an understanding of how each part contributes to the whole of cultural maintenance and change. But seeking to determine "the status" of individuals in any society on the basis of one or a couplet of institutional rules obscures the interaction of the parts, as is required for any system to work; it also presupposes a ranking or value system that places greater emphasis or value on one part as *opposed* to another.

In examining the history of San Juan Pueblo, questions concerning "women's place" and "men's place" in society reveal that, until very recently, there was no general scale that could support any consideration of women as being subordinate to men[2] or women's work and other roles inferior to men's. This means that the issue of women's and men's statuses is an elusive one, fluctuating over time, and, when it occurs, depending on annual changes in the political organization. I intend to demonstrate that there is no gender-based status differential among the Tewa at San Juan Pueblo.

Tewa ideology emphasizes maintenance of balance and harmony within and between the natural and supernatural worlds. The domestic and public domains are emic categories here located (epistemologically and, until recently, spatially) on a continuum: each leads to the other and beyond to the cosmos. No single individual, and no class or cohort of people, can be said to be inferior or superior to another. Still there is a hierarchy of social organization that has its origins in Tewa cosmology. Based in the presumed religious structure of antiquity, reinforced and in part re-created through successive colonial periods, the theocratic order defines responsibilities for the individuals who accept a "calling" to traditional sodalities as well as the roles and responsibilities expected of individuals within each moiety and within the

---

2. Ortiz has said there has been a tendency for the reverse to be true within the pueblo, or village center, and the region lying immediately adjacent to this area, all of which are considered to "belong" to women, while the far hills and other portions of the outlying areas "belong" to men (pers. comm. 1982).

community as a whole (see Ortiz 1969 for a thorough discussion of this theocratic order). When one examines the systems of reciprocity between members of the community, one clearly comes to understand how a theocratically based hierarchical government can coexist over a long period with a value for nonhierarchical ordering of individuals, regardless of gender or place of role performance (for early basic information on this issue, see Aberle 1948; Bandalier 1910; Bandalier and Hewett 1937; Harrington 1916; Parsons 1929; for more recent information, see Ford 1968; Ortiz 1969, 1972). Recent economic and technological intrusions into Tewa culture, however, threaten to break the continuity of these traditions and therefore threaten the traditional (emically defined) statuses and roles of women at San Juan Pueblo and may lead to the emergence of a public/private distinction and dichotomization in role performances.

The materials presented below provide information necessary to answer five questions: What tasks are performed to meet the cultural imperatives? By whom are they performed? Where are they performed (domestic/public? inside/outside? private/public? domains)? To which domain(s) is (are) the tasks directed? Are the task performances governed by cultural values concerning gender roles and statuses (i.e., are there variations in authority and social control which are directly related to task performances)? The answers to these questions provide the basis for generalizing about continuity and change in gender roles at San Juan Pueblo in the context of the above described theoretical problems.

SELECT ETHNOGRAPHIC AND ETHNOHISTORICAL INFORMATION

In organizing oral histories and ethnographic and ethnohistorical information, I use the time markers provided by individuals (rather than publicly documented intrusions and their subsequent impacts) because the markers for these periods reflect either individual or family turnings (Langness and Frank 1981). The periods are of uneven duration. Because of space limitations and to dramatize quantitative and qualitative changes in life over the eighty-two-year period, information on only two of these periods is presented in any detail: Life before the atomic age will provide a baseline of information to which the period 1972 to 1982 will be compared and contrasted. There will be brief contextual references to some changes that took place during the intervening years (late 1930s to 1972) when these are important to understanding the more recent scenarios. The following discourse covers, roughly in this order, domains of activities (see Gronhaug 1978; Barth 1978; Blom pers. comm.; Kent 1984); economics (food acquisition, employment, arts and crafts production); education, childbirth, child rearing, and accoutrements of home life.

"LIFE BEFORE THE ATOMIC AGE": 1900 TO CA. 1940

Many changes occurred at San Juan Pueblo between 1900 and the late 1930s which can be attributed to outside forces. But in recounting life and work during this period, individuals refer only to those changes that are considered to be of personal or familial significance, while recognizing the larger effects of these changes on Pueblo people and the organization of San Juan Pueblo. Consider, for instance, the statement of RCB (born in 1900):

> We used to live so happy in the old days. The men's [sic] would go to the fields every day. We ladies would cook our food, take care of our houses, and make a little pottery to sell to the tourists. Life was very good then. (RCB 1983)

People in RCB's generation remember their childhoods being filled with events related to three major activities: farming, schooling, and Tewa religious ceremonies. For the most part, life was lived within and centered around the pueblo or village center. Friends and family lived in homes that were connected in typical Pueblo fashion, with entrances facing the plazas. A number of elders have told me that life was lived outside of their homes more than inside, even in winter.

> You always knew what people were doing because you could see them when they came out of their houses. The ladies were always making bread outside, or they were making pottery, or they were watching the children. Your friends and family were always close by for talking and visiting or helping. (MA 1980)

> The men who had planted their fields would go out very early in the morning. They would hitch up their horses, if they had them, and go to the fields. My grandfather had a barn back of where the well used to be and he would go every morning to take water from the well. By noon, my grandmother would have lunch made and she and I or my sister and I would take lunch to our men in the fields. (RCB 1978)

During spring and summer, many people were engaged in farming activities. In the spring, they began with cleaning of the irrigation ditches, a process that all men were supposed to help with. Discussion of ditch cleaning invokes memories of picnicking, storytelling, and singing.

> The men would take their hoes and rakes early in the morning, sometimes before the sun came up and follow the *cacique* [one of the religious elders; a sodality leader] to the mother ditch. Then they would start. We would fix their lunches and take it to them by noon or maybe ten o'clock. We always knew where they were because we could see the smoke from the line of the fire they used to burn up all the trash. Then they would sit with us under a tree and we would all eat, and they would tell stories, and rest. Sometimes they would sing or tell jokes. After we rested, we would come back to the pueblo [village] and the men would work until it was dark. Then they would come home and we would have supper. The next day it was the same, and the next, until the whole ditch was cleaned. (RCB 1978)

Religious ceremonials accompanied the various phases of farming (see Ortiz 1969 for discussion and description of ceremonials performed during these phases). Children and their parents and other relatives participated in the dances and other activities within these ceremonies to help assure a good harvest. Memories of these times include happiness and a sense of bounty associated with the coming together of friends and family to eat at the feasts prepared in various homes as part of the religious celebrations. RCB, her husband, SM, their children, and her sister and brother-in-law and their children moved to their "summer house," which was located in one of their large fields, following the Feast of San Juan (held on June 24).

> We would get our bedding together and all the things we would need, and the next day after our feast day, we would go to the summer house, in the

field where we had our little orchard. We got apples and plums from the trees, and we grew corn, chili and squash along with our wheat and hay. When we left, we would close the pueblo [house] by just putting a stick at the door. We would sleep out on the roof at night and were never afraid that anybody would bother us. (RCB 1978)

While the family members lived in their summer homes, they attended to irrigation and cultivation of their crops. SM also carved wood, creating sculptures of various *kachinas* and animals. He also made "flower-sticks" and the paired sticks with birds and animals carved on them that are used as rasps over baskets in specific ceremonial dances. RCB made pottery at this and other times. Both of these activities led to possibilities for cash income, and both required forays into outer regions of the reservation for raw materials.

RCB and her sister, along with other women, would go into the fields to collect manure that had been deposited by cattle during the winter, early spring, and late fall. Using a gunnysack and their shawls, the women would "carry a full backload" of the dried manure to their storage areas to be used later for firing their pottery. They also dug up sand and clay from various locales. If these resources were close by, several women would go together; if they were "in the far little hills," their husbands, brothers, sons, or sons-in-law usually went along to help. Likewise, collection of wood (a chore that had to be done throughout the year) for cooking, boiling water, and pottery firing was an activity RCB and her sisters-in-law have said was fun.

We would pack up a lunch and go over to the little hills across the highway. In those years, there used to be little trees on those hills. We would take a gunnysack and our shawls. First we would get those little animals [an insect of some type] in our sacks; then we would gather our little sticks, the branches that were dead on the trees or lying around on the ground. When we got home, we would fry those little animals. They tasted so good; just like french fries. (RCB 1978)

Pottery making takes a considerable amount of time but has scheduling advantages, since the work can be interrupted for child care, preparation of meals, and other activities. The pottery made by RCB and her women friends and relatives was used by them for storage of processed food, for cooking, for trade, and as a source of cash income.

In late summer, the families moved back to their homes in the pueblo, and harvesting of food sources became intensified. Drying was the main technique used for processing harvested food. Apples, peaches, and some squash and pears were cut into thin slices, then laid out in the sun to dry. Chili and beans were laid out on flat surfaces or tied into strings and hung to dry. In the late 1930s, U.S. government agricultural extension agents introduced techniques of storage referred to as "cold-packing." With this technique, storage jars and the fruit or vegetable to be "canned" are boiled. The jars are sealed airtight after being "packed." Some fruits and vegetables are processed more quickly using this technique, and if done properly, there is less loss due to spoilage than there was with drying of certain foods. Ears of corn were blanched in outdoor ovens, then braided together and hung to dry in the sun. Wheat was brought by the men of the family into a "corral" area where the women cleaned it. When this was completed, women and men drove in their wagons or walked to the miller in an adjacent community. Some of the meat from butchered pigs, sheep, and cows was cut into strips and hung to dry inside the homes. The rest of the meat that was to be stored was cured with salt and hung in larger chunks inside the homes or in a well-guarded barn (in an effort to keep the meat safe from dogs and other predators). Once the various foods were dried and otherwise processed, they were stored for use during the remainder of the year. Fruits, grains, and vegetables were stored in pottery and glass jars, in "tins," or in cloth sacks; dried meat was wrapped in burlap and other cloth. There were storage pits in the floors of the houses as well as storage shelves that had been etched into the thick adobe walls.

Food that required cooking for daily meals was cooked mainly in pots, pans, and skillets of iron on a wood-burning stove or over a wood fire in a pit oven or fireplace in the corner of one room of the house or outside the house. Beans were often cooked in pottery jars made of micaceous clay.[3] Corn was ground by hand using a classic stone *mano*

---

3. A form of clay that contains metal particles, giving a "shiny" appearance after it is fired.

and *metate* or a coffee bean grinder, then made into either a gruel or dough for tortillas. "Wild spinach" and other edible weeds were collected in the spring and most often consumed shortly thereafter. Other plants used for making tea or medicine were either collected in the fall when they were dry or dug up in spring, summer, and fall and hung to dry for use over the next year.

Some families relied on the purchase of all their foods from local farms and the various produce stores in the area. Not all individuals held arable land, not all individuals who held arable land farmed it, and not all individuals who farmed depended for their food on the products of their labors. Before explaining this statement, it must be pointed out that, technically, no individual can "own" Pueblo land. Any married adult enrolled member of San Juan Pueblo can request land for farming or housing. Land belonging to the Pueblo is assigned to families on the basis of several factors: need or desire to farm or build a home; the customary rights of the individual and others in the land being requested; and the overall availability of land (i.e., the amount of usable land divided by population density). Before the Pueblo Lands Board decisions in the 1920s and later and the subsequent court decisions, many of the best farming acres were occupied and used by non-Indians who had by various means ensconced themselves on San Juan Pueblo's land grant.[4] Once lands were returned to the Pueblo, a lottery system was set up so that all enrolled individuals, at least those who understood what was going on and so desired, could have farming land assigned to them by the Pueblo authorities.[5] Some individuals who had "won" good farming land in the lottery drawing did not begin to farm immediately, for one reason or another. In addition to these individuals, there were others who did not farm their assigned lands because they did not have sufficient help with the intensive work required to make it economically worthwhile or because they did not

---

4. Although much of this land was returned to San Juan Pueblo, RCB's family lost more than 40 acres that had been transmitted through her "grandfather's line" over several generations.

5. The complexities involved in regaining land during this period and other aspects of land and water rights faced by San Juan Pueblo over the years are developed in Jacobs (n.d.).

have the strength for or interest in doing the necessary labor involved or because they were employed full-time in wage labor activities off the reservation.

It was difficult to devote full attention needed for successful farming if the size of one's family or other conditions made it necessary to work off the reservation to obtain enough food, clothing, and other necessities. Some families managed to combine both farming and wage labor, but their crop production was not enough to both meet the complete food needs of their families and market their produce for cash or trade it for other necessities. The personal and economic needs of the families required some cash income and the most certain way to obtain cash was to work off the reservation. Partially because of limited education, in spite of Bureau of Indian Affairs (BIA) mandatory education rules, off-reservation employment for individuals who wanted to live at home (i.e., on the reservation) was limited largely to low-wage nonskilled jobs.

Employment for women outside of the reservation included helping to build, refurbish, and clean homes for families in the local (predominantly) Hispano homes; working as domestics in homes in more distant communities (e.g., Santa Fe and Albuquerque); working as "cleaning ladies" or janitors at Boys Ranch (a private boarding school) in Los Alamos and other institutions and businesses; and occasionally working as crop harvesters in other New Mexico areas as well as in communities in southern Colorado alongside their husbands or fathers. Off-reservation employment for men included digging trenches and laying pipelines for the gas company; building railroads in New Mexico and Colorado; and working as ranch hands, as general maintenance workers for various institutions and businesses in New Mexico, and as migrant crop farmers. When Los Alamos was chosen as the site for the Manhattan Project in 1941, some individuals who had been working at the Los Alamos Boys Ranch (which was taken over for the atomic research projects) were hired in support services. (RCB and several of her agemates worked as "cleaning ladies" in the security guards' dormitory, commuting to and from Los Alamos three to five days each week.)

Most children were sent to school by their parents, although some parents hid their children from officials because they did not believe the formal schooling would be good for them. (SM was "protected" from going to school by his mother. As a young man, he had been initiated into one of the religious sodalities. According to him, his mother was determined to keep him as close to traditional Tewa culture as possible.) In the BIA day school at San Juan Pueblo, children were taught arithmetic and how to read, write, and speak English. Children were not allowed to speak Tewa at school. At the boarding school in Santa Fe, the 3 Rs were reinforced and other normal school subjects were taught (e.g., geography and civics). Additionally, high school girls were taught "domestic arts" (they were required to work in the kitchens and laundry, mend clothes, and clean the dormitories), while boys were taught "extra-domestic crafts" (while they were allowed to learn carpentry skills, they were also required to work in the fields and to clean the campus grounds, mend fences, and do other outdoor chores). The BIA emphasized vocational training for the students at Santa Fe Indian School because many BIA personnel believed that Indians did not have the mental capacity to succeed in college or the professions (this in spite of the fact that there were many Indians who had demonstrated the falsehood of this belief). Consequently, emphasis was placed on development of manual skills as well as arts and crafts. So that they could attend feast days during the school year, children who were attending either the BIA or private (St. Catherine's) boarding school in Santa Fe were brought home by means of the transportation most accessible to their families, horse-drawn wagon or train.

RCB and her best school friend, who was from Picuris Pueblo, had dreams of becoming lawyers when they were in high school. They knew that other high school graduates had gone to Haskell College and other universities and colleges to prepare for later entrance into professional schools. But her family believed that women should marry and raise families. So her parents refused to let her finish her last year in high school. She married SM shortly thereafter.

In those years they were very strict with our rules. I had to go live with my mother-in-law. There was so much work to do, but I learned how to make tortillas outside on the big round stone she had and I learned more about

189

pottery making from her. She was very kind to me, but still I worked very hard. Then my husband and I lived for awhile with my parents, but then we moved back to live with his and stayed there until just before my first child was born. (RCB 1975)

Childbirth took place at home, with a Tewa midwife in attendance and other women who could be supportive or otherwise helpful before, during, and after delivery. Most often these helpers were relatives and friends. A clean sheepskin was placed on the polished earthen floor of the home. A rope was hung from a viga or attached to the wall. When the woman's "water broke," the mother-to-be was told to lie down on the sheepskin and to pull hard on the rope every time she felt a contraction. Sometimes there was a special chair available for the expectant mother to sit in during most of the birthing time. Once the infant was born, it was bathed by the midwife, wrapped in a blanket, passed around the attending friends and family members, then placed in the mother's arms. Shortly after the placenta was expelled by the mother, the midwife would bury the placenta in a corner of the house or she would take it to the river and cast it in to be carried away by the current. After full delivery was completed, the mother was given an herbal tea "to give her strength" and reminded that she should avoid certain foods for a minimum of four days. If she felt strong enough, the mother would get up shortly after her baby was born and walk around the house. However, she was not supposed to go outside for four days. With no plumbing in the houses at this time, water had to be brought to her for cooking, and human waste receptacles had to be carried from the house. When the four days had passed, the mother could resume use of the community toilet facilities and obtain water from the well. Early in the morning of the fourth day, before sunrise, the "naming mother" would take the infant outdoors to perform the first naming ceremony. The full ritual from home birthing to naming of the infant, although perceived to be painful and dangerous, is still considered by some elders to be the "best way" to have a child that will turn out "right."

We never questioned having children. We took what God gave us. I had 3 boys and 4 girls. I lost two of my boys. . . . When my sister died [in childbirth] I took all of her children to raise and that was six more—and of course their Dad. . . . The people came and told me that I should go on welfare, especially since [the baby] was so sick. I asked them "Why should I go on welfare? God gives me the strength to do my work to care for these children." And to this day, I've never gotten those checks. (RCB 1979)

Infants were breastfed for up to four years of age, depending on circumstances (whether the mother became pregnant during this time or simply wished to stop breastfeeding earlier). RCB said, "I nursed all of mine for three or four years, but not all ladies wanted to do that." Supplemental food for infants included sugar water, maize or cornmeal water, and a variety of herb "teas." Depending on the mother's desires, her general health, and her infant's needs, the cornmeal water was made progressively thicker over the months so that by the age of "six to eight months we would be giving him real food," although on the whole full weaning did not occur until about age three or four.

Child care included holding, feeding, talking with, teasing, transporting, cleaning, clothing, singing to, and laughing with as well as feeding the child, plus the many other things people everywhere do to encourage their children to grow to maturity. Sibling caretaking as well as paternal caretaking is referred to in the literature for San Juan Pueblo. The impression I have from these sources is that child rearing was at least an extended family affair, if not a full community responsibility. Children, as well as their parents and other relatives, were subject to daily critical and nurturing attention of their community members because of the public/outside quality of life. The Pueblo elders could officially reprimand any child, as well as scold their parents, publicly. In addition, at Christmas time, when the *abuelos,* or "old ones," came into the village with their whips, wearing masks and the other adornments of kachinas, they might (gently) whip both children and adults who had misbehaved since their last visit.

Religious practitioners were also political leaders. Most of the individuals in these leadership roles were men, but women were also "called" to serve in the various sodalities as "clan Mothers." The role of clan Mother has been described to me as being highly important: "Without a Mother, we would not exist" (SM 1980). Women also had roles in the Catholic church: "In the old days, we used to go to pray in the Chapel every morning, very early. Now only a few of the old women do this" (HM 1982).

Within the village homes, there was no electricity and no gas for lighting, cooking, or heat. Kerosene lamps and candles purchased at the trading post or other store, or made at home, provided light in the homes at night. Wood fires provided the heat and cooking sources and some light. RCB and other women made the families' everyday clothing by hand or on treadle sewing machines with fabric purchased from one of the mercantile stores. Ceremonial clothing was also made by hand: women embroidered their own and some of the men's garments, and SM and other men made moccasins and other leather items, headdresses, and other adornments. Some of this work was done outside (in warm weather) the home. People ate, slept, and sat on the floor of the largest room in the home. But in spite of what some might perceive as hardship during these years, RCB always refers to them by saying, "We used to live so happy in those days."

1972 TO 1982 FIELD DATA

By the summer of 1972, there were roughly 170 consanguineal, affinal, and *compadrazco* (godparents, co-madres, co-padres, and sometimes their children) kin, plus an uncounted number of people involved directly in the everyday life of RCB and SM. By 1982, this number had grown to about 250. During this ten-year period not only has the kinship network expanded exponentially but so have the changes in the quality and quantity of interpersonal interactions, subsistence and other economic activities, housing styles and patterns, acquisition and maintenance of material goods, and participation in both on-reservation and off-reservation activities.

Except for those individuals who have reached retirement age (60–65), most adult members of this family rely on wages for meeting their family and individual needs for food, housing, clothing, transportation, recreation, and other essentials. This means that in most households at least one person is gainfully employed throughout the year, but many households have several employed adults. There are a few households where the income is dependent on sale of work produced by one or more artists (e.g., pottery, clothing, jewelry, wood carvings and other sculpture, and paintings). Additionally, there are a few households dependent on government (state and federal) subsidies; a few that are dependent on workman's compensation funds (payment for forced early retirement from the labor force because of a permanent injury), and many where income is produced through a combination of several activities, including farming and ranching.

When giving accounts of how and why community members have become so dependent for their livelihood on wage labor and other nonfarming activities, people refer to the changes brought about during and following World War II. During that war, a relatively large number of men were drafted or enlisted in the military. In their absence, women grew "victory gardens" and learned "modern" canning techniques and other skills associated with home economics. Women increased their wage labor efforts during this time, working as domestics in the homes of Los Alamos scientists or as janitors in the research and development centers; they also took jobs according to their academic preparation in local schools, hospitals, and businesses or at some distant location (Albuquerque, Santa Fe, and various cities in Colorado, Arizona, and California). Those engaged in such activities did so out of an expressed sense of loyalty to their family, their community, and to the nation—"to help with the war effort."

After World War II, many of the men who returned to their pueblo were unable to find employment compatible with the skills they had acquired during their military service, and their incentive for farming had essentially been eradicated by the military experience and the socioeconomic changes that had taken place in the Española Valley during their absence. In an effort to provide training that could secure employment for Indians, and still operating with the forced assimilation model begun in the late 1800s, the BIA developed the so-called Relocation Program. Several younger families within this extended family participated in the program, which promoted expectations that the overall economic condition of the relocated families would be improved through skills development in on-site training programs. Some individuals perceived an opportunity to develop skills that could be used on their reservation after completion of the training. For the most part, this was not the case. The families were relocated in specific urban places and wound up learning how to be factory workers and other laborers whose contributions to industry were in the forms of specific tasks. Most of the families who tried this experimental program became totally dissatisfied and returned home without completing the training. In the cities where they had been located, there was little in the way of cultural support. Housing conditions were poor, the general morale of many individuals plummeted, and drinking problems arose. Several families decided to remain in the cities, where they found jobs following their training period. Other individuals became military careerists. Many who have made successful careers away from the reservation found a way to combine Tewa values with their new urban life. These individuals routinely return home during their vacations (which they often take to coincide with traditional ceremonial occasions at San Juan Pueblo) and express a strong sense of being part of their home community, even though separated for economic and educational purposes.

Capital improvements on the reservation were dramatically increased during the 1950s. Electricity was brought in by the Jemez Electric Cooperative, following a short period of gas lighting and heating installed by the Gas Company of New Mexico. Housing programs were developed, and people began to move into single-family dwellings some distance from the pueblo or village proper. The Mercantile Store expanded to include a kiln for firing pottery, since many women had some difficulty obtaining enough quantities of cow manure for the traditional means of firing their work. The U.S. Post Office was built on the site of a barn (which "belonged" to RCB through inheritance from her "grandfather") that had collapsed. Indoor plumbing and sewage lines were installed to improve sanitation.

In the 1960s and 1970s, pueblo officials were able to procure federal monies through grants to improve housing, educational, social, and health services on the reservation. Local men were employed for the building of homes from the ground up and from inside out. Federal regulations regarding the construction of homes built with federal monies meant that homes to be built of adobe had to be made with stabilized adobe. No longer could a woman and her kin (both female and male) and friends set out adobe bricks made from the earth adjacent to her homesite and build her house from scratch. The yearly task of scraping and replastering homes with "mud" was reduced greatly by 1977, and most existing homes were plastered with semipermanent stucco. Electricity, gas lines, and indoor plumbing were redone to conform to new federal regulations.

At the same time that the housing programs were being started, bilingual education, Head Start, senior citizen programs, and dental, prenatal, mother-infant, and other health clinics were established on the reservation. These and other programs provided new, on-reservation employment for many Tewa. There were improved incentives to finish high school and attend college, through scholarships and grants provided by the Tribal Council and other Indian politicoeconomic units, as well as through the many grants and fellowships available for higher education from the U.S. government at that time.

Some men enlisted or were drafted into the military during the 1960s and early 1970s. Of these, a few were sent to Vietnam. When some of these men returned home, they brought many of the destructive values decried in other communities throughout the United States: anger over the specific history of discrimination against members of their community, fueled by the use of illegal drugs, alcohol, and fiery speeches from civil rights activists. For those men who had been exempt from the military service, who had remained at home and learned the skills and knowledge needed to participate in the new programs of development on the reservation, the returning Vietnam veterans (and those youth who were quick to follow their lifestyle) brought a series of unwanted values and behaviors. For others, these new values and accompanying behaviors appeared to be a form of salvation from their confusion over the loss of valued traditions. For the majority of women with whom I have talked, regardless of their age, these new behaviors and values were just one set more in a series of disruptive male actions that had to be incorporated into the fabric of everyday life.[6]

At the same time, many of the on-reservation programs proved to be a means that allowed a semblance of an older order to return to everyday life. Men could contribute to the maintenance of their familial units without having to leave the reservation for extended periods of time. Commuting to off-reservation jobs was made easier because minimum wage and fair employment legislation provided sufficient income for individuals to have their own vehicles (although most commuters to Los Alamos, Santa Fe, or other now relatively close cities do so in carpools). However, the work of many men employed on the reservation in federally funded programs is seasonal and dependent on the annual preparation of grant applications, the awarding of these grants, and the effect of inflation on the amounts awarded. Because of these externally controlled variables, only 50 percent of the potential labor force within this family is employed on average for any given year. This percentage includes women, since it is generally women who are employed on a regular, full-time basis, even though their overall incomes tend to be less than men's when these figures are compared on an hourly basis (e.g., a woman who had a clerical job might make $3.75 an hour, while her husband who was a construction laborer might make $7.25 an hour [1982 figures]).

The kinds of employment women find now includes clerical work (receptionist, secretary, bookkeeper, etc.) for the Eight Northern Indian Pueblos Council, Inc. offices (located at San Juan Pueblo) and San Juan Pueblo Tribal Council offices; teaching in the public school or the BIA day school on the reservation; various occupations at Los Alamos (from working as household domestics to working as clerical staff and janitors within the atomic laboratory facilities); employment at various public and private institutions in Española and Santa Fe (including work as clerks in supermarkets and various occupations at the U.S. Public Health Service Indian Hospital); and others generally

6. To my knowledge there is only one woman veteran among enrolled members of San Juan Pueblo. She entered the army during World War II and retired during the Vietnam war. She has not lived on the reservation since entering the army.

classified as women's primary occupational categories in American society. Men's employment includes management of the Eight Northern Indian Pueblos Council offices and programs; management of the San Juan Pueblo Tribal Council offices and programs; management of the San Juan Pueblo General Stores; management of various divisions of the Indian Hospital in Santa Fe and in subdivisions of the Los Alamos laboratory and other facilities; working as managers and day laborers in the adobe factory located on the reservation or with the construction firm owned and operated by the Eight Northern Indian Pueblos Council; and various other manual labor and service jobs that follow traditional American definitions of men's jobs.

On the reservation, the sexual division of labor for income is controlled largely by the values of the surrounding society. These values are reflected in the prevalent sex segregation patterns still operating in the United States, which implicitly (through hiring and placement practices) classifies jobs according to sex. Although these external values are understood, there are women who say that they would engage in the higher-paying "men's" occupations if they could do so in the company of women friends or kin. The main reasons given for this are that they prefer to work with people with whom they share common interests and experiences—as they put it, "so we'll have something to talk about, because we'll already understand [each other]." Traditions that involve manual labor are still important aspects of Tewa values; and in this, women and men are both considered to be capable of and necessary to the performance of such tasks as a part of everyday life. It is equally true that men and women are both considered to be important for proper and balanced child rearing, and these gentler, less laborious (though generally more time-consuming) tasks of everyday life can be performed equally by men and women. In this respect, the work of women and men who compose many domestic units within this extended family tends to follow older, traditional Tewa values: within stable households women and men work cooperatively to maintain a harmonious interactive everyday life oriented toward the maintenance of family and Pueblo culture. Irrespective of gender, people do whatever is necessary in these arenas to meet the daily and long-term needs of their families and community. This does not mean that conflicts do not arise but that they are resolved within the family or with help from family and friends. Even where intense conflicts often arise, the adult members of the households work diligently to keep the household functioning harmoniously.

In homes where the mother works in a full-time wage labor job and the father is employed part-time or is a farmer, men perform many roles now associated with the expression "househusband." These men do the laundry, clean house, cook meals (including having meals ready when their wives get home from work), pick children up at school or at the bus stop, transport children to after-school activities, and perform other family responsibilities. In homes where the father works full-time and the mother is either employed sporadically or not at all, women perform the majority of roles associated with the expression "house-wife." Where both wife and husband are employed full-time, there is a sharing of domestic chores. During the workday, children are cared for by female kin (who now are usually paid for this work), the schools, or a combination of these. In homes where both husband and wife have retired, women usually do most of the cooking, cleaning, and other inside work, and men do most of the yard work (including gardening, in which women are also involved), chopping or otherwise obtaining wood, some major home repairs, and other largely outside activities. Artists work past the official retirement age, and both women and men engage in the production and sale of pottery, jewelry, and woven articles. More women than men make clothing, and more men than women do sculpturing and painting for sale.

It does not matter who makes the most money over the course of a year in a job. The income earned goes toward the maintenance of the primary family unit (which may extend beyond the household to include other consanguineal and affinal kin) and is put into a common pool for that purpose. Examined over the course of any year, women and men both contribute what they can to household finances. From the common pool of funds (usually held in a bank or credit union), women decide more often than men how the money is to be spent since they have the primary responsibility for maintaining the domestic unit. The sources of money within this large extended family include salaries earned at jobs; rental of farmland or sale of hay, which grows wild on individually owned land; the sale of pottery, jewelry, wood carvings, oil and watercolor paintings, fabric items (aprons, dresses, men's "kilts," which are embroidered, leggings, shawls, woven blankets and belts, etc.) and other crafts and artworks; cutting and hauling firewood; profits earned from selling food and drink at various public events (e.g., the Eight Northern Indian Pueblos Arts and Crafts Show and the Santa Fe Indian Market). Decisions regarding expenditures of funds take into account whether there is a mortgage payment or rent due on the home; electric, gas, and telephone bills; the supply of firewood on hand; clothing, transportation, education, recreation, and other needs; bills of credit at department or furniture stores; gas, tires, insurance, and so forth, needed for the family car(s); and everyday food requirements as well as food needed for specific events (e.g., feast days, weddings, funerals, and the death anniversaries of deceased family members). The main responsibility for purchase and other acquisitions of food remains with women, even in households where men cook most of the meals during the workweek.

Most of the members of RCB and SM's large extended family share the elders' strong work ethic. RCB's attitude toward work is partially reflected in these comments:

> It's those checks that have caused so much trouble. Those boys [referring to a few specific young men] never have to work. They just sit and wait for their checks and when they come, they drink them up, never thinking about their families. (RCB 1979)

Although she may verbally "blame the welfare [programs]" for the fact that some of her grandchildren "don't even bother to look for work," there is a clear recognition by RCB and others that there is very little opportunity for full-time employment in and around the Española Valley (a recounting of some aspects of the harsh economic circumstances of this area can be found in Jacobs [1979]). Consequently, whenever she needs help, RCB employs young men and women to work for her. The men chop wood, trim trees, rake the grounds surrounding the house, cut weeds, mend fences, help SM plant the garden adjacent to their home, and do other outdoor chores (as well as moving furniture and other heavy tasks inside the house). Women clean house, cook, sand pottery, wash clothes, and take her grocery shopping or on other errands in town (Española, Santa Fe, Albuquerque). Some of the young people perform their work without accepting money, saying that either they "don't need any right now" or that they "did it because they wanted to" or "owed work" for money advanced earlier. During the women's work time, they talk with RCB, as she works along with them, about school, work, or family matters. RCB usually talks about the same matters with the young men after they have finished their work, either sitting with them in the living room of her home or in the kitchen.

RCB and her family moved from the pueblo (village) in the early 1940s, to a home that she, her husband, and family helpers built of adobe bricks they had made. There are now six rooms in this house (including the kitchen and bathroom). The land on which they built this home was assigned on their request by the tribal council to their eldest son when he was married and his wife was expecting their first child. As RCB and SM's children grew up and married, homes were built for them by family members in close proximity to them. The home in the pueblo has been used as a "starter home" for most married children and grandchildren who later moved into their own homes after the birth of their first or second child. The homes of grand-children have largely been built by the construction teams hired by pueblo officials through the BIA- and HUD-funded housing projects. Most of these homes are made of concrete blocks or wood and stucco. They are fully wired and plumbed and many have piped-in gas for stoves and hot water heaters. They usually have baseboard electric heat, but some newer houses have central heating and air condition-ing. RCB still relies on her wood-burning stoves for heating and cooking, but she also cooks on a two-burner hotplate that sits on top of her large freezer. The bathroom in her home has a toilet, sink, shower, and tub. She also has a laundry area in the small room between the bath and kitchen, and although she uses this on a weekly basis, she prefers to go to a specific laundromat in Española where she can visit with relatives and other friends who also use that facility.

In 1982, RCB was still making pottery, but, as she said, "not nearly as much as I used to," and SM continued to carve wood sculptures to some extent. Each spring, a small garden (consisting of corn, chili, and squash) was grown to supplement food bought at the grocery stores in town. RCB still "cold packs" certain foods, dries others (including various herbs and vegetables collected in nearby areas, corn and chile grown in their garden, and meat), freezes various vegetables and meats, and bakes bread in her outside ovens. RCB makes some of her clothing, but most is made by one of her nieces because she feels required to wear "traditional clothing" since she promised her husband (a religious elder) she would do so as long as he lived. RCB and SM's home and the grounds around it take considerable time to clean and maintain, as do the homes of their children and their children's children and others. Some of their children do the same kinds of work that RCB and SM do, but few of their grandchildren do.

All of RCB's children were born at home; many of her children's children were born at home. She has many grandchildren and great-grandchildren. (She says, "Don't ask me to count them, there are just too many.") Birth control was rarely practiced among women of RCB's and her children's generations. But many of her grandchildren and their spouses have made conscious decisions to limit the size of their families (one granddaughter has decided to have no children, another has decided to have only one, another to have only two). Prenatal care, hospital births, and postpartum care of mothers and infants are all routine aspects of the birth process now. The four-day naming ceremony is performed soon after the mother and child return home from the hospital. Many infants are not breastfed but are bottle fed from the outset since most mothers will return to the workforce after a short maternity leave from their jobs. In these younger families, parents strive to wean their children from the bottle by age two or three.

In homes where both of the child's parents are employed, it is often the parents' mothers or grandmothers who assume the primary roles involved in infant day care, but older siblings, cousins, aunts, and uncles who are out of school, unemployed, and at home may take care of infants; in either case, the child caretakers are paid for this work either directly by the parents or through the "day care payment program." Even with this assistance, parents take primary responsibility for meeting their children's and their own needs. However, since the range of socioeconomic support extends far beyond any single nuclear family or beyond any household (which may be composed of a simple extended family), one readily observes the support provided by grandparents and great-grandparents in the nurturance of the younger generations. This additional support is made possible by the transportation of individuals between the now widely scattered domestic units.

Genuine interest in children's affairs is expressed by relatives throughout their lives, as is interest in the goings-on of other kin and friends. Children receive a considerable amount of attention and are encouraged to engage in conversation with adults from their earliest days. When families get together to share a meal or celebrate a birthday or other special occasion, cousins, aunts, grandparents, great-grandparents, and others all give the youngest family members verbal (in Tewa, Spanish, and English) and nonverbal attention, often interrupting other conversations to do so.

Most of the men in the family are, or have been, officers in the tribal government. About once a month, the men who are officers must attend a meeting of the tribal council. Those who have their own transportation drive to the Council Hall for these meetings; those who do not are picked up by the sheriff or one of the other officers and transported to and from the meeting place. When the men return home, they explain (in Tewa) what went on at the meeting to their wives and other family members. Matters related to public or community issues are discussed with family members (e.g., progress on land claims, the need to build an additional water tower to accommodate the growing demands on the community water supply, the new houses that are to be built, and employment of a geologist/planner to help with overall assessment of community development needs, the scheduling of ritual ceremonials, and the need to fence certain sections of land to keep cattle out of the hay patches). In this way, women are brought into the tribal decision-making process, since the women in the households usually express an opinion about the matters relayed to them in these discussions, and the men generally respond favorably to what the women have to say.

DISCUSSION

When one compares the activities described for the two time periods, it is abundantly clear that the constellation of gender roles has changed markedly for the Tewa at San Juan Pueblo during the past eighty or so years. Caught up in the changes introduced by the movement of Tewa society toward greater participation in the socioeconomics of U.S. society at large, yet at the same time working diligently to maintain Tewa culture (through language, specific ceremonials, and a daily life that encourages intense familial interactions), life can appear to be frenetic at times, as individuals strive to maintain a balance between the apparently conflicting demands of two worlds. Yet at the heart of Tewa culture there are those elements that have been refined through many generations, allowing the blending and, at the same time, separation of these two worlds so that for the personally integrated individuals, life flows in a relatively smooth pattern that accommodates the differences in the non-Indian and Tewa communities and ethos.[7] This is most easily seen in the dynamics of interaction between women and men within a given household and within a given large extended family; it is also seen, however, by moving between those two

---

7. Details on this issue will be provided in Jacobs (n.d.). People with whom I have worked and talked have mentioned many aspects of the "outside world" that cause some stress in their lives, as they try to live close to Tewa cultural practices and belief. Among those relevant to this discussion are meeting time and work expectations of schools and non-Indian employers; speaking, reading, writing, understanding, and therefore "thinking in English;" using various banking procedures; establishing credit and meeting contract conditions for automobile, furniture and other time purchases; use of new technologies at work, school, and home; and voting and other aspects of participation in county, state, and federal political processes. Some individuals have described how they learned to balance the two worlds, while others have explained in detail their difficulties in achieving a balance between the outside and inside worlds. Some of these latter individuals have said that they have given up trying to integrate the two worlds, preferring to "leave the outside world to others."

worlds (and others) on a daily basis with individuals and asking them how they handle seeming "conflicts."

As in all modern urban-oriented societies, work today goes far beyond the need to satisfy the basic cultural imperatives discussed at the outset of this chapter. The size of modern housing is generally greater than that needed to provide only sleep and minimal shelter space. Clothing ranges widely in style, form, and function. Pregnancy, childbirth, and child rearing are less dangerous now than they were before the 1940s. No one within this family, or within their full reference group, goes hungry because crops failed or because there is not enough income for the household. People did suffer hunger prior to the 1940s in spite of the sharing ethic of the community, simply because there was not enough money and food produced to prevent hunger. Now there are government and private subsidies for all households in which hunger might be felt without this support. But today it is the rare household that can get by with farming as the primary means of subsistence.

When comparing the activities undertaken in the two periods, one notes that there have been minimal shifts in gender roles that are specifically aimed at satisfying cultural imperatives. These shifts are a function of (1) those technological and socioeconomic changes that have affected most people in the United States and that have been incorporated into the Tewa world; (2) change in population dynamics, namely, dispersal of community members into single-family dwellings located away from the reservation center (the old pueblo or village) and resulting in less public performance of all activities than when people lived side-by-side in the pueblo proper; and (3) the readiness of women and men to perform any task required to meet their individual and familial needs. In this last regard, it must be added that there is a cohort of young men who seem to have acquired what is referred to by others in San Juan Pueblo as "the macho image." These men express clear disdain for any domestic chore they deem "women's work" (e.g., stating that they "will never be caught cooking," or, as in one instance, "There goes L taking the laundry. Ho boy, you'll never see me doing that. He should make his old lady [wife] do it"). I have heard them shout at and otherwise disrespectfully address women as well as make deprecating remarks about women in general but never about specific women.[8] It is primarily their male kin who rebuke this behavior and strive to incorporate them into more traditional roles within their families (an uncle recently told one of these men that he had better "relearn respect for women" because "you have to remember that all women are Mothers and you wouldn't be here without them").

It must also be added that although women do not exercise formal religious or political leadership, they are nonetheless active in the maintenance of religious and political organization. This is accomplished through their participation in the many religious ceremonies conducted throughout the calendrical year, the performance of their roles in the remaining sodalities (see Ortiz 1969 for a full description of these roles), and the informal but definite influence women have on the men in their lives who serve on the tribal council or work in the various tribal offices.

Carol R. Ember (1983) has presented a compelling evolutionary case concerning changes in women's tasks, roles, and statuses when a society replaces extensive agriculture with intensive agriculture. Her evidence leads to the conclusion that where intensive agriculture is the primary mode of subsistence production, women are constrained from performance in public or outside activities because (1) the nature and amount of work required to process agricultural products is highly time-consuming and generally carried out in private or indoors; (2) a large amount of time is required for child care because intensive agriculturalists tend to have relatively large families; and (3) intensive agriculture tends to lead to an increase in material possessions and a potential for exponential growth in desire for both nonessential and essential goods as these goods are acquired. In this chapter, I have provided some evidence to indicate that in changing from intensive agriculture to nearly full participation in wage labor economies, a portion of the population at San Juan Pueblo have (1) altered the quality and reduced the quantity of work directly involved in acquisi-

---

8. They may do this outside of earshot of any woman, however.

tion and processing of food for storage and consumption; (2) decreased the amount of time spent in child care activities with an increase in formally assigned caretakers (women and men) who do this work inside more than outside; and (3) increased the amount of time and work necessary to acquire material goods that are both necessary for basic survival (per the cultural imperatives) and desired for aesthetic and personal reasons, which go far beyond those needed to satisfy basic biophysiological needs of individuals, their families, and the community.

If the predictive model implicit in Ember's study holds true, one would expect to find an increase in women's public roles as they experience a decrease in food processing and child-care activities. This is true if we use "public" to mean outside the home. If we use "public" to mean "social good" and the regulation of community affairs (following Ortner and Whitehead 1981:7–8), specifically in reference to women's roles in political or religious leadership, it is more difficult to find validity in the prediction. At one Rio Grande pueblo, women have been selected to serve as governors, but I have been told that to date (1989) no woman has been "considered" for this position at San Juan Pueblo. Neither have women been selected for other one-year public official roles. Nor has a woman been hired in the position of tribal manager (a relatively new five-year appointment at San Juan Pueblo).

The director of the Pueblo's nutrition and commodity program is a woman; secretaries, a few bookkeepers and accountants, computer programmers, and administrative assistants employed by the tribal office are mostly women. Their work is performed in public (outside the home) for public (social good/communal) purposes, but their roles seem to lack the authority and power held by the men who work in public for public purposes. The place of work is a *public* world seen by all who enter their offices. To those who do not see beyond the physical and interactional similarities of this world when compared to other urban office complexes throughout much of the United States, it appears as though women are in "the usual inferior positions." However, when traditional Tewa women and men leave their workplace and reenter their homes (the private, inside, domestic domain), there are other factors marking their respective statuses and roles (see Ortiz 1981). But even before that, a closer look at the subtleties of interactions between women and men in the offices reveals the same reciprocal playing out of deference and demeanor within specific social fields,[9] based on respect for the special attributes of each gender, as is seen in home life. Sometimes a dramatic marking of this reciprocity occurs.

In spring 1982, I worked in the San Juan Pueblo Tribal Office on matters related to potential land claims. At one point, the tribal manager asked me who might be good to have on a community advisory committee to address the land issues (he also asked everyone else in the office). I commented on the "qualifications" of several men who immediately came to mind. After we had discussed these men, he asked, "Now, which of the women should we ask?" I was embarrassed because I could not as readily give an accounting of women elders, nor did I fully understand *in that context* how to assess various women's qualifications. He taught me how to do this: "Remember, the women *know* the land in all its forms, and they know it fully. So we have to ask them too which is the most important to fight for and how we should do this." He sought out two of the women elders to be on the proposed committee of six.

CONCLUSION

At San Juan Pueblo, as in many other cultures of the world, the dualistic division of labors that tends to be examined along gender identification lines (by social scientists) is not as clear-cut as an itemization of tasks might imply. Women and men must work together for any society to survive. In Tewa culture, the essential focus is on maintenance of a harmonious integration of human, nonhuman, and spiritual components of life. This focus leads to what may appear to be an overlapping of gender roles, though not necessarily an overlapping of actual tasks. But there are traditions within Tewa culture that create a near-androgynous mind-set about participation of individuals in

9. See Mitchell (1966:57), who defines a social field as follows: "A social field may be thought of as a series of interconnecting relationships of all of which in some way influence one another."

achieving cultural goals. Women are encouraged to see the world as men see it, and men are encouraged to see the world as women do. Each is expected to possess some characteristics of the other and to be integrated within themselves. Yet gender identification is clear, and each knows which roles are primary for them to fulfill. As Van Ball (1975:85) found in investigating Australian aboriginal cultures, "The sexes are complementary to one another and it is impossible to understand the position of women without paying due attention to that of men," and vice versa. When such attention is given, one finds that the range of normative social behaviors that work to keep the social fabric intact has little to do with the quality of roles but rather with the possibility of roles. When acted out on an everyday basis, the roles exercised by members of the large extended family who are the focus of this chapter are seen to extend along a continuum of variance (graph-ically demonstrated below) that leaves only a few roles that are predominantly performed by women or men.

Some would argue that these few characteristics are the most significant, since they are the standard roles that, in Western societies, are used to disparagingly separate women and men. Among those at the extreme ends of the continuum would be childbearing and primary activities associated with and responsibilities for management of their households by women at the X_o end and political and religious leader-ship roles that are primarily filled by men at the Y_o end. The actual range of role *possibilities* is such that the only empirical certainty for sex role differences is at the end point X_o: childbearing.

"In the old days," but still forming part of the Tewa ethos, the public and domestic domains were interwoven more clearly than they appear to be today; that is, in the past there was very little distinction between the two, while today some distinctions are emically made between them. The former interweaving was facilitated by the physical struc-tures that comprised the living and working areas of the pueblo. Women and men were engaged in daily chores that maintained community order and met individual and community needs. The focus was on communal life rather than on individual needs, and the participation of community members in meeting these objectives was

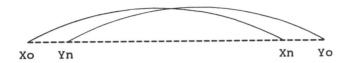

X = women's roles
Y = men's roles
-------- = range of possible roles from o to n

Fig. 11.1

readily observed. Child rearing was a community as well as a family endeavor. Children played in the plaza or in the fields (when the community adults were tending to crops) under the watchful eye of the majority of their elders. This has changed markedly during the past twenty years or so, but the elders whom I know remember well this communal focus and live a life aimed toward satisfying the larger community needs. Some individuals within their extended family have moved away from this objective and live more like their white and His- pano counterparts. They do not speak Tewa or participate in cere- monials, and although they are genetically Tewa, they have largely given up their Tewa identities. The children of some of these individu- als seek to participate in Tewa culture, having been introduced to specific cultural elements in the bilingual program at the elementary school, yet they find this a hardship, which is made keener by the demands of the off-reservation world in which they must participate if they are to be economically successful. This other world, of which they are a genuine part, is the "outside" world in the sense that many of the values and aspects of everyday life "out there" are not found in the "inside" world of the reservation. The hardship is, however, softened by the encouragement of family members who live closer to traditional culture.

It is through the regular reinforcement of cultural values and the encouragement of elders to participate in traditional cultural affairs that Tewa culture has been able to survive the many intrusions from societies with values that are seen by many older Tewa as antithetical to their own. There is a familial orientation in the stablest households that extends beyond biological kin to compadrazco and others. But this is not to be contrasted with communal orientation. Working toward social good and familial good are, on the whole, part of the same process. In this regard, virtually all women and men are concerned with basic everyday socioeconomic activities that lead to satisfaction of the cultural imperatives (some men, but few women, seek to satisfy only their own needs).

Most women and most men are ordinary social persons who do not engage in daily Tewa political or religious activities. Some women, but more men, are both religious and social persons. A few men and fewer women are political, religious, and social persons; they are involved in daily political and religious activities. Some men, but no women, are political and social persons, in that they hold political office, exercise limited political authority, yet retain their identity as an "ordinary" member of the community.

There is no doubt that the Tewa world has changed and continues to change in response to both external and internal pressures, as all dynamic living cultures must do if they are to survive. For the most part, the changes that have occurred over the past eighty years or so have not caused intense tensions to arise between the sexes. Consequently, there has been no concerted feminist movement at San Juan Pueblo as there has been among other Native Americans (see Green 1980:248–67 for a consideration of this point and review of scholarship concerning Native American women). This is not to say that women here have not had to be alert and responsive to men's occasional efforts to either deny women their traditional rights (e.g., home ownership and control) or *assign* women to stereotyped roles in the local workforce.[10]

---

10. It was because of an endogenously perceived denial of women's rights that I became involved in research at San Juan Pueblo. Members of the arts and crafts cooperative, which has been largely a women's economic enterprise for about fifty years, felt that the San Juan Pueblo Tribal Council was placing undue demands on them for funds that the cooperative

A number of women have told me that they would happily accept employment in one of the higher-paying jobs at which men work—but *only* if other women worked with them. The camaraderie that women enjoy with each other cannot be measured in terms of income. It grows among women in age cohorts from shared daily experiences begun early in childhood. Friendships among children, regardless of kin relatedness, is encouraged by their parents. Consequently, sets of loyal, sharing, and caring women emerge from this socialization to friendship formation, and, as a result, women prefer to work with other women (and, as well, men prefer to work with other men). There are a few individuals who have stated a willingness to give up the comfort of gender companionship on the job to work in a predominantly other-gender situation either to earn a higher income (in the case of a few women) or to pursue an occupational ambition (e.g., a man who wished to become a registered nurse). On the whole, individuals who are employed in jobs within the pueblo find themselves working in what social scientists call "sex-segregated" situations, but according to the individuals I have questioned on these matters, the above factors are what make their situation ideal. Still, they are open to alternative futures.

When women and men are permitted by cultural norms to experience a full sense of personhood, to have clear confidence in the equal value of their roles in society, and to understand that they may explore the full range of role possibilities in their society, there is no need for a full-scale social movement, the objective of which is to strike a balance between the sexes. There are, however, some women in this extended

---

had accumulated through sales of their work, in 1970. Some women perceived the problem in feminist terms and asked me if I could help them figure out "when and why we lost our status in this pueblo." However, they were able to negotiate their way through the financial issue and the immediacy of their interest in this question was prolonged, becoming a larger research interest that would require long-term querying. Since that time, several other instances have occurred that have raised the question again and again. In each instance that I know of, the issue has been resolved or is currently being negotiated with the tribal council or through other local means. It is likely, from my point of view, that instances of seeming "sexism" are going to continue to occur and, it is hoped, will continue to be settled through internal negotiations. This point is further developed in the monograph referred to above.

family who have engaged in feminist activism directed against the outside system that stereotypically and negatively segregates women's and men's work and career opportunities. With a grounding in Tewa culture and in collaboration with non-Tewa women, they are striving to change working conditions and career opportunities outside of the pueblo, realizing that since the larger American society affects their own culture, they need to forestall or eradicate adverse working and other conditions at home.

In the 1970s, the first clear efforts to establish feminist anthropology began to appear in the important work of Michelle Z. Rosaldo and Louise Lamphere et al. (1974), Kay Martin and Barbara Voorhies (1975), and R. R. Reiter et al. (1975). At that time, the ethnographic record on women was scant. There were two major tasks before us: conducting fieldwork designed specifically to study women in the world's cultures and building theories to account for women's statuses and roles cross-culturally. Using what was available to them (including their own field experiences), some feminist anthropologists (and other social scientists) argued that they had found some universals: for example, "women everywhere are subordinate to men," and "women's work (and therefore women) is considered less valuable than men's (and therefore men)." For many scholars, these statements rang true because of their personal and field experiences. For others, these "universals" would not hold because they had worked in egalitarian societies where cultural norms did not devalue women or women's work. Now there is a large body of data available for further development of the theoretical debates on women's statuses cross-culturally; these data include the case studies cited at the outset of this chapter. Yet as early as 1975, Susan Carol Rogers posited a model of female/male interaction that reveals "female forms of power and the myth of male dominance." Others have found that reference to universal male dominance constitutes "an ethnological illusion" (Poewe 1980:11–125). Furthermore, cross-cultural studies show that there can be no generalized statements about *the* status of women, since there is great variability in women's statuses cross-culturally (see Whyte 1978).

One of my aims here is to contribute to the debates about women's statuses cross-culturally. I hope I have demonstrated the relative absence of a gender-based status differential among the Tewa at San Juan Pueblo, thereby supporting others who argue against the *universal* subordination of women and devaluation of women and their work. In meeting my second objective, contributing to the ethnographic record of life at San Juan Pueblo, I am also adding to the growing number of case studies that support a notion of balanced reciprocity in gender roles and relationships.

Theories used to account for sex and gender differences ought to be grounded in empirical fact, rather than used as a priori means to personal or political ends. Gordon H. Orians (1983:3) warns that "the main abuse to be avoided is to become so emotionally involved with theories . . . that acceptance of those theories is so highly preferred over their rejection that observations [and interpretations] are not objective." Research ought not to be directed or framed by questions that *lead* us to find dominating men and submissive women, "cultural devaluations of women's work," and inequality in the statuses and roles of women and men. Research held open for discoveries of and explanations for a range of human conceptual and behavioral possibilities may in some instances reveal inequality of statuses and roles between women and men, while in other instances it will reveal dyadic, complementary, and reciprocal interactions between women's and men's roles that are defined *emically* to be of *comparable worth*. On the whole, this latter is the Tewa case as revealed through the daily life activities of a significant portion of the population at San Juan Pueblo.

12

The Southeast

WOMEN'S STATUS AMONG
the Muskogee and Cherokee

Richard A. Sattler

Descendants of the earlier Mississippian cultures, the American Indians of the Southeast were organized into numerous medium to large chiefdoms at the time of contact with Europeans in the sixteenth century. Most of these people lived in medium to large villages and practiced intensive riverine agriculture mixed with hunting, fishing, and some gathering. Most of the societies in the region had a ranked social organization. Despite sharing similar overall patterns, they displayed marked variability in the particulars of social organization and culture. This variability included the presence of highly developed clan systems among most eastern groups and their absence among western groups, the extent of ranking, and the size and degree of integration of sociopolitical groups.

Under the pressures of European colonization, chronic warfare, and widespread depopulation from epidemic disease, many of these southeastern chiefdoms consolidated into large-scale confederacies (such as the Creek, the Cherokee, and the Choctaw) during the eighteenth century. Consolidation and centralization of power within these confederacies continued until they emerged as unified nations in the early nineteenth century. By the mid-nineteenth century, five of these—the Cherokee, Creek, Choctaw, Chickasaw, and Seminole—had acquired the accoutrements of modern nation-states. Combined with the presence of sizable mixed-blood, partially acculturated elites, this development led to their designation as the Five Civilized Tribes. These mixed-blood elites emerged as the result of the tribes' extensive involvement in the eighteenth-century deerskin trade.

During the 1830s, these tribes came under President Andrew Jackson's removal policy. As a result, most of the American Indians in the Southeast (except for the tribes of Louisiana, the coast and piedmont of the Carolinas and Virginia, and fragmentary remnants of the others) were removed to what is now eastern Oklahoma. They soon reestablished their lives and societies in this environment and prospered there until they fell victim to the General Allotment Act in the late 1890s. The allotment process proceeded between 1898 and 1906, at which time all tribal lands had been divided and the tribal governments were dissolved by federal decree. By 1910, the southeastern American Indians in Oklahoma were a minority in what were once their exclusive territories.

Those who remained in their homelands also attempted to maintain their cultures, with varying degrees of success. Most were confined to relatively isolated reservations, largely created in the mid-nineteenth century, or submerged into the larger Euro-American and African-American populations. Owing to their greater marginalization, those remaining in the East did not enjoy the relative prosperity of those in Oklahoma during the nineteenth century.

Today, most southeastern American Indians, both in Oklahoma and in the East, live interspersed among the larger American population, though often maintaining separate communities in predominantly rural areas. Despite submersion in Euro-American society and concerted efforts at assimilation by the federal government, many of the tribes, particularly those in Oklahoma and the larger eastern groups, have remained culturally conservative. These people retain their languages, much of their traditional religious beliefs and practices, and some elements of indigenous social and political organization. Economically, however, all are integrated into marginal positions within the larger American economy, and most experience significant degrees of poverty. Even where Euro-American practices and beliefs have been adopted, considerable syncretism is evident and the most acculturated groups in the East retain a distinctive social identity.

GENDER IN THE SOUTHEAST

During the last twenty years, anthropology has turned increasingly to the examination of gender status and roles, particularly the position of women in a variety of cultures. In part, this renewed interest derives from the feminist movement, but it also derives from the increased sophistication of anthropological research and models as well as from expanded knowledge of these cultures. This new research has refined and amplified our understanding of gender systems and their relationships to larger cultural systems. The cultural definition of gender, along with the accompanying statuses and roles, has been tied intimately to other aspects of the culture, particularly to economic and political/prestige systems. In many cases, we now know that gender statuses serve to maintain and replicate these systems through a variety of complex operations (Ortner and Whitehead 1981; Reiter 1975).

Despite increased anthropological interest in gender, our knowledge of this topic remains spotty and incomplete for Native North America. Researchers have undertaken relatively few systematic efforts to understand the cultural construction of gender among American Indians and the relationship of gender to other aspects of the cultural systems. Some researchers have been struck by the apparent similarities among the various groups (Whitehead 1981), but the wide diversity of cultural patterns, particularly of political and economic systems, would indicate a similar disparity of gender systems for the area.

This chapter examines gender status among two southeastern Indian groups, the Muskogee and the Cherokee, who differ markedly in this as well as other aspects of their cultures, despite many general similarities. These two groups are felt to represent the two extremes regarding gender status in the Southeast. The discussion focuses primarily on the Muskogee (Creek), with comparisons to the better-known Cherokee. Factors contributing to the differences are also discussed. I attempt to show how differences in the political/prestige and economic systems have produced systematic differences in gender status systems. This analysis thus amplifies our understanding both of the internal operations of these two cultures and of the nature and range of gender status systems in Native North America.

The cultural practices and beliefs described here generally pertain to the eighteenth and early nineteenth century, though many have continued in some form into the present. The data for this study are, therefore, largely ethnohistorical, with the predictable problems of observer biases and incompleteness. This documentary evidence is informed by extensive personal observation and reconstructive ethnography among Seminole and Creek traditionalists in Oklahoma conducted since 1981, as well as more limited research among conservative Oklahoma Cherokee during the 1970s.

THE MUSKOGEE

The term "Muskogee" is used here to refer to the eastern Muskogean-speaking peoples who occupied Georgia, Alabama, and northern Florida from the sixteenth through the early nineteenth century. These include groups such as the Upper and Lower Creek, the Yamasi, the Alabama, the Koasatl, the Apalachl, and the Seminole. Though these groups spoke several distinct but related languages, they shared general cultural patterns and most were amalgamated into either the Creek Confederacy or the Seminoles during the eighteenth and early nineteenth century.

Several general features of Muskogee culture need to be mentioned. The economy combined intensive riverine agriculture, hunting, and trade, which generated considerable surpluses. Politically, the Muskogee were organized into local chiefdoms (*italwa*), generally consisting of several permanent villages and/or hamlets. Each italwa was governed by a hereditary chief (*mikko*) and a variety of hereditary and appointed officials. The italwa were further organized into a number of larger, regional chiefdoms under paramount chiefs until the eighteenth or nineteenth century when these were supplanted by still larger groupings such as Upper Creek, Lower Creek, and Seminole. All of the Muskogee were matrilineal and matrilocal and possessed corporate moieties, phratries, clans, and lineages. All of these descent groups, except the moieties, were exogamous. Each italwa contained several clans, generally representing six to nine phratries, and all were preferentially endogamous (Sattler 1987; Swanton 1922, 1928).

MUSKOGEE WOMEN

The position of Muskogee women is somewhat problematic. They enjoyed considerable freedom and respect but endured rather onerous constraints and generally lacked direct, formal access to power. The overall picture is one of limited self-determination within a generally male-dominated and male-controlled system.

The control of female sexuality aptly illustrates this situation. Unmarried women generally enjoyed complete sexual freedom, and no onus was attached to sexual affairs or to children resulting from such liaisons. Likewise, all forms of sexual assault, not just rape, against women were capital crimes (Bartram 1853:31; Swanton 1928:355–56). Marriage drastically altered this situation. Complete fidelity was expected from married women, and any familiarity, even nonsexual, with an unrelated male was grounds for accusations of adultery. The penalty for adultery consisted of the offended husband and his male clansmen beating the woman and her lover senseless with switches and then cropping off their hair, ears, and sometimes noses. The husband generally then divorced his wife. Great disgrace attached to a woman who was divorced by her husband for any cause, and such women often found it difficult to remarry. Many were forced into prostitution (Swanton 1928:346–56, 384). Widowhood did not immediately free women. Their mourning period extended for up to four years, during which they were secluded and remained unkempt and under the control of their deceased husband's female relatives. The adultery penalty applied during this entire period. At the end of the mourning period, which could be abridged by the women of the husband's clan, the widow was offered a clan brother of her dead husband as a replacement husband. The couple had to spend the night together, after which either could refuse the match. If the remarriage was refused, then the woman regained her unmarried status and its freedoms. Even divorce did not immediately free a woman from the marriage constraints. Divorced women remained bound to their husbands and subject to the adultery penalty until after the next Green Corn Ceremony (Apuskita), which generally occurred in mid-July (ibid., 377–83).

The control of female sexuality contrasts markedly with that of men. Polygyny, though not common, was permitted in any degree.[1] While a man required the permission of his first wife to take additional wives, she had little recourse other than divorce if he was committed to this course. The adultery penalty for men was much less severe than that for women. The man and his lover were simply beaten senseless by the offended wife and her female relatives, with no cropping. Likewise, little onus attached to the man under such circumstances. Additionally, invoking the adultery penalty automatically instituted a divorce for the woman, while a man might choose to retain an adulterous wife (Adair [1775] 1986:149–52; Hawkins 1848:73–74). Similarly, a man became free immediately after a divorce or permanent separation. The mourning period for men was also abbreviated to only four months, under conditions similar to those for women (Swanton 1928:377–83). While clan elders *(achulaki)* arranged all first marriages, men might institute such proceedings by approaching the elders with a personal choice. Women, at best, had only the right of refusal of an arranged match (Spoehr 1942:78, 90–91).

Several other features of Muskogee culture also illustrate a subordinate status of women. Such features cover a wide range of attitudes and behaviors. The most revealing are attitudes toward women's characters, women's political position, and differential mortality among children.

The Muskogee characterize women as immature, excessively emotional, and unduly parochial in their outlook. They are believed to be incapable of calm, reasoned discussion that emphasizes the interests of the group as a whole over those of family and clan, all qualities esteemed in positions of responsibility (Hawkins 1848:72; Swanton 1928:297–98). Muskogees also often assume that women are inherently irresponsible and immoral, as exemplified in the ceremonial harangues given to the women of the italwa during the Apuskita.

---

1. There is considerable difference of opinion in the historical documents as to the prevalence of polygyny among the Muskogees, but the quantitative data do not indicate that more than 5 percent of married men were polygamous during the nineteenth century. This lower rate also finds support in some direct statements (Bartram [1775] 1928:403, Hawkins 1848:42, 73; Romans 1775:97–98; Swan 1857:273; Swanton 1928:370–76).

Therefore, women are blamed for the bad luck of the town considered ultimately responsible for the excesses and transgressions of the men.[2]

Women were expressly excluded from participation in political affairs. They held no exclusive offices and were eligible for none of those held by males. Even the clan elders were exclusively male.[3] For a woman to enter either the ceremonial plaza (square ground) or the "rotunda," the two locations where all direct political activity occurred, constituted a capital crime except under special circumstances (Bartram [1789] 1853:27). Any man who was known to listen to the opinions or advice of a woman became subject to ridicule and accusations of being either "henpecked" or effeminate, effectively excluding women from informal participation as well (Hawkins 1848:8; Sprague 1847:297).

Census data also indicate a degree of preferential treatment for male children. While infanticide and primary nurturing were controlled by the mother, sex ratios for children under ten years from the Second Seminole War and mortality figures from a smallpox epidemic among the Oklahoma Seminoles in 1899 indicate a preference for male offspring. During the Second Seminole War, American observers reported widespread infanticide. The male to female sex ratios of 1.4:1 or higher during this period, as compared to 0.98:1 at other times, indicates either some preferential female infanticide or differential treatment of male children (Sattler 1987:134). During the 1899 smallpox epidemic, the crude death rate for females under ten was 129.23/1,000, while that for males was only 65.69/1,000. Such a disparity cannot be accounted for by differential effects of the disease itself. Further, in 1900 and 1901, the crude death rates for males and females were nearly equal (44.45:45 and 21.46:33.2, respectively), while in 1903 and 1904, male mortality exceeded that of females

2. This is certainly the case today, when women are frequently blamed for bad luck and dissension within the italwa. The harangues and injunctions to women differ markedly from those given to young men, in that the assumption of immorality is absent in the latter. Similar statements and attitudes appear throughout the eighteenth and nineteenth centuries as well (Adair [1775] 1986:112–14; U.S. Congress 2:631–32).

3. The Muskogee word translated as "elder," *achuli,* literally means "old man." The word for "old woman" is *imhoktalwa.*

(13.51:4.29 and 13.64:4.29, respectively). Overall estimated life expectancy for males and females during the period 1898 to 1905 showed a four- to five-year advantage for males under five years. After five years of age, female life expectancy began to exceed that of males by one to two years until about age thirty, after which the sexes achieved near-equality in life expectancy.[4] This clearly indicates preferential treatment of male children, particularly during periods of stress.

THE CHEROKEE

The Cherokee were far more homogeneous than the Muskogee and represent a single ethnic group speaking a single language living in the southern Appalachians of western North and South Carolina, eastern Tennessee, and northeastern Georgia. The Cherokee bordered the Muskogee to the south and west. The Cherokee language possessed at least three major dialects during the eighteenth century: Eastern (Elati), Middle (Kituhwa), and Western (Otall). Similarly, the Cherokee were divided into three or four major geographic divisions: Lower, Middle, and Valley and Overhills towns. These divisions were culturally homogeneous, despite dialect differences.

The geographic divisions showed varying degrees of political unity within themselves, and the extent to which these divisions represented political entities is problematic. Regardless of the existence of any larger confederacies or chiefdoms, Cherokee towns showed far greater autonomy and less cohesion than did the Muskogee italwa (Gearing 1962; Perisco 1979:92–95). As in the case of the latter, Cherokee towns often consisted of a central settlement with outlying hamlets. These outlying hamlets, however, never seem to have achieved the size of some Muskogee outliers. Like the Muskogee, the Cherokee were matrilineal and matrilocal, with a preference for town endogamy. The Cherokee possessed corporate, exogamous clans and lineages but lacked phratries or moieties. The Cherokee also had fewer clans

---

4. This is based on a demographic analysis of data contained in the Seminole Census Cards (1898). In general, these patterns are unusual, since women generally enjoy a higher life expectancy at birth and during early childhood.

(seven) than the Muskogee (thirty-four). Theoretically, each Cherokee town contained households representing each of the seven clans.

Cherokee Women

The position of Cherokee women contrasts sharply with that of Muskogee women. Premarital sexual freedom among the Cherokee extended to some degree to the postmarital state. While adultery constituted grounds for divorce, neither sex had recourse to any greater sanction for this transgression. Indeed, the extent to which Cherokee women cuckolded their husbands elicited frequent comments from European observers (Adair [1775] 1986:152–53). Married Cherokee women also enjoyed greater freedom of association than did their Muskogee counterparts. Likewise, the mourning period for the Cherokee was the same for both sexes and limited to no more than one year. And divorce was complete for both sexes immediately on formal separation (Gilbert 1943:339–40, 347–48). Clearly, little effort went into the control of female sexuality among the Cherokee.

Politically, Cherokee women fared better as well. The status of Beloved Woman or War Woman conferred considerable status and power on Cherokee women. This group of offices belonged to the senior women of the clans and had considerable influence in beginning or ending warfare as well as determining the fate of prisoners. In addition to this official authority, Cherokee women frequently and openly made their opinions known on political issues, with no shame attached to the man who listened and considerable peril of severe and public tongue-lashings to one who did not (Fogelson 1977).

Cherokee attitudes toward women's characters similarly show no great discrepancy with those toward men's. In both cases, maturity, reliability, and other positively valued characteristics developed with age and seniority (Gearing 1962). Thus relative age carried greater weight than did sex in determining moral character among the Cherokee.

COMPARISON AND EVALUATION

How, then, do we evaluate and reconcile such marked differences in women's status between neighboring peoples who shared much of their cultural patterns? I propose that general differences between the two groups both subsume and account for the differences in gender status. Differences in economic organization and sociopolitical organization are particularly important in this regard.

Economic Factors

While generally similar, the two groups differ significantly in one economic feature. Among the Cherokee, as among northern tribes in the eastern United States, women did almost all agricultural labor. Men only cleared the fields and assisted in the planting and harvesting (Grant 1980:7). Among the Muskogee, while women cultivated small garden plots adjacent to the households (in-fields), most subsistence came from the large town fields (out-fields) at some distance from the settlements, which were worked by the men with occasional assistance from the women (Bartram [1789] 1853:39–40). Among both groups, titular ownership of the fields and land rested with the women, but among the Muskogee, men "owned" or controlled the produce of the town fields, whereas among the Cherokee, women retained control over the produce as well as the land.[5]

Access to land and agricultural produce came to men in both groups through women, but among the Cherokee, marriage conferred no greater access or control over this area of economic production than could be gained through mothers, aunts, and sisters. Among the Muskogee, after marriage a man gained direct control over the produce of his wife's fields. Men had no similar control over the produce of their female relatives' fields, which were under the control of their husbands. Since generosity was a primary requisite of high status and political

5. Among both the Muskogee and the Cherokee, marriage conferred no control to the husband over his wife's property (Grant 1980:321). It may be misleading, therefore, to say that women owned the town fields among the Muskogee. Rather, it may be that ownership was vested in the town and that marriage conferred rights in them to the men. Certainly, only married men held such rights. Male control is inferred from the fact that Muskogee men traded corn to Europeans during the eighteenth century and that they resisted efforts by the Americans to trade with women or to introduce innovations that would provide women with direct access to trade (Bartram 1928:63, 71; Boyd 1941: 20:308, 326 and 21:48; Boyd and Latorre 1953:106, 112–13; Grant 1980: 1:63, 354).

power, such as direct control over agricultural produce, including the right to dispose of surplus production, represented an important resource to Muskogee men. Since such control derived only from marriage among the Muskogee, men in that group had great incentive to control the sexuality and other activities of their wives, thereby guarding against the alienation of their affections and maintaining access to primary politicoeconomic resources. Among the Cherokee, where men gained no economic advantages from marriage, no such incentive existed.

Sociopolitical Factors

While both groups show general similarities in regard to sociopolitical features, important differences appear as well. The most important relate to the distribution of power and authority in the two groups and to the nature and development of status hierarchies within each. These factors are interrelated and connected with the previously mentioned economic differences.

Seniority played an important role in the status hierarchies of both groups, but greater elaboration characterized the Muskogee. Among the Cherokee, seniority was personal and derived primarily from genealogical position and relative age within each localized clan segment. Clans generally were not ranked on the basis of seniority. The lineage and possibly the clan of the town chief (*uku*) may have been ranked slightly senior to the others (Fogelson 1977; Gearing 1962). Structural seniority played a more important role in the Muskogee status hierarchy. Within each phratry, one clan was considered senior to the others and referred to as "uncle" (*pawa*) or "elder brother" (*'L'aha*). The lineages within the clans were ranked, and the phratries were also implicitly ranked to some extent (Spoehr 1942:53; Swanton 1928:122–23). Thus groups as well as individuals enjoyed seniority in the Muskogee system.

In congruence with the minimal development of ranking among the Cherokee, most prestige statuses in that society were achieved and often subject to popular election. Demonstrated success in warfare, hunting, oratory, and similar activities all contributed to prestige for men. Old age, which may be viewed as partially achieved, also conferred prestige. With the exception of the office of uku, few high-status positions relied primarily on hereditary succession or other ascriptive factors among the Cherokee (Fogelson 1977). This contrasts strongly with the Muskogee, where most high-prestige positions depended on either clan membership or appointment by the mikko (Sattler 1987:45–59). Even such nominally achieved statuses as those in the war organization depended partially on clan membership (Swanton 1928:433, 436–37). The more open status hierarchy of the Cherokee, with its emphasis on achievement rather than on ascription, contributed to the greater equality of Cherokee women. Conversely, the more closed hierarchy of the Muskogee, with its emphasis on ascription, made status differences based on gender more important.

Among the Muskogee, a relatively few clans controlled virtually all of the positions of authority. The "royal" clan (that of the mikko) in fact controlled the vast majority of offices, either directly or indirectly through patronage. A second clan, that of the *hinihaki* ("second chiefs" or councillors), also enjoyed considerable authority. In most italwa this clan and one or two others constituted the "noble" rank. In the italwa of the so-called White division, the clan or group of clans that provided the war chiefs *(tastanakaki)*, also controlled positions of authority. Among the so-called Red towns the post of paramount war chief *(tastanuki 'L'akko)* belonged to the royal clan. The remaining positions of authority, the clan heads, were divided equally among all of the clans (Sattler 1987:45–59; Swanton 1928:276–306). Among the Cherokee, authority was more evenly distributed. Authority was divided among the hereditary uku, the clan heads (the senior men in each clan), and the war leaders (whose status was achieved) (Fogelson 1977).

Power was distributed similarly to authority in each group. Control of offices conferred the most power for both individuals and clans among the Muskogee. Since members of the royal clan occupied most offices among them, it enjoyed considerable power. Additionally, the mikko appointed or confirmed most other officials. This control of patronage conferred additional power both to the mikko and to his clan. Magicoreligious power and ability translated into political influ-ence as well, but since this attribute attached to many of the offices, it primarily expanded the power of officials (Sattler 1987:45). Success in trade, hunting, warfare, and oratory also affected personal power and influence among both the Muskogee and the Cherokee. Numerical strength likewise contributed to the power of clans in both groups. Power among the Cherokee derived far more from personal achieve-ment and the numerical superiority of clans (Fogelson 1977; Gearing 1962). Among the Muskogee, numbers conferred less power than seniority and ranking among the clans. The senior clan in any phratry was seldom the largest and often the smallest (Swanton 1928:145–49).

The Muskogee tended to concentrate power and authority in the hands of a few men who occupied positions of structural seniority. Junior men (in both structural and chronological terms) were generally excluded from the political process.[6] While these men attended councils, they did not actively participate or speak unless asked. Significantly, the ascribed attributes of young (and structurally junior) men closely paralleled those of women. However, while the former could shed these attributes with age and achievement, women could not (Sattler 1987:48). Senior men exerted control over both groups and excluded both from direct participation in decision making.

Marriage also played an important role in political relations among both groups, though perhaps more particularly among the Muskogee. Marriage established alliances between clans and lineages and served to extend relations of dominance and subordination beyond the clan. Within the clan a man owned deference and suport to his elder brothers and his mother's brothers. He also owed similar deference and support to members of his father's clan. After marriage these respect relations extended to the men of his wife's clan and her father's clan. Particular respect and support (both economic and political) were owed to senior members of the wife's clan. Direct support tended to be limited, however, to the actual father-in-law, with only a diffuse

---

6. In the present, the idiomatic expression for structural inferiority or ignorance among Creek and Seminole men in Oklahoma is, "I am too young." This can be somewhat disconcerting when said by an eighty-year-old man.

respect attaching to other men of his clan (Gilbert 1943:153; Spoehr 1942:86–87). Among the Cherokee, these relations primarily reflected the deference owed by a younger man to an elder, whereas the additional factor of ranking also influenced the Muskogee system.

Under the Muskogee marriage system, a man was structurally inferior to his in-laws, a fact exploited at least by elite and senior lineages. Mikkos routinely married their sisters and nieces to other prominent men within the italwa, in part to ensure the support and cooperation of these men. Likewise, paramount chiefs arranged similar marriages to their subordinate chiefs (Sattler 1987:140–43). This pattern of binding subordinates through marriage indicates a degree of institutionalized hypogamy, at least among elite lineages or clans. As the Cherokee clans and lineages were not ranked, no such pattern pertained among them.

Two anomalies attach to marriage patterns in regard to the Muskogee mikko. Normally a couple built a house adjacent to the wife's mother's home after marriage, in typical matrilocal fashion, but this did not always apply to the mikko. In those recorded cases where his bride belonged to a different italwa, she always came to live in her husband's village. Most men had no say in the marriages of their children, these being arranged by the clan elders (achulaki) of the latter's clan. There are numerous recorded examples, however, of a mikko arranging his daughter's marriages, particularly to traders and other potentially useful or influential men. These facts seem to emphasize the power and structural superiority of the mikko and the extent of his control and influence through his ability to override the normal rules governing marriage relations. They also support the hypothesis of institutionalized hypogamy, since the wife of a mikko, in most cases, did not marry hypogamously. The structural superiority of the mikko relative to his wife's clan and lineage under these circumstances can account for the anomalies.

The marriage patterns outlined here have further implications for gender relations. Marriage among the Cherokee joined clans of equal status, and the husband and wife enjoyed equal status. Muskogee marriages, however, established and perpetuated relations of inequality between clans, with the husband subordinate to his wife's clan and her father. Within the marriage, however, the husband was structurally superior to his wife, as indicated by the differential control he exercised over his wife. This superiority is further emphasized by the injunction given a woman by her clan elders at marriage that she obey her husband (Spoehr 1942:78–79, 91–92). This creates a discrepancy between the greater prestige of the wife's clan and her own subordination. This discrepancy can be resolved if women did not share the same status as men in their clan but rather occupied a lower status equivalent to or slightly below that of men in their husbands' clans.[7]

CONCLUSION

Significant differences in gender status existed between the Cherokee and the Muskogee, reflecting more general differences in political and economic organization and in prestige systems. Complementarity of gender roles and statuses among the Cherokee reflect a more open, egalitarian system in which differences in prestige and power reflect individual achievement and age, rather than ranking of descent groups and ascriptive hierarchies. Gender inequality and subordination of women among the Muskogee derive from a more general pattern of inequality and an ascriptive hierarchy that concentrated power in a few structurally senior men. While women served to create political links between men of different clans among both the Cherokee and the Muskogee, the inequality of those relations among the latter acted to lower the status of women relative to men in their own clans. The control of women in Muskogee society likewise followed general patterns of dominance and subordination wherein senior men also controlled junior men and largely excluded them from active participation in political affairs.

7. This also contrasts with the strongly hierarchical Polynesian systems. The difference here derives from the nature of the descent systems. Among the bilateral (or ambilineal) Polynesians, women can recruit members to the descent group through marriage, but there is an element of choice. Under these circumstances, women contribute directly to the power of the descent groups through their choices and influence and therefore share in its prestige. Among the matrilineal Muskogee, no choice exists, so such incentives are not offered to women (see Ortner 1981).

Certain caution should be exercised, however, in interpreting this situation, and the degree of inequality and dominance in Muskogee society should not be overemphasized. Structural inequality and subordination do not imply total powerlessness, nor are these features as highly developed among the Muskogee as in many other cultures. Junior men could and did assert a degree of power and even control at various times during the history of the Muskogee peoples. Similarly, under certain circumstances, women could assert their independence and influence the course of events.

An additional caveat derives from the nature of the data. Virtually all accounts of gender roles and status were written by European and American men who derived much of their information from other (Muskogee) men. This certainly introduces into the data a bias that must be accounted for in the analysis. The continuation of many earlier patterns of interaction between the sexes, particularly a degree of sexual segregation, also limits the ability of present-day male ethnographers to redress this bias. Research by female ethnographers with modern Muskogee women may therefore require some revisions of this model as informed by the female perspective. Despite these reservations, the available data do support significant differences between the Cherokee and the Muskogee. Complementarity of the roles and statuses implies very different relations of power and mechanisms for its acquisition and expression than does structural inequality and subordination. Even if the relative power differential between the sexes is essentially similar in both groups, the structural differences profoundly influence its operation in each. Our understanding of social and cultural processes can progress only by recognizing and accounting for these differences and their effects in society.

13

GENDER AND POWER IN NATIVE NORTH AMERICA
CONCLUDING REMARKS

DANIEL MALTZ AND JOALLYN ARCHAMBAULT

Even within a single field of inquiry such as the study of gender, different theoretical issues become more or less relevant in different areas of the world. For those who study gender in Native North America the most compelling issues have been (1) the strong distinction between gender and sexuality as cultural domains, (2) the impact of European colonialism and conquest on gender roles, and (3) the relation between gender and power.

It is the third of these issues that is the central focus of this volume. Two concepts, "complementarity" and individual "autonomy," dominate these essays as they do the literature on Native American gender relations in general. In the 1970s the debate over whether or not women are universally subordinate to men was a central theme in the anthropology of gender. In the 1990s this debate is no longer as compelling as it once was. Continued discussions about egalitarian versus nonegalitarian societies, about complementarity versus inequality, can sometimes make it seem as if North Americanists are one or two decades behind the rest of the field of anthropology in defining their theoretical problems. But it is worth remembering that from the early years of this debate in the 1970s through the present, the discussion has been propelled largely by North Americanists such as Louise Lamphere (1974), Eleanor Burke Leacock (1981), and Alice Schlegel (1977a) who drew heavily on their own Native American field experience as well as by scholars such as Judith K. Brown (1970) and

Jane Fishburne Collier (1987, 1988) who have chosen to reinterpret North American data. In an era in which little of the general theoretical discussion within anthropology has originated in the ethnography of Native North America, it is important to examine the topic of gender and power, not as a leftover from the 1970s, but as a topic to which North American ethnography and ethnographers have made and still can make a major theoretical and ethnographic contribution.

What makes the Native North American case so interesting for the study of gender and power is that it is a region in which gender is central to the cultural system but not closely linked to either biology or power. This point is made most clearly by comparing Native North American gender concepts to those of other world regions. Like Southeast Asia, North America is noted for complementary gender relations, but whereas gender distinctions are muted in Southeast Asia (Atkinson and Errington 1990), they are elaborated in much of North America. As in Melanesia and the Mediterranean, gender is culturally elaborated in Native North America, but unlike these regions, in which gender concepts are closely tied to the notions of biology and sexuality, the gender concepts of North America are tied to behavioral as opposed to biological differences. Finally, whereas many of the ideologies stemming from world religious systems, such as Christianity and Islam, elaborate patriarchal gender systems in which gender relations are expressed in terms of authority, the ideologies of Native North America rarely express the relation between the genders in political terms.

Cultural Variations

Each of the chapters in this volume makes a case that the women in a particular cultural area of aboriginal North America had more power than many previous observers have claimed. But the relation between gender and power is different in different regions, and the kinds of arguments being made vary from one region to the next depending on the ways in which power was characterized and distributed and gender relations were defined in each region. Within Native North America, basic cultural differences in political systems lead to at least four different kinds of arguments concerning the relation between gender and power: (1) arguments for egalitarian gender relations in societies in which hierarchical relationships in general are noticeably weak (Plateau, Basin, parts of California, and the eastern Subarctic); (2) arguments for female power in societies that allocate comparatively high degrees of informal or even formal power to women (Iroquois, Cherokee, Hopi, Navajo); (3) arguments that male power is culturally limited even in societies usually characterized as dominated by male authority (Arctic, Northern Athapaskan, Plains, Creek); and (4) arguments that even very hierarchical societies may not use gender as a major dimension for the distribution of power and prestige (Tlingit). Each of these arguments is important both ethnographically and theoretically. Ethnographically, each frames gender relations in a particular region of North America and helps define the relation of gender to other aspects of aboriginal society. Theoretically, different culture areas help refine different arguments concerning the nature of gender, of power, and of the relationship between them.

The first kind of argument for relative female power is really an argument about a lack of power by everyone, both male and female. In certain societies, few, if any, hierarchical distinctions are made between people. If no one has power over anyone else, then men as a group have little or no power over women. This is part of a more general argument for the relatively egalitarian nature of male/female relations in small-scale hunting and gathering societies. Arguments of this type have been made for Australia, tribal Southeast Asia, the Amazon, and the Kalahari Desert and the Ituri Forest of Africa, but not all such societies allow equally strong arguments for gender complementarity rather than gender hierarchy. In general, even when the economic contributions of men and women are relatively equal, high-prestige male activities such as the hunting of large animals, frequent warfare, headhunting, or male-dominated ritual activities may give greater prestige and power to men. The case for egalitarian gender relations in hunting and gathering societies is probably strongest for parts of Native North America. It has been made most forcefully by Eleanor Leacock, especially for the Montagnais-Naskapi.

The dispersal of authority in band societies means that the public-private or jural-familial dichotomy, so important in hierarchically organized society, is not relevant. . . . With regard to the autonomy of women, nothing in the structure of egalitarian band societies necessitated special deference to men. There were no economic and social liabilities that bound women to be more sensitive to men's needs and feelings than vice versa. (Leacock [1978] 1981:140)

Lillian A. Ackerman's analyses of the Plateau and Martha C. Knack's analyses of the Great Basin follow in this tradition. But not all hunting and gathering societies, even in North America, present equally strong cases for egalitarian gender relations. The strong case made for the Plateau and the Great Basin has not been made for the Arctic, Northern Athapaskan societies such as the Chipewyan or the buffalo hunters of the high Plains.

The most valuable contribution of these ethnographic cases is not to prove or disprove the universal subordination hypothesis but rather to help refine the argument for relative gender equality in certain hunting and gathering societies. No matter what one's theoretical orientation, one would agree that the societies described by Ackerman and Knack were among those with the least hierarchical relations between the sexes.

The second kind of argument concerns the often complex relationship between formal authority and political power in general, including indirect or behind-the-scenes power. The distinction between authority and influence and its critical relationship to gender has been made most clearly by Lamphere.

Women's strategies are a response to the distribution of power and authority and will differ, I suggest, depending on whether women are able to make decisions or whether decisions are made by men. Since women are often not in positions of authority, a key concept in understanding their strategies is that of influence. (Lamphere 1974:99)
Where men hold positions of authority, a woman (in her role as wife, mother, or sister) may be able to influence a man's decision . . . by persuading him that such a decision is in his own interests or perhaps in the interests of his children or other kin. (Ibid., 100)

Thus authority involves the holding of formal political office, whereas influence (equally a form of power) involves the ability to affect decisions but without the need of an office.

It is in the ethnography of Mediterranean Europe that this relation between male authority and indirect female influence has been analyzed most carefully. In a classic article, Ernestine Friedl (1967:97) has argued that the greater prestige given to male activities in the public sphere may create an "appearance" of a male monopoly on power in rural Greece that masks the "reality" of real female power particularly "in the life of the family." Others such as Susan Harding (1975) have responded that Friedl's argument "isolates the village from the larger structural context from which men derive much of their economic, political, and ideological power in the village" (306) and "seriously overestimates the power in women's hands by not recognizing the nature, limits, and consequences of that power" (307).

Friedl's analysis of women's indirect power combined with Harding's critique and modification provide a general three-step strategy for analyzing the relation between gender and power that includes examining (1) apparent power as determined by ideology and formal institutions, (2) real power as determined by indirect influence, and (3) the limitations on different types of power based on the structural relationships between different power domains. For Mediterranean Europe, this approach reveals a pattern of a strongly male-dominant ideology, significant indirect female power, particularly in the domestic domain, and strong limitations on this power based on the nonequivalence of domains.

For many of the matrilineal societies of Native North America (including the Iroquois, Cherokee, Navajo, and some of the Pueblo peoples), the structural pattern is very different from that of Mediterranean Europe, but a parallel type of argument can be made. In these societies, ideology emphasizes substantial female power, often characterized as "matriarchy" or "petticoat politics." The reality, however, often reveals that access to decision-making and political offices is primarily in the hands of men. The limits of female influence in these societies is even more complex than in the Mediterranean, in part because of the lack of a strong public/domestic distinction. Where the distinction between internal and external social affairs is associated with gender, as among the Iroquois, it makes sense to ask questions about the inequality between these two political arenas and the relation of this inequality to gender. In other societies, more like the Tlingit, in which both internal and external relations are controlled by lineages and not gender distinguished, questions about gender and power focus not on the inequality of domains but on differences in the power of men and women within particular domains.

The Iroquois are among the best known and most analyzed of American Indian societies and certainly the most likely to be labeled "matriarchal" in popular literature. Numerous scholars, for example, such as Cara Richards (1957), Judith K. Brown (1970), and Elisabeth Tooker (1984), have discussed the relatively high political influence of Iroquois women but also acknowledged their exclusion from major positions of formal political power. What is unusual about the Iroquois case is the extent to which this power was "socially recognized and institutionalized" (Brown 1970: 155). Theoretically, this is a very important point. The difference between influence and authority is not simply one of legitimacy or cultural recognition, since among groups like the Iroquois influence is culturally legitimized but is still not the same thing as authority.

Joy Bilharz, in this volume, continues in the tradition of these other scholars and summarizes the case for women's power and status as being based on their relative control over land, horticultural production, nomination of chiefs, and the fate of war captives as well as their participation in village and tribal decision making. The male/female opposition of forest/clearing can be seen as one of complementarity rather than inequality, particularly with men frequently absent while hunting or at war. But women's political power was the ability to influence who held office, not the more direct ability to hold office, and the culturally recognized distinction between internal and external social relations worked to create an inequality between men's and women's arenas of power, particularly with the increasing importance of relations with the outside world.

Among the Cherokee, Richard A. Sattler describes a similar pattern of relative female autonomy and even power in homogeneous matrilineal, matrilocal communities with little restrictions on female sexuality and some political offices open to senior women. But here again, "in general, authority outside the domestic household was vested in men. Men held political offices; men were the formal decision makers. Women participated in making political decisions through informal channels, however, especially through their influence on brothers, sons, and other male members of their matrilineage" (Fogelson 1990:172).

Similarly among the matrilineal Pueblo, relative female autonomy and major economic contributions allow Sue-Ellen Jacobs, like Schlegel (1977*b*), to make a strong argument that women's roles were complementary to, rather than subordinate to, those of men despite limited access to formal positions of authority. As Schlegel argues for the Hopi, "to say, therefore, that women have no positions in the formal authority structure is to say very little. As the mothers, sisters, and wives of men who make community decisions, the influence of women cannot be overestimated. These women, after all, control the houses that the men live in" (Schlegel 1977*b*:254).

The Navajo, although they were more dispersed and less centralized, resembled these other societies in the relative autonomy of women, egalitarian domestic relations, and comparatively undifferentiated public and domestic domains. As described by Mary Shepardson, there was comparatively little indigenous ideology of female inferiority as opposed to male/female complementarity, but again there was a relative exclusion of women.from the formal political domain because mythology was thought to justify the idea that "Navajo women could not be trusted in politics."

The general conclusion to be reached from examining these societies is that even in settled and somewhat centralized societies women have more power when descent is matrilineal, residence is matrilocal, restrictions on female sexuality are limited, men are frequently absent due to involvement in activities such as warfare, or women have some veto power, if not control, over formal political, military, or religious offices.

The third kind of argument concerns societies in which men are basically dominant but certain aspects of female power can be seen as limiting the power of men. In a variety of Native American societies including the Plains, the Northern Athapaskan, the Inuit, the Creek, and much of the Eastern Woodlands, the case for male power over women is fairly strong. The question then becomes, what is it about these societies that allows women to place limitations on male power over them? Some answers to this question include cultural values on individual autonomy, alternative roles such as that of the "manly-hearted woman" open to at least some women, and mythological charters for women's status. In societies of this type, men control most power, but women have a variety of options for limiting it or gaining access to some of it.

For the Inuit, Lee Guemple describes a society in which men possess domestic authority, especially in the Central Arctic, and control community decision making, especially in Greenland. Males are socialized to be aggressive and women to be deferential, and the male economic activity of hunting is highly valued by the community as a whole. But this pattern of male dominance is partially counter-balanced by a spatial separation of men's and women's work in which neither gender impinges on the work of the other and a person's worth is expressed in terms of their work performance, not the type of work they do. Female skills in sewing and processing foods are likewise valued. Women's lack of formal authority is partially balanced by indirect power through gossip or influence over men, the shamanic role is equally open to women and men, and the basic cultural notion of the person is gender neutral. Even personal names are not divided into men's and women's names.

For the Chipewyan, Henry S. Sharp reports a distinction between an innate female status as dependent and an achieved male status as provider and controller. But rather than accepting the idea of male dominance, he argues that these ideas were embedded in a basic notion of gender complementarity, not hierarchy. He notes that definitions of maleness placed an obligation and vulnerability on men that was apt to wane with increasing age. The male role as protector and provider may have been manipulated by women to escape from unwanted men or play off some men against others rather than simply being examples of male assertions of power over women.

For the Blackfoot, representing the high Plains, Alice B. Kehoe describes a society in which male roles are more flamboyant, visible, and assertive than those of women, who are generally characterized as "submissive, docile, and quiet." Balancing this pattern of male dominance are the major contribution of women to subsistence, the participation of married women in the sodalities of their husbands, the availability of the assertive "manly-hearted" role to fully one-third of elderly women, and an ideology that stresses personal autonomy and greater innate spirituality of women. And an ideology in which the innate nature of men is more foolish and that of women more spiritual results in a system of religious practice in which men, not women, are involved in actions such as vision quests aimed at increasing their spirituality.

Among the Creek, as analyzed by Sattler, women were viewed as immature, emotional, parochial, irrational, irresponsible, and immoral. They were given no direct political power, and men were ridiculed for even listening to them. Relations were hierarchical, status was hereditary, power was in the hands of a few older men, and marriages were used to create bonds with individuals of different status. But even here, women possessed personal freedom and respect, if not power.

The fourth kind of argument concerns hierarchical societies in which status distinctions are relatively independent of gender. Laura F. Klein's analysis of the matrilineal societies of the Northwest Coast, particularly the Tlingit, is one of the most unusual and original recent contributions to the ethnographic discussion of gender and power in Native North America. Margaret Blackman's analysis of the position of Haida women is more typical of the way in which gender is understood on the Northwest Coast.

Though aboriginally Haida women occupied a relatively high status as demonstrated in their access to numerous domains of the culture, Haida society was still a male dominated one. Men were the final authorities of

238

the household and the holders of positions of political authority. They alone were the hosts of the most important types of potlatches, the owners of the most important property (houses and totem poles), the performers of the most prestigious rituals (dances), the creators and monopolizers of an art form whose symbols represented the matrilineal groups they dominated. (Blackman 1981:75)

But Klein approaches the problem in a fundamentally different way, distinguishing between gender inequality and social hierarchy. Hierarchy need not be expressed in terms of men's control over women, and among the Tlingit, she argues, wealth and kinship rather than gender are the bases for establishing rank and status. She argues for a definition of women among the Tlingit that was not tied to either nurturance or the public domain but rather to the status of the matriclan. In her more recent writings, Blackman (1991:182–84) herself has presented a new interpretation of the public power of one Haida woman that more closely resembles the Klein's portrayal of the Tlingit.

COLONIAL CONTEXT

In addition to sharing the cultural characteristics that come from being a single world area, all Native North American cultures experienced a similar pattern of colonial encounter. While this experience varied in details that were frequently critical to the lives of those involved, it broadly consisted of conquest by and partial assimilation to the culture of eighteenth- and nineteenth-century Western Europe.

Economically, warfare was ended, migratory groups were forced to settle, tribes were displaced, some multiple times, and many groups were involuntarily resettled far from their original home area. Settled residence altered the level of social contact among groups such as the Chipewyan and the end of warfare decreased the autonomy of women among groups such as the Iroquois, as men increased their presence in the local community. Control over local resources was largely lost, native economies were destroyed or significantly reduced, and labor was incorporated into a larger capitalist system, first as equal participants in exploration and trade, then as unequal labor on local white enterprises such as mines, ranches, and farms, and finally as incorporated elements in an urban-centered national economy. Among some groups, such as the Paiute, both men and women equally lost control over local resources. Among others, such as the Chipewyan, "sustained residence in villages reduced the need for traditional products of women's labor" (Sharp, this volume), thus decreasing the status of women more than that of men. The distribution of labor opportunities was based on location, education in skills relevant to the larger society, and white-defined gender roles. As groups were absorbed into the national economy, employment opportunities were often more available for women than for men. As described for the Pueblo and the Paiute, greater incorporation into the dominant economy meant that outside forces, not local cultural traditions, determined which economic tasks were assigned to men and which were assigned to women, "Euro-American employers determined for which sexually stereotyped tasks [women as opposed to men] would be hired" (Knack, this volume).

Politically, Indian groups lost local autonomy, many were confined to reservations, and all were increasingly incorporated into the larger nation-states of the United States and Canada. Even changing residence patterns changed the social and political positions of men and women so that among the Chipewyan, for example, "the nature of the ties of friendship and being neighbors opened new opportunities for mutual support between women and created a new category for political and economic activities" (Sharp, this volume). Increasingly, power came from relationships, economic, sexual, and marital, not to insiders but to outsiders. Thus, with continually expanding degrees of contact, the power of Pomo women "within their own communities increased as their knowledge of English and white behavior grew as a result of their intimacy with white households, goods, and habits. . . . Pomo women had a separate relationship with white men. The victims of rape, sexual exploitation, and abuse, they also received favors and money from the white men who often fathered their children" (Patterson, this volume). External laws redefined individual authority and rights over people and property. Particularly in matrilineal societies such as the Iroquois and Navajo, Euro-American definitions of male household heads increased the power of men and of nuclear families at the expense of women and of matrilineal kin groups. In these cases women actually lost both domestic rights and voting authority in the larger community. The colonial experience has transformed tribal cultures and created tensions between men and women that may have increased wife beatings (e.g., the White Shawl Society at Rosebud).

Ideologically, Euro-American culture introduced a variety of notions that strongly influenced gender ideology, including Christian redefinitions of gender complementarity and gender hierarchy. Changing notions of sexual propriety decreased the autonomy of women, particularly in societies such as the Cherokee that tolerated high degrees of sexual freedom. As described for several groups including the Plateau Indians, the Pomo, and the Pueblo peoples, the distinction between public and domestic, which characterizes gender relations throughout much of the Old World, was introduced to American Indian societies and served to replace the complementary notion of gender difference with a more hierarchical one. As argued by Sharp, cultural notions of egalitarianism and autonomy were sometimes altered radically with the introduction of "Western ideas of individualism and the family" and changing political and economic realities. Thus, among the Chipewyan, the increasing economic autonomy of women in the late 1960s allowed traditional notions of egalitarianism to be expressed through the ideological concept of "romantic love" in opposition to arranged marriages.

THE DANGER OF UTOPIAN FANTASIES

It is in the nature of colonizing societies to create images of those they colonize, images of noble savages and of lowly heathens, images they use to help tell them who they are and who they are not. So for the last five hundred years, Europeans and European Americans have created images of American Indians. It is left to Indian peoples to respond to these images, to be amused by them, confused by them, or angered by them, to deflect them, accept them, or to exploit them for their own benefit. Negative images present one kind of obstacle. They must be challenged and rejected. But positive, romantic, even utopian images can be even more dangerous. They are more seductive, more likely to confuse you about the relation between who you are and who others think you to be. The danger of having your culture romanticized is that you expect too much of yourself by trying to live up to a past that never really was.

Scholars have frequently discussed the stereotypes of the late nineteenth and early twentieth century, of Indian men as brave, war-bonneted, horse-riding warriors and Indian women as drudgelike squaws or noble princesses. These are images created in part by Wild West shows and Hollywood movies and widely accepted in popular culture. But these are not the only images of the last three decades of the twentieth century. Increasingly, another different image of American Indians has emerged, again an image to satisfy the needs of non-Indian Americans to imagine who they are not and who they could have been. In a time of ecology movements, New Age religious movements, alternative health movements, feminist movements, and gay rights movements, the American Indian has once again captured the imagination of those people who are exploring who it is they wish they were. Popular culture has been captivated by images of Indians as ecologists in harmony with nature, as holy men, as Iroquois matriarchs, and as berdaches free to explore and express their individual sexual and gender identities.

These images of a utopian past in which everything was peaceful, beautiful, and harmonious until contact with whites destroyed this pristine perfection can be as problematic as negative images. Despite their apparent anti-European bias, these fantasies about the past are as much a product of Euro-American imaginings as are notions of slavelike squaws and noble Indian princesses, and they are at least as dangerous to Indian self-conceptions and probably more important.

The danger of these utopian fantasies is that they are, almost by definition, partial images of human society, lacking the complexity of the true human condition. They focus on single aspects of society and portray individuals who are perfect rather than human. As they influence contemporary American Indians, particularly younger non-reservation Indian people, these fantasies seem to come in two varieties, both products of white society's desires to think about Indians as idealized others. The first is the image of spiritual holy men and occasional holy women, a world of warriors and hunters, constantly communing with nature and with holy spirits, removed from the dirty realities of politics, of economics, of conflict, and of domestic life. It is a world of spiritually pure men and some women, unencumbered by spouses, children, or everyday mundane life. The second is the fantasy of an aboriginal matriarchy, a world in which women are the centers of the universe, controlling all power and resources. It focuses on a romanticized version of the Iroquois polity, popularized by such writers as Paula Gunn Allen.

Definitions of gender, like definitions of ethnicity, are part of an ongoing dialogue, with different groups of people vying to define themselves and to define one another. Scholars such as anthropologists and historians struggle to discredit popular stereotypes of American Indians that misrepresent social realities and cultural process. In response, many American Indian activists, inspired by the intentionally antiacademic writings of the Lakota writer Vine Deloria, Jr., dismiss these scholarly definitions of themselves.

> The massive volume of useless knowledge produced by anthropologists attempting to capture real Indians in a network of theories has contributed substantially to the invisibility of Indian people today. . . . Not even Indians can relate themselves to this type of creature who, to anthropologists, is the "real" Indian. Indian people begin to feel that they are merely shadows of a mythical super-Indian. Many anthros spare no expense to reinforce this sense of inadequacy in order to further their influence over Indian people. (Deloria 1969:86).

To discredit academic depictions of Indians, Deloria proceeds to create his own caricature of the other, in his case, anthropologists.

> They are the most prominent members of the scholarly community that infests the land of the free, and in the summer time, the homes of the braves. . . . While their historical precedent is uncertain, anthropo-

gists can readily be identified on the reservations. Go into any crowd of people. Pick out a tall, gaunt white man wearing Bermuda shorts, a World War II Army Air Force flying jacket, an Australian bush hat, tennis shoes, and packing a large knapsack incorrectly strapped to his back. He will invariably have a thin, sexy wife with stringy hair, an IQ of 191, and a vocabulary in which even the prepositions have eleven syllables. . . . This creature is an anthropologist. (Ibid., 83–84)

Clearly, Deloria is engaged in discrediting others by creating simplistic stereotypes and denying the legitimacy of any but the most subjective ways of defining oneself or others. It is clear that he is attempting to stifle a white male monopoly on defining the "true Indian," but what is somewhat more subtle is his move to turn the whole debate over defining "Indianness" into a contest or battle between posturing male egos, an observation best made by his cousin, the Lakota anthropologist Beatrice Medicine.

Perhaps female anthropologists should be grateful that they are not part of this native typology or perhaps Vine Deloria, Jr. did not have sufficient empirical evidence to portray the female of the anthropological species. Be that as it may, the foregoing description has been the rallying cry for many tribal communities and militant groups since the original description appeared in *Playboy,* August, 1969, and later in Deloria's book, *Custer Died for Your Sins* (1969). (Medicine 1978:13)

What Deloria and those who follow him are clearly doing is discrediting not only white scholars who attempt to define Native American culture but also anthropologists such as Medicine and Ella Deloria, his own father's sister, who are neither white or male. They are discrediting the use of historical and ethnographic methods even by Indians, particularly women, who are attempting to define their own communities. To quote Bea Medicine once again:

Native societies and the males in them have continued their attempts to restrict [Native] women. Phrased differently, Indian males are chauvinistic! They are the first to admit this fact. However, they justify their stance by saying that certain behavior and proofs of self-sufficiency in an Indian female is "Not the Indian way!" Whatever that may mean! This flies in the face of fact, of reality . . . [so a scholarly] examination of sex roles is imperative. (Ibid., 4)

What American Indian people need to have is a vision of themselves that is realistic. They need to see themselves as part of the human condition, not as images of utopia. They need to have a vision of themselves and their history that is genuinely human and not always flattering. It is important for Indian students to learn to do a critical reading of historical documents as opposed to simply rejecting them, to learn to see biases and look through them as opposed to rejecting some biases and simply replacing them with others. They must overcome the problem of historical egocentrism, the assumption that "I know how my grandmother felt and thought," the idea that simply because of one's spiritual or genetic identity one can read the past without identifying historical objects or their meanings. One's culture gives perspective, but genetics does not enable one to know the past: the past is, in a sense, "another country." Critical understanding of all claimed realities affects others. Self-interest and bias are part of the human condition, but there is a need not to glorify the past or to assume its superiority to the present.

THE GENERAL ARGUMENT AND ITS LIMITATIONS
The major argument of this volume has been to demonstrate that for at least one world culture area, that of Native North America, "domination" and "inequality" are not the most useful concepts for examining the nature of gender or the relationship between gender and power, that "autonomy," "complementarity," and even "egalitarianism" are more useful. It is a compelling argument that is both well demonstrated in this volume and compatible with the previous research of such major scholars as Eleanor Leacock, but it is also important not to overstate or misunderstand the nature of the argument. It is not so much an argument for the lack of any power differential between men and women as an argument for the importance of certain themes, economic, political, and ideological, stressing complementarity rather than inequality.

We find it useful to distinguish four major themes in the ethnography of Native North America that contribute significantly to our understanding of gender complementarity in the region, each of which possesses certain problems and limitations. First is a cultural notion of the self that stresses individual autonomy and relative freedom independent of one's gender. Second is a relative lack of social domination and submission in defining interpersonal relations, including relations between men and women, with some significant exceptions such as the Northwest Coast. Third is a cultural elaboration and valuation of feminine principles in mythology and belief. Fourth is relative availability of positions of power to women as well as men.

The first theme is the importance of autonomy in Native American concepts of the self. Kehoe's description of the Blackfoot is fairly typical:

> What really matters to a Blackfoot is autonomy, personal autonomy. Blackfoot respect each person's competence, even the competence of very small children, and avoid bossing others. People seek power to support the autonomy they so highly value. Competence is the outward justification of the exercise of autonomy. (Chap. 7, this vol.)

It is the contrast between this notion of autonomy and Western notions of individualism that is most useful for helping us understand the culturally specific nature of gender and power in the cultures of Native America. This distinction is most clearly explained by Anne S. Straus in her analysis of Cheyenne ethnopsychology:

> Individuality is by no means peculiar to modern Western society. . . . But the meaning of individuality differs in different cultural contexts. In Western society the valued self is independent, internally driven, "self-actualizing"; the dependent, other-directed person is defined as having an unhealthy self. In Northern Cheyenne culture, individuality does occur and is respected unquestioned, but (as one woman stated it) "the individuals are like the poles of a tipi—each has his own attitude and appearance but all look to the same center [heart] and support the same cover." For Cheyennes, individuality supports a tribal purpose, a tribal identity. Individual freedom does not consist in distinguishing oneself from the group. Indeed, without the tribe there is no freedom; there is only being lost. (Straus 1982: 125)

In other words, in Western thought, the individual and society tend to be seen in opposition to one another. The assertion of individual autonomy is seen as opposed to social commitment, and social relations are seen as inherently threatening to one's autonomy. In Native North American thought, in contrast, individual autonomy is not threatened by social relations; relationships between people do not imply that one is in any sense controlled by the other. Whereas autonomy in contemporary Western thought is equated with independence, in Native North American thought it is compatible with interdependence. This distinction is one of the major reasons why "gender complementarity" makes more sense in Native American society than it does in Western society.

The second theme of relevance to gender and power in American Indian culture is a relative deemphasis on domination and submission in all social relations. Even in cultures in which prestige is important and hierarchy is a major issue, the ability to dominate others does not tend to be the major basis for determining status. If control over other people is relatively unimportant in all social relations, then the control of men over women is not a major theme.

A less frequently discussed aspect of domination and control is the issue of interpersonal violence. In a cross-cultural comparison of violence against women. D. Alan Aycock (1976) finds traditional American Indian societies to be significantly less male dominant with respect to violence than African societies. In large part, this distinction is a result of frequent male absence from the community and the direction of violence outside of the community. While American Indian cultures devalue issues of domination, they often do not deemphasize violence or warfare and in many cases devalue intervention to prevent interpersonal violence. In many American Indian societies, men were traditionally warriors, trained to killing and intimidation. What needs to be asked is how violence was used to intimidate, control, and embarrass when it is brought home from the battlefield, to what extent man the hunter and man the warrior was also the man the wife beater and man the rapist. There is also the question of whether a high valuation on individual autonomy implied an unwillingness to interfere with the behavior of others even in cases of interpersonal violence. Clearly violence, including violence against women, was a part of the Native North American experience, including wife beating in the Arctic (Wagner Sorenson 1990:94), gang rape and nose cutting as punishment for adultery in the northern Plains (Kehoe 1970:102), and interethnic violence including killing of Indian men and raping of Indian women (Knack 1986:86, 94). Women who lived away from their own relatives were more vulnerable to wife beating. This is an area that deserves more research but may be difficult because it is not flattering to Native groups.

The third theme is a frequent pattern of gender balance in Native systems of belief. From Holy Woman of the Blackfoot and White Buffalo Calf Woman of the Lakota, both of the northern Plains, to Changing Woman, Spider Woman, and White Shell Woman of the Navajo in the Southwest, Native North American cultures are characterized by mythological images of women that are complementary rather than subordinate to those of men. Several contributors to this volume argue that male/female ideological dichotomies such as wolf/dog (Chipewyan), forest/clearing (Iroquois) and even lascivious and aggressive/chaste and compliant (Pomo) imply difference but need not imply hierarchy. Even recent reinterpretations of menstrual taboos by Thomas C. T. Buckley (1988) for the Yuroks, R. D. Fogelson (1990:175) for the Cherokee, and Victoria Patterson (this volume) for the Pomo have stressed the theme of female power rather than subordination.

But not all male/female distinctions in Native North American thought and action point to the ideological equality of men and women. Jacobs's discussion of contemporary San Juan Pueblo in this volume, for example, includes reports of young "macho" males expressing disdain for "women's" tasks. And this kind of disparaging use of femaleness in Native American thought is not entirely recent. Since at least the early eighteenth century, the Iroquois have referred to the neighboring Delaware as women. It is unclear how this ideological theme originated, whether it was originally meant to be insulting, or to what extent the Delaware themselves interpreted it as negative or positive (Miller 1974; Speck 1946; Wallace 1947). But it does seem clear that despite their high reverence for women, by the middle to the late eighteenth century "the expanding and relatively well integrated Iroquois came to despise the Delawares" (Wallace 1947:30) and to view their female status as a representation of their inferiority.

The fourth theme is the availability of certain positions of power to women in many Indian cultures. In some cultures, there were specific positions allocated to women such as Pueblo clan mothers and Cherokee war women. In others, women were granted a degree of indirect power surprising to Western observers. In still others, institutions such as that of the Manly-Hearted Woman among the Blackfoot allowed flexibility in the definition of gender roles. Each of these variations implies a culture in which the political possibilities of women are not as limited as they might have been, but access to male roles for a limited number of women is a double-edged sword. As Kehoe observes for the Blackfoot, the availability of high-status male roles to some elderly women implies the superiority of male roles and makes women who occupy them the exception rather than the rule.

What has been demonstrated by the essays in this volume is the importance of complementarity and autonomy in defining the position of Native North American women and a comparative deemphasis on hierarchy and interpersonal dominance. But these themes need not imply either equivalence or equality. Native North American cultures, like all cultures, are characterized by inherent tensions, tensions that define the status of individuals and the relation of individuals to social groups. Among these tensions are personal independence versus social responsibility, complementarity versus hierarchy, and personal preferences versus innate capacities. Together they define the universe in which gender roles are acted out.

REFERENCES

Aberle, David F.
1966 *The Peyote Religion Among the Navaho.* New York: Wenner-Gren Foundation for Anthropological Research.

Aberle, Sophia D.
1948 "The Pueblo Indians of New Mexico: Their Land, Economy and Civil Organization." American Anthropological Association Memoirs no. 70:1–93 (*American Anthropologist* 50: 4, 2).

Abler, Thomas S., and Elisabeth Tooker
1978 "Seneca." In *Handbook of North American Indians.* Vol. 15, *Northeast,* 505–17. Washington, D.C.: Smithsonian Institution Press.

Ackerman, Lillian
1971 "Marital Instability and Juvenile Delinquency among the Nez Perces." *American Anthropologist* 73(3):595–603.
1982 "Sexual Equality in the Plateau Culture Area." Ph.D. dissertation, Department of Anthropology, Washington State University, Pullman.
1987 "The Effect of Missionary Ideals on Family Structure and Women's Roles in Plateau Indian Culture." *Idaho Yesterdays* 31:64–73.

Adair, J.
[1775] 1986 *The History of the American Indians.* New York: Promontory Press.

Adams, Ben Q., and Richard Newlin
1987 *R. C. Gorman: The Graphic Works.* Taos, New Mex.: Taos Editions.

Aginsky, B. W., and E. G. Aginsky
1934–46. Unpublished field notes collected under the aegis of the Columbia University Social Science Field Laboratory in Ukiah. Notes housed at

the Cultural Resources Facility, Sonoma State University, Rohnert Park, California.

Albers, Patricia

1983 "Introduction: New Perspectives on Plains Indian Women." In *The Hidden Half: Studies of Plains Indian Women*," ed. Patricia Albers and Beatrice Medicine, 1–26, Washington, D.C.: University Press of America.

1989 "From Illusion to Illumination: Anthropological Studies of American Indian Women." In *Gender and Anthropology*, ed. Sandra Morgen, 116–31. Washington, D.C.: American Anthropological Association.

Albers, Patricia, and Beatrice Medicine (eds.)

1983 *The Hidden Half.* Washington, D.C.: University Press of America.

Allen, Paula Gunn

1986 *The Sacred Hoop: Recovering the Feminine in American Indian Tradition.* Boston: Beacon.

Anastasio, Angelo

1972 "The Southern Plateau: An Ecological Analysis of Intergroup Relations." *Northwest Anthropological Research Notes* 6(2):109–229.

Anonymous

1924 "Stories from a Real Home." *Women and Missions* 7:257–59.

Arrington, Leonard J.

1966 *Great Basin Kingdom: An Economic History of the Latter-Day Saints, 1830–1900.* Lincoln: University of Nebraska Press.

Atkinson, Jane

1982 "Review Essay: Anthropology." *Signs* 8:236–58.

Atkinson, Jane Monnig, and Shelly Errington, eds.

1990 *Power and Difference: Gender in Island Southeast Asia.* Stanford: Stanford University Press.

Aycock, D[aniel] Alan

1976 "Violence, Strategic Resources, and the Exploitation of Women." *Western Canadian Journal of Anthropology* 6(3): 8–23.

Bailey, Flora L.

1950 *Some Sex Beliefs and Practices in a Navaho Community.* Papers of the Peabody Museum of American Archaeology and Ethnology 40, no. 2. Harvard: Harvard University.

Balikci, Asen

1970 *The Netsilik Eskimo.* Garden City, N.J.: Natural History Press.

Bandalier, Adolph F. A.

1910 *Documentary History of the Rio Grande Pueblos of New Mexico.* Papers of the School of American Archaeology, Santa Fe, New Mex.

Bandalier, Adolph F. A., and Edgar Hewett
1937 *Indians of the Rio Grande Valley.* Albuquerque: University of New Mexico Press.

Barrett, S. A.
1917 *Pomo Bear Doctors.* University of California Publications in American Archaeology and Ethnology, vol. 12, No. 11. 443–465. Berkeley: University of California.
1933 *Pomo Myths.* Bulletin of the Public Museum of the City of Milwaukee, 15: 1–608. Milwaukee: Board of Trustees.

Barth, Frederick
1978 "Conclusions." In *Scale and Social Organization,* ed. Frederick Barth, 253–73. Oslo: Universitetsforlaget.

Bartram, W.
[1789] 1853 "Observations on the Creek and Cherokee Indians." *Transactions* 3:1–81. American Ethnological Society.
[1775] 1928 *The Travels of William Bartram.* Edited by M. Van Doren. New York: Dover.

Bataille, Gretchen M. (ed.)
1993 *Native American Women.* New York: Garland.

Bataille, Gretchen M., and Kathleen Mullen Sands
1984 *American Indian Women: Telling Their Lives.* Lincoln: University of Nebraska Press.
1991 *American Indian Women: A Guide to Research.* New York: Garland.

Blackman, Margaret
1981 "The Changing Status of Haida Women: An Ethnohistorical and Life History Approach." In *The World Is as Sharp as a Knife: An Anthology in Honour of Wilson Duff,* ed. Donald B. Abbott, 65–77. Victoria: British Columbia Municipal Museum.
1982 *During My Time: Florence Edenshaw Davidson, A Haida Woman.* 2d ed. rev. Seattle: University of Washington Press.
1989 *Sadie Brower Neakok, An I'nupiaq Woman.* Seattle: University of Washington Press.

Boas, Franz
1901 "The Eskimo of Baffin Land and Hudson Bay." *Bulletin of the American Museum of Natural History* 15(1).

Bonvillain, Nancy
1980 "Iroquoian Women." In *Studies on Iroquoian Culture,* ed. Nancy Bon-

villain, 47–58. Occasional Papers in Northeastern Anthropology, no. 6. Peterborough, N.H.: Peterborough Transcript.

Boyd, M.F. (ed.)

1941 "From a Remote Frontier: San Marcos de Apalache, 1763–1769." Pt. 2. *Florida Historical Quarterly* 19:179–212, 402–12; 20:82–90, 203–5, 293–308, 382–88; 21:44–50, 136–46.

Boyd, M. F., and Latorre, J. N.

1953 "Spanish Interest in British Florida and in the Progress of the American Revolution." I: "Relations with the Spanish Faction of the Creek Indians." *Florida Historical Quarterly* 32:92–130.

Boyer, Ruth M., and Narcissus, D. Gayton

1992 *Apache Mothers and Daughters.* Norman: University of Oklahoma Press.

Briggs, Jean L.

1970 *Never in Anger: Portrait of an Eskimo Family.* Cambridge: Harvard University Press.

1974 "Eskimo Women: Makers of Men." In *Many Sisters: Women in Cross-Cultural Perspective,* ed. C. J. Matthiasson, 261–304. New York: Free Press.

Brody, H.

1981 *Maps and Dreams: Indians and the British Columbia Frontier.* Bungay, Suffolk: Chaucer Press.

Brooks, Juanita (ed.)

1972 *Journal of the Southern Indian Mission.* Western Text Society, no. 4, Logan: Utah State University Press.

Brown, Jennifer

1980 *Strangers in Blood: Fur Trade Company Families in Indian Country.* Vancouver: University of British Columbia Press.

Brown, Judith K.

1970 "Economic Organization and the Position of Women Among the Iroquois." *Ethnohistory* 17:151–67.

Buckley, Thomas C. T.

1988 "Menstruation and the Power of Yurok Women." In *Blood Magic: The Anthropology of Menstruation,* ed. Thomas Buckley and Alma Gottlieb, 187–209. Berkeley, Los Angeles, and London: University of California Press.

Buckley, Thomas, and Alma Gottlieb (eds.)

1988 *Blood Magic: The Anthropology of Menstruation.* Berkeley, Los Angeles, and London: University of California Press.

Bunzel, Ruth
[1929] 1972 *The Pueblo Potter.* New York: Columbia University Press.

Burch, Ernest
1975 *Eskimo Kinsmen: Changing Family Relationships in Northwest Alaska.* American Ethnological Society Monograph, no. 59. St. Paul, Minn.: West Publishing Co.

Burns, Robert Ignatius, S. J.
1966 *The Jesuits and the Indian Wars of the Northwest.* New Haven: Yale University Press.

Carter, R. M.
1974 "Chipewyan Semantics: Form and Meaning in the Language and Culture of an Athapaskan-speaking People of Canada." Ph.D. dissertation, Department of Anthropology, Duke University. Ann Arbor: University Microfilms.

Cesara, Manda
1982 *No Hiding Place: Reflections of a Woman Anthropologist.* New York: Academic Press.

Chazanof, William
1970 *Joseph Ellicott and the Holland Land Company: The Opening of Western New York.* Syracuse: Syracuse University Press.

Chisholm, James S.
1983 *Navajo Infancy: An Ethological Study of Child Development.* New York: Aldine.

Chittenden, Hiram Martin
1905 *Life, Letters and Travels of Father Pierre-Jean DeSmet, S.J., 1801–1873.* 4 vols. New York: Francis P. Harper.

Cleland, Robert Glass, and Juanita Brooks (eds.)
1983 *A Mormon Chronicle: The Diaries of John D. Lee, 1848–1876.* 2 vols. Salt Lake City: University of Utah Press.

Clignet, Remi, and Joyce A. Sween
1981 "For a Revisionist Theory of Human Polygyny." *Signs* 6(3):445–68.

Cline, Walter
1938 "Religion and World View." In *The Sinkaietk or Southern Okanagon of Washington,* ed. Leslie Spier, 131–82. Menasha, Wisc.: George Banta.

Collier, Jane Fishburne
1974 "Women in Politics." In *Women, Culture, and Society,* ed. Michelle Z. Rosaldo and Louise Lamphere, 89–96. Stanford: Stanford University Press.
1987 "Rank and Marriage: Or, Why High-Ranking Brides Cost More. In

Gender and Kinship: Essays Toward a Unified Analysis, Jane Fishburne Collier and Sylvia Junko Yanagisako, 197–220. Stanford: Stanford University Press.

1988 *Marriage and Inequality in Classless Societies.* Stanford: Stanford University Press.

Collier, Jane Fishburne, and Sylvia Junko Yanagisako (eds.)

1987a *Gender and Kinship: Essays Toward a Unified Analysis.* Stanford: Stanford University Press.

1987b "Introduction." In *Gender and Kinship: Essays Toward a Unified Analysis,* ed. Jane Fishburne Collier, and Sylvia Junko Yanagisako. 1–13 Stanford: Stanford University Press.

Colson, Elizabeth

1974 (ed.) *Autobiographies of Three Pomo Women.* Berkeley: University of California Archaeological Research Facility.

n.d. *Acculturation Among Pomo Women.* Unpublished manuscript.

Commons, Rachel

1938 "Diversions." In *The Sinkaietk or Southern Okanagon of Washington,* ed. Leslie Spier, 183–94. Menasha, Wisc.: George Banta.

Condit, James H.

1926 "Woman's Place in Alaska's Development." *Women and Missions* 3: 257–58, 265.

Crow Dog, Mary, and Richard Erdoes

1991 *Lakota Woman.* New York: Harper Perennial.

Cruikshank, Julie

1990 *Life Lived Like a Story: Life Story of Three Yukon Native Elders.* Vancouver: University of British Columbia Press.

Dauenhauer, Nora Marks, and Richard Dauenhauer (eds.)

1990 *Haa Tuwunáagu Yís, For Healing Our Spirit: Tlingit Oratory.* Seattle: University of Washington Press.

Deloria, Vine, Jr.

1969 *Custer Died for Your Sins: An Indian Manifesto.* New York: Macmillan.

di Leonardi, Micaela

1991 "Introduction: Gender, Culture, and Political Economy." In *Gender at the Crossroads of Knowledge,* ed. Micaela di Leonardi, 1–48. Berkeley, Los Angeles, and London: University of California Press.

Divale, William Tulio, and Marvin Harris

1976 "Population, Warfare, and the Male Supremacist Complex." *American Anthropologist* 78(3):521–38.

Dorais, Louis-Jacques
1986 "Agiter l'homme pour attraper la femme: La sémantique des sexes en langue Inuit." *Études Inuit Studies* 10(1–2):171–78.

Douglas, Mary
1970 *Natural Symbols*. New York: Vintage/Random House.
1975 *Implicit Meanings*. London: Routledge and Kegan Paul.

Drury, Clifford Merrill
1936 *Henry Harmon Spalding*. Caldwell, Id.: Caxton.

Dunning, R. W.
1962 "A Note on Adoption Among the Southhampton Island Eskimo." *Man* 259:163–67.

Durlach, Theresa Mayer
1928 *The Relationship Systems of the Tlingits, Haida, and Tsimshian*. Publications of the American Ethnological Society 11. Washington, D.C.: Smithsonian Institution.

Dyk, Walter
1938 *Son of Old Man Hat: a Navaho Autobiography*. New York: Harcourt, Brace.

Eisler, Diane
1987 *The Chalice and the Blade: Our History, Our Future*. San Francisco: Harper and Row.

Ember, Carol R.
1983 "The Relative Decline in Women's Contribution to Agriculture with Intensification." *American Anthropologist* 85:283–304.

Emmons, George T.
1907 "The Chilkat Blanket." *Memoirs of the American Museum of Natural History* 3:329–404. New York.

Engels, Friedrich
1972 *The Origin of the Family, Private Property and the State*. Edited by Eleanor Leacock. New York: International Publishers.

Etienne, Mona, and Eleanor Leacock (eds.)
1980 *Women and Colonization: Anthropological Perspectives*. New York: Praeger.

Farella, John
1984 *The Main Stalk: A Synthesis of Navajo Philosophy*. Tucson: University of Arizona Press.

Farrow, E. A.
1917 Superintendent's Annual Report, Kaibab Agency. U.S. National Archives, Record Group 75, Microfilm Series 1011, roll 68, no frame

numbers.

Fenton, William N.

1949 "Seth Newhouse's Traditional History and Constitution of the Iroquois Confederacy." *Proceedings of the American Philosophical Society* 93(2):141–58.

1967 "From Longhouse to Ranch-type House: The Second Housing Revolution of the Seneca Nation." In *Iroquois Culture, History, and Prehistory: Proceedings of the 1965 Conference on Iroquois Research*, 7–22. Albany: University of the State of New York, State Education Department, New York State Museum and Science Service.

1968 "Editor's Introduction." In *Parker on the Iroquois*, ed. William N. Fenton, 1–47. Syracuse: Syracuse University Press.

Fogelson, R. D.

1977 "Cherokee Notions of Power." In *The Anthropology of Power*, ed. R. D. Fogelson and R. N. Adams, 185–94. New York: Academic Press.

1990 "On the 'Petticoat Government' of the Eighteenth-Century Cherokee." In *Personality and the Cultural Construction of Society: Papers in Honor of Melford E. Spiro*, ed. David K. Jordan and Marc J. Swartz, 161–81. Tuscaloosa: University of Alabama Press.

Ford, Richard I.

1968 *"An Ecological Analysis Involving the Population of San Juan Pueblo, New Mexico."* Ph.D. dissertation, University of Michigan.

Foreman, Carolyn

1954 *Indian Women Chiefs*. Muskogee, Okla.: Hoffman.

Foucault, M.

1980 *The History of Sexuality*. Vol. 1. New York: Vintage.

Fowler, Catherine S.

1989 "Ethnographic Field Notes as Historical Documents: Isabel Kelly's Southern Paiute Work, 1922–1932." Paper delivered at Southwestern Anthropological Association, Riverside, Calif.

Fowler, Catherine S., and Lawrence E. Dawson

1986 "Ethnographic Basketry." In *Handbook of American Indians*. Vol. 11, *Great Basin*, 705–37. Washington, D.C.: Smithsonian Institution Press.

Franciscan Fathers

1910 *An Ethnologic Dictionary of the Navaho Language*. St. Michael's Ariz.: Franciscan Fathers.

Freuchen, Peter

1935 *Ivalu: The Eskimo Wife*. New York, Lee Furnam.

1961 *Peter Freuchen's Book of the Eskimos*. Edited by Dagmar Freuchen. New York: World.

Friedl, Ernestine
1967 "The Position of Women: Appearance and Reality." *Anthropological Quarterly* 40(3): 97–108.
1975 *Women and Men: An Anthropologist's View.* New York: Holt, Rinehart and Winston.

Frisbie, Charlotte Johnson
1967 *Kinaaldá: A Study of the Navaho Girl's Puberty Ceremonial.* Middletown, Conn.: Wesleyan University Press.
1982 "Traditional Navajo Women: Ethnographic and Life History Portrayals." *American Indian Quarterly* 6 (1–2): 11–33.
1987 *Navajo Medicine Bundles or Jish: Acquisition, Transmission, and Disposition in the Past and Present.* Albuquerque: University of New Mexico Press.

Gardner, Peter M.
1991 "Foragers' Pursuit of Individual Autonomy." *Current Anthropology* 32(5): 543–72.

Gearing, F.
1962 *Priests and Warriors: Social Structures for Cherokee Politics in the 18th Century.* American Anthropological Association Memoirs no. 93.

George, D. M.
1991 "Dancing with Myths." Letter, *Washington Post*, April 13, 1991.

Gewertz, Deborah
1981 "A Historical Reconsideration of Female Dominance among the Chambri of Papua New Guinea." *American Ethnologist* 8:94–106.

Giago, T. [Nanwica Keiji]
1991 "Dancing with Myths." Letter, *Washington Post*, April 13, 1991.

Gidley, M.
1979 *With One Sky Above Us.* New York: G. P. Putnam's Sons.

Giffen, Naomi
1930 *The Roles of Men and Women in Eskimo Culture.* Chicago: Department of Anthropology, University of Chicago.

Gifford, Edward W.
1926 *Clear Lake Pomo Society.* University of California Publications in American Archaeology and Ethnology, vol. 18, no. 2:287–390. Berkeley: University of California.

Gilbert, W. H., Jr.
1943 *The Eastern Cherokees.* Bureau of American Ethnology Bulletin no. 133,

paper 23:169–413.

Gillespie, B. C.

1975 "Territorial Expansion of the Chipewyan in the 18th Century." In *Proceedings: Northern Athapaskan Conference, 1971.* Mercury Series, Canadian Ethnology Service Paper no. 27:350–88. Ottawa: National Museum of Man.

1976 "Changes in Territory and Technology of the Chipewyan." *Arctic Anthropology* 13(1):6–11.

Graburn, Nelson

1964 *Taqagmiut Eskimo Kinship Terminology.* Northern Coordination and Research Council, Department of Northern Affairs and National Resources, NCRC 64–1.

Grant, C. L. (ed.)

1980 *Letters, Journals and Writings of Benjamin Hawkins.* 2 vols. Savannah: Beehive Press.

Green, Rayna

1975 "Pocahontas Perplex." *Massachusetts Review* 16 (Autumn): 698–714.

1980 "Native American Women." *Signs* 62:248–67.

1983 *Native American Women: A Contextual Bibliography.* Bloomington: Indiana University Press.

1984 "The United States: Honoring the Vision of Changing Woman." In *Sisterhood Is Global,* ed. Robin Morgan, 705–13. Garden City, N.Y.: Anchor Press/Doubleday.

Griswold, Gillett

1954 *"Aboriginal Patterns of Trade between the Columbia Basin and the Northern Plains."* M. A. thesis, Montana State University.

Gronhaug, Reidar

1978 "Scale as a Variable in Analysis: Fields in Social Organization in Herat, Northwest Afghanistan." In *Scale and Social Organization,* ed. Frederick Barth, 78–121. Oslo: Universitetsforlaget.

Ground, Mary

1978 *Grass Woman Stories.* Browning, Mt.: Blackfeet Heritage Program.

Guemple, Lee

1961 *Inuit Spouse Exchange.* Occasional Paper, Department of Anthropology, University of Chicago.

1965 "Saunik: Name Sharing as a Factor Governing Eskimo Kinship Terms." *Ethnology* 4(3):323–35.

1972 "Eskimo Band Organization and the 'D P Camp' Hypothesis." *Arctic*

Anthropology 9(2): 80–113.

1975 "Marking and Sex Classification in Inupik Eskimo." *Proceedings of the Second Congress, Canadian Ethnology Society,* National Museum of Man Mercury, Series no. 28:183–96.

1980 *Inuit Adoption.* Mercury Series, Canadian Ethnology Service Paper no. 47: 121. Ottawa: National Museum of Man.

1986 "Men and Women, Husbands and Wives: The Role of Gender in Traditional Inuit Society." *Études Inuit Studies* 10(1–2): 9–24.

Haile, Father Berard

1938 *Origin Legend of the Navaho Enemy Way.* New Haven: Yale University Publications in Anthropology.

1948 *Navaho War Dance.* St. Michael's, Ariz.: St. Michael's Press.

Hall, C. F.

1879 *Narrative of the Second Arctic Expedition Made by C. F. Hall.* Edited by J. E. Norse. Washington, D.C.: Government Printing Office.

Halpern, Katherine Spencer

1957 *Mythology and Values: An Analysis of the Navajo Chantway Myths.* Philadelphia: American Folklore Society.

Hamamsy, Laila

1957 "The Role of Women in a Changing Navajo Society." *American Anthropologist* 59:101–11.

Harding, Susan Friend

1975 "Women and Words in a Spanish Village." In *Toward an Anthropology of Women,* ed. Rayna Rapp Reiter, 283–308. New York: Monthly Review Press.

Harrington, John P.

1916 "The Ethnogeography of the Tewa Indians." In *Twenty-ninth Annual Report of the Bureau of American Ethnology, 1907–08.* Washington, D.C.: U.S. Government Printing Office. Pp. 37–636.

Hartsock, Nancy

1983 Money, Sex and Power: Toward a Feminist Historical Materialism. New York: Longman.

Hawkins, B.

1848 *A Sketch of the Creek Country in the Years 1798 and 99.* Georgia Historical Society, *Collections* 3.

Hearne, S.

[1791] 1971 *A Journey from Prince of Wales Fort in Hudson's Bay to the Northern Ocean.* Edmonton: M. G. Hurtig.

Heinrich, Albert

1972 "Divorce as an Alliance Mechanism Among Eskimos." In *Alliance in Eskimo Society,* ed. L. Guemple. Proceedings of the American Ethnological Society, 1971, Supplement.

Heizer, Robert F.

1978 *Handbook of North American Indians.* Vol. 8, *California.* Washington, D.C.: Smithsonian Institution. Pp. 274–324.

Helm, June

1993 "'Always With Them Either a Feast Or a Famine': Living Off the Land with Chipewyan Indians, 1791–1792." *Arctic Anthropology* 30:46–60.

Hertzberg, Hazel W.

1966 *The Great Tree and the Longhouse: The Culture of the Iroquois.* New York: Macmillan.

Hill, W. W.

1936 *Navaho Warfare.* New Haven: Yale University Publications in Anthropology.

Hobart, M.

1985 "Anthropos through the Looking-Glass: Or How to Teach the Balinese to Bark." In *Reason and Morality,* ed. J. Overing, 104–34. New York: Tavistock.

Holm, Gustov

1916 "Ethnological Sketch of the Angmjagsalik Eskimo 1911." *Meddelelser Om Gronland* 82(2).

Hughes, Richard E., and James A. Bennyhoff

1986 "Early Trade." In *Handbook of North American Indians.* Vol. 11, *Great Basin,* 238–55. Washington, D.C.: Smithsonian Institution Press.

Hunn, Eugene S.

1981 "On the Relative Contribution of Men and Women to Subsistence among Hunter-Gatherers of the Columbia Plateau: A Comparison with Ethnographic Atlas." Summaries. *Journal of Ethnobiology* 1(1): 124–34.

Hurtado, Albert L.

1988 *Indian Survival on the California Frontier.* New Haven and London: Yale University Press.

Illich, Ivan

1982 *Gender.* New York: Pantheon Books.

Irimoto, T.

1981 *Chipewyan Ecology: Group Structure And Caribou Hunting System.* Senri Ethnological Studies no. 8. Osaka: National Museum of Ethnology.

Irving, Theodore

[1869] 1971 *The Conquest of Florida by Hernando de Soto.* New York: Kraus Reprint Co.

Jacobs, Sue-Ellen

1979 "Top-Down Planning: Obstacles to Community Development in an Economically Poor Region of the Southwestern United States." *Human Organization* 38:120–33.

n.d. *As If in a Dream: Images of Change at San Juan Pueblo.* Unpublished manuscript.

Jake, Lucille, Evelyn James, and Pamela Bunte

1983 "Southern Paiute Woman in a Changing Society." *Frontiers* 7(1):44–49.

Jameson, Elizabeth

1988 "Toward a Multicultural History of Women in the Western United States" *Signs* 13(4):761–91.

Jarvenpa, R.

1976 "Spatial and Ecological Factors in the Annual Economic Cycle of the English River Band of Chipewyan." *Arctic Anthropology* n.s. 18(1):45–60.

1977 "The Ubiquitous Bushman: Chipewyan–White Trapper Relations of the 1930's." In *Prehistory of the North American Subarctic: The Athapaskan Question.* Proceedings of the Ninth Annual Conference. Calgary: Archaeological Association of the University of Calgary.

Jenness, Diamond

1922 The Life of the Copper Eskimo. *Report of the Canadian Arctic Expedition.* vol. 12. Ottawa: F. A. Ackland.

Jones, Livingston

1914 *A Study of the Tlingets of Alaska.* New York: Fleming H. Revell.

Jorgensen, Joseph G.

1971 "Indians and the Metropolis." In *The American Indian in Urban Society,* eds. Jack O. Waddell and Michael Watson, 66–113. Boston: Little, Brown.

Joset, Joseph, S.J.

n.d. The Joset Papers. Mss., box 1351, Folder M, XXI, XV. Oregon Province Archives, Crosby Library, Gonzaga University, Spokane, Washington.

Kamenskii, Fr. Anatolii

[1906] 1985 *Tlingit Indians of Alaska.* Trans. Sergei Kan. Fairbanks: University of Alaska Press.

Kan, Sergei

1989 *Symbolic Immortality.* Washington, D.C.: Smithsonian Institution Press.

Kaplan, Victoria
1984 *Sheemi Ke Janu: Talk from the Past: A History of the Russian River Pomo of Mendocino County.* Ukiah, Calif.: Ukiah Title VII Project, Ukiah Unified School District.
Kastengren, G.E.
1920 "Among the Alaskan Tlinkats." *Mid-Pacific Magazine* 20:421–25.
Kearney, Michael
1984 *World View.* Novato: Chandler and Sharp.
Kehoe, Alice
1970 "The Function of Ceremonial Intercourse among the Northern Plains Indians." *Plains Anthropologist* 15(48):99–103.
1976 "Old Women Had Great Power." *Western Canadian Journal of Anthropology* 6:68–79.
1983 "The Shackles of Tradition." In *The Hidden Half: Studies of Plains Indian Women,* ed. Patricia Albers and Beatrice Medicine, 53–73. Washington, D.C.: University Press of America.
1991 "Home on the Range." Paper presented at the annual meeting of the American Anthropological Association, November 20, 1991, Chicago, Ill.
1993 "How the Ancient Peigans Lived." *Research in Economic Anthropology* 14:87–105.
Kelly, Isabel T.
1964 "Southern Paiute Ethnography." *Anthropological Papers* no. 69, University of Utah, Salt Lake City.
Kelly, Isabel T., and Catherine S. Fowler
1986 "Southern Paiute." In *Handbook of North American Indians.* Vol. II, *Great Basin,* 368–97. Washington, D.C.: Smithsonian Institution Press.
Kent, Susan
1984 *Analyzing Activity Areas: an Ethnoarchaeological Study of the Use of Space.* Albuquerque: University of New Mexico Press.
Kidwell, Clara Sue
1992 "Indian Women as Cultural Mediators." *Ethnohistory* 39(Spring):97–107.
Klein, Alan
1983 "The Political-Economy of Gender: A 19th-Century Plains Indian Case Study. In *The Hidden Half: Studies of Plains Indian Women,* eds. Patricia Albers and Beatrice Medicine, 143–74. Washington, D.C.: University Press of America.

Klein, Laura F.
1975 "Tlingit Women and Town Politics." Ph.D. dissertation, Department of Anthropology, New York University. Ann Arbor: University Microfilms International.
1980 "Contending with Colonization: Tlingit Men and Women in Change." In *Women and Colonization: Anthropological Perspectives,* ed. Mona Etienne and Eleanor Leacock, 88–108. New York: Praeger.

Kluckhohn, Clyde
1967 Navaho Witchcraft. Boston: Beacon Press.

Kluckhohn, Clyde, and Dorothea Leighton
1948 *The Navaho.* Cambridge: Harvard University Press.

Kluckhohn, Clyde, W. W. Hill, and Lucy Wales Kluckhohn
1971 *Navaho Material Culture.* Cambridge: Belknap Press of Harvard University.

Kluckhohn, Clyde, and Leland C. Wyman
1940 *An Introduction to Navaho Chant Practice.* American Anthropological Association Memoirs no. 53. Menasha, Wisc.

Knack, Martha C.
1973–74 Unpublished field notes. In possession of the author.
1980 *Life Is with People: Household Organization of the Contemporary Southern Paiute Indians.* Ballena Press Anthropological Papers no. 19, Socorro, New Mex.
1986 "Newspaper Accounts of Indian Women in Southern Nevada Mining Towns, 1870–1900." *Journal of California and Great Basin Anthropology* 8:83–98.
1987 "The Role of Credit in Native Adaptation to the Great Basin Ranching Economy." *American Indian Culture and Research Journal* 11: 43–65.
1989 "Contemporary Southern Paiute Women's Economic and Political Role and the Measurement of Women's Status." *Ethnology,* 28:233–48.
n.d. "Nineteenth-Century Great Basin Indian Wage Labor." In *Early Native American Wage Labor,* ed. Alice Littlefield and Martha C. Knack. Forthcoming.

Knapp, Frances, and Rheta L. Childe
1896 *The Thlinkets of Southeastern Alaska.* Chicago: Stone and Kimball.

Koolage, W. W.
1975 "Conceptual Negativism in Chipewyan Ethnology." *Anthropologica* n.s. 18(1):45–60.

Krause, Aurel

1956 *The Tlingit Indians.* Trans. Erna Gunther. Seattle: University of Washington Press.

Krech, S.

1980 "Northern Athapaskan Ethnology in the 1970's." *Annual Review of Anthropology* 9: 83–100.

Kroeber, A. L.

1899 "The Eskimo of Smith Sound." Bulletin of the American Museum of Natural History 12.

1947 *Cultural and Natural Areas of Native North America.* Berkeley: University of California Press.

1953 *Handbook of the Indians of California.* Berkeley: California Book Co.

Kuhns, Eileen P.

1947 "Institutional Participation of Women Members of Population Sub-Groups in Ukiah, California, as Affected by Their Group Memberships." Unpublished manuscript. Social Science Field Laboratory, Ukiah, Sonoma State University, Department of Anthropology, Rohnert Park, Calif.

de Laguna, Frederica

1960 *The Story of a Tlingit Community.* Bureau of American Ethnology. Bulletin 172. Washington, D.C.: Smithsonian Institution.

1965 "Childhood Among the Yakutat Tlingit." In *Context and Meaning in Cultural Anthropology,* ed. Melford E. Spiro, 3–23. New York: Free Press.

1972 *Under Mount Saint Elias.* Washington, D.C.: Smithsonian Institution Press.

Lamphere, Louise

1974 "Strategies, Cooperation and Conflict Among Women in Domestic Groups." In *Women, Culture and Society,* ed. Michelle Z. Rosaldo and Louise Lamphere, 97–112. Stanford: Stanford University Press.

1977 "Review: Anthropology." *Signs* 2(3):612–27.

Landes, Ruth

[1938] 1977 *The Ojibwa Woman.* New York: Columbia University Press.

Langness, L. L., and Gelya Frank

1981 *Lives: An Anthropological Approach to Biography.* Novato, Calif.: Chandler and Sharp.

Lantis, Margaret

1946 The Social Culture of the Nunivak Eskimo. *Transactions of the American Philosophical Society* 35(3):153–323.

Leacock, Eleanor Burke
1955 "Matrilocality in a Simple Hunting Economy (Montaignais-Naskapi)."
    Southwest Journal of Anthropology 11:31–47.
1975 Introduction to *The Origin of the Family, Private Property and the State*, by
    F. Engels, 7–67. New York: International Publishers.
[1978] 1981 *Myths of Male Dominance*. New York: Monthly Review Press.
Leacock, Eleanor Burke, and Richard Lee, eds.
1982 *Politics and History in Band Societies*. Cambridge: Cambridge University
    Press.
Lee, Richard
1982 "Politics, Sexual and Non-Sexual in an Egalitarian Society." In *Politics
    and History in Band Societies*, ed. Eleanor Burke Leacock and Richard
    Lee, 37–59. Cambridge: Cambridge University Press.
Levene, Bruce (ed.)
1976 *Mendocino County Remembered: An Oral History*. Vol. 1, A–L. Men-
    docino County, Calif.: Mendocino County Historical Society.
Lévi-Strauss, Claude
1967 "Do Dual Organizations Exist?" In *Structural Anthropology*, by Claude
    Lévi-Strauss, 128–60. Garden City, N.Y.: Doubleday.
Levy, Jerrold E., Eric B. Henderson, Tracy J. Adams
1989 "The Effects of Variation and Temporal Change on Matrilineal Elements
    of Navajo Social Organization." *Journal of Anthropological Research*
    45(4):351–77.
Levy, Jerrold, Raymond Neutra, and Dennis Parker
1987 *Hand Trembling, Frenzy Witchcraft and Moth Madness*. Tucson: University
    of Arizona Press.
Levy-Bruhl, L.
[1923] 1967 *Primitive Mentality*. Boston: Beacon Press.
[1926] 1979 *How Natives Think*. New York: Arno Press.
Lewis, Oscar
1941 "Manly-Hearted Women Among the North Piegan." *American Anthro-
    pologist* 43(2):173–87.
Lewis, Oscar, and Ruth Lewis
1939 Field Notes: Brocket Reserve, Alberta (North Piegan). Columbia Uni-
    versity project directed by Ruth Benedict.
Linderman, Frank
[1932] 1974 *Pretty Shield, A Crow Medicine Woman*. New York: John Day and
    Co. (Original title, *Red Mother.*)

Loeb, E. M.

1926 *Pomo Folkways.* University of California Publication in American Archaeology and Ethnology, vol. 19. Berkeley: University of California.

Lombard, Juliette

1942 "The Migration of Women From the Ukiah Valley in California to the San Francisco Bay Region." Master's thesis, Faculty of Political Science, Columbia University.

Lowie, Robert

1924 "Notes on Shoshonean Ethnography." *Anthropological Papers* 20:191–314. American Museum of Natural History.

[1935] 1956 *The Crow Indians.* New York: Holt, Rinehart and Winston.

[1922] 1967 "A Crow Woman's Tale." In *American Indian Life,* ed. Elsie Clews Parsons, 35–40. Lincoln: University of Nebraska Press.

Luckert, Karl W.

1975 *The Navajo Hunter Tradition.* Tucson: University of Arizona Press.

Lunt, Henry

n.d. "Personal Pioneer History." Typescript. WPA Federal Writers' Project Collection, Utah State Historical Society, Salt Lake City, Utah.

Lurie, Nancy O.

1961 *Mountain Wolf Woman.* Ann Arbor: University of Michigan Press.

1972 "Indian Women: A Legacy of Freedom." In *Look to the Mountain Top,* ed. Robert L. Iacopi, 29–36. San Jose, Calif.: Gousha Publications.

McClintock, Martha K.

1971 "Menstrual Synchrony and Suppression." *Nature* 229, no. 5282 (January 1971): 244–45.

McClintock, Walter

1910 *The Old North Trail.* New York: Macmillan.

McKee, Charlotte Ruth Karr

n.d. *Mary Richardson Walker, Her Book.* Typescript in Holland Library, Washington State University, Pullman. 2 vols.

McLendon, Sally

1977 "Cultural Presuppositions and Discourse Analysis: Patterns of Presupposition and Assertion of Information in Eastern Pomo and Russian Narrative." In *Linguistics and Anthropology,* ed. Muriel Saville-Troike, 153–89. Georgetown University Round Table on Language and Linguistics, 1977. Washington, D.C.: Georgetown University Press.

MacNeish, J. H.
1956 "Leadership Among the Northeastern Athabascans." *Anthropologica* II:131–63.

Mahon, W.
1991 "Dancing With Myths." Letter, *Washington Post,* April 13, 1991.

Mandelbaum, May
1938 "The Individual Life Cycle." In *The Sinkaietk or Southern Okanagon of Washington,* ed. Leslie Spier, 103–29. Menasha, Wisc.: George Banta.

Mangum, David Newton
1939 *History of David Newton Mangum.* Typescript, Works Projects Administration Writer's Project Files, Utah Historical Society, Salt Lake City.

Mankiller, Wilma, and Michael Wallis
1993 *Mankiller: A Chief and Her People.* New York: St. Martin's Press.

Martin, C.
1991 "Dancing with Myths." Letter, *Washington Post,* April 13, 1991.

Martin, Kay, and Barbara Voorhies
1975 *Female of the Species.* New York: Columbia University Press.

Medicine, Beatrice
1975 "The Role of Women in Native American Societies: A Bibliography." *Indian Historian* 8:51–53.
1978 *The Native American Woman: A Perspective.* Austin: National Educational Laboratory Publishers.

Michelson, Truman (ed.)
1925 "The Autobiography of a Fox Indian Woman." *U. S. Bureau of American Ethnology Papers* 40:295–349.
1932 "Narrative of a Southern Cheyenne Woman. *Miscellaneous Collections* 87. Washington, D.C.: Smithsonian Institution.
1933 "Narrative of An Arapaho Woman." *American Anthropologist* 35:595–610.

Miller, [Julius] Jay
1974 "The Delaware as Women: A Symbolic Solution." *American Ethnologist* 1(3): 507–14.

Mitchell, Frank
1970 *Navajo Blessingway Singer.* Tucson: University of Arizona Press.

Mitchell, J. Clyde
1966 "Theoretical orientations in African urban studies." In *The Social*

Anthropology of Complex societies, ed. Michael Banton, 37–68. London: Tavistock.

Moore, Henrietta
1988 *Feminism and Anthropology.* Minneapolis: University of Minnesota Press.

Morgan, Lewis Henry
[1851] 1962 *League of the Ho-de-no-sau-nee, Iroquois.* Seacaucus, N.J.: Citadel.

Morgen, Sandra (ed.)
1989 *Gender and Anthropology.* Washington, D.C.: American Anthropological Association.

Mukhopadhyay, Carol C., and Patricia J. Higgins
1988 "Anthropological Studies of Women's Status Revisited: 1977–1987." *Annual Reviews of Anthropology,* ed. Bernard J. Siegel, 17:461–95. Palo Alto, Calif: Annual Reviews.

Murdock, George Peter
1934 *Our Primitive Contemporaries.* New York: Macmillan.
1949 *Social Structure.* New York: Macmillan.

Nash, Jill
1981 "Sex, Money and the Status of Women in South Bourgainville." *American Ethnologist* 8:107–26.

Needham, R.
1972 *Belief, Language, and Experience.* Oxford: Basil Blackwell.
1975 "Polythetic Classification: Convergence and Consequences." *Man,* n.s. 10:349–69.

Nelson, Richard
1983 *Make Prayers to the Raven: A Koyukon View of the Northern Forest.* Chicago: University of Chicago Press.

Newcomb, Franc J., and Gladys Reichard
1975 *Sandpaintings of the Navajo Shooting Chant.* New York: Dover.

Niethammer, Carolyn
1977 *Daughters of the Earth.* New York: Collier Books.

Oberg, Kalvero
1934 "Crime and Punishment in Tlingit Society." *American Anthropologist* 36:145–146.

Olson, Ronald L.
1956 "Channeling of Character in Tlingit Society." In *Personal Character and Cultural Milieu,* ed. Douglas G. Haring, 675–87. Syracuse:

Syracuse University Press.

1967 "Social Structure and Social Life of the Tlingit of Alaska." *Anthropological Records* 26. Berkeley: University of California Press.

Olson, Wallace M.

1991 *The Tlingit.* 2d ed. Auke Bay, Alaska: Heritage Research.

Oosten, Jaarich

1986 "Male and Female in Inuit Shamanism." *Étude Inuit Studies* 10(1–2):115–32.

Orians, Gordon H.

1983 "The Uncertain Quest for Scientific Generalization." Address to the Centennial Celebrations of the American Ornithologists' Union, New York. Excerpted in *Environmental Outlook* 2:1–3.

Ortiz, Alfonso

1969 *The Tewa World.* Chicago: University of Chicago Press.

1972 (ed.) *New Perspectives on the Pueblos.* Albuquerque: University of New Mexico Press.

1981 "Cosmological Correlates of Tewa Sex Role Classifications." Paper presented at the American School of Research Seminar on the Tewa, Santa Fe, New Mex.

Ortner, Sherry

1974 "Is Female to Male as Nature Is to Culture?" In *Woman, Culture and Society,* ed. Michelle Z. Rosaldo and Louise Lamphere, 67–88. Stanford: Stanford University Press.

1981 "Gender and Sexuality in Hierarchical Societies: The Case of Polynesia and Some Comparative Implications." In *Sexual Meanings: The Cultural Construction of Gender and Sexuality,* ed. Sherry Ortner and Harriet Whitehead, 359–409. Cambridge: Cambridge University Press.

Ortner, Sherry, and Harriet Whitehead (eds.)

1981 *Sexual Meanings: The Cultural Construction of Gender and Sexuality.* Cambridge: Cambridge University Press.

Oswalt, Robert L.

n.d. "Retribution for Mate Stealing: A Southern Pomo Tale." Unpublished manuscript.

1964 *Kashaya Texts.* University of California Publications in Linguistics, vol. 36. Berkeley: University of California Press.

Oswalt, W.

1967 *This Land Was Theirs.* San Francisco: Chandler.

Overing, J.
1985 *Reason and Morality.* New York: Tavistock.

Parezo, Nancy
1982 "Navajo Sandpaintings: The Importance of Sex Roles in Craft Production." *American Indian Quarterly* 6 (1–2): 431–34.

Parker, Arthur C.
1968a "The Code of Handsome Lake." In *Parker on the Iroquois,* ed. William N. Fenton, Part 2, 1–148. Syracuse: Syracuse University Press.
1968b "The Constitution of the Five Nations." In *Parker on the Iroquois,* ed. William N. Fenton, Part 3, 1–158. Syracuse: Syracuse University Press.
1968c "The Iroquois Constitution." In *Parker on the Iroquois,* ed. William N. Fenton, 7–13. Syracuse: Syracuse University Press.

Parkin, D.
1985 "Reason, Emotion, and the Embodiment of Power." In *Reason And Morality,* ed. J. Overing, 135–51. New York: Tavistock.

Parsons, Elsie C.
1929 *The Social Organization of the Tewa of New Mexico.* American Anthropological Association Memoirs no. 36:1–309.

Patterson, Victoria
1988 Unpublished field notes. In possession of the author.

Perisco, V. R., Jr.
1979 Early Nineteenth-Century Cherokee Political Organization. In *The Cherokee Indian Nation: A Troubled History,* ed. D. H. King, 92–109. Knoxville: University of Tennessee Press.

Poewe, Karla O.
1980 "Universal Male Dominance: An Ethnological Illusion." *Dialectical Anthropology* 5:111–25.

Point, Nicholas, S.J.
1967 *Wilderness Kingdom: Indian Life in the Rocky Mountains. 1840–1847.* New York: Holt, Rinehart and Winston.

Post, Richard H.
1938 "The Subsistence Quest." In *The Sinkaietk or Southern Okanagon of Washington,* ed. Leslie Spier, 9–34. Menasha, Wisc.: George Banta.

Powers, Marla N.
1986 *Oglala Women: Myth, Ritual, and Reality.* Chicago: University of Chicago Press.

Randle, Martha Champion
1951 "Iroquois Women, Then and Now." *Bureau of American Ethnology*

Bulletin 149(8):167–80.

Rapp, Rayna
1979 "Review Essay: Anthropology." *Signs* 4:497–513.

Rasmussen, Knud
1929a *Intellectual Culture of the Iglulik Eskimos*. Report of the Fifth Thule Expedition 1921–24. Vol. 7, no. 1.
1929b *The Netsilik Eskimos: Social Life and Spiritual Culture*. Report of the Fifth Thule Expedition 1921–24. Vol. 8, no. 1–2.

Ray, Verne F.
1932 *The Sanpoil and Nespelem*. University of Washington Publications in Anthropology, vol. 5:1–237. Seattle: University of Washington Press.
1939 *Cultural Relations in the Plateau of Northwestern America*. Los Angeles: Publication of the Frederick Webb Hodge Anniversary Publication Fund, Southwest Museum.

Reichard, Gladys A.
1928 *Social Life of the Navajo Indians*. Columbia University Contributions to Anthropology, vol. 7
1950 *Navaho Religion: A Study of Symbolism*. 2 vols. Bollingen Series XVIII. New York: Pantheon.

Reiter, R. R. (ed.)
1975 *Toward an Anthropology of Women*. New York: Monthly Review Press.

Richards, Cara
1957 "Matriarchy or Mistake: The Role of Iroquois Women through Time." In *Cultural Stability and Cultural Change*, ed. Verne F. Ray, 36–45. Seattle: University of Washington Press.

Rides At The Door, Darnell Davis
1979 *Napi Stories*. Browning, Mont.: Blackfeet Heritage Program.

Robert-Lamlin, Joëlle
1986 "Influence de l'éducation sur l'identité sexuelle, un exemple chez les Inuit." In *Côté femmes, approches ethnologiques*. Paris: L'Harmattan, coll. Connaissance des Hommes.

Robin, Enid Fenton
1943 "Indian Girl, White Girl." Master's thesis, Faculty of Political Science, Columbia University.

Roessel, Ruth
1981 *Women in Navajo Society*. Rough Rock, Navajo Nation, Ariz.: Navajo

Resource Center, Rough Rock Demonstration School.

Rogers, Susan Carol

1975 "Female Forms of Power and the Myth of Male Dominance: A Model of Female/Male Interaction." *American Ethnologist* 2:727–56.

1978 "Women's Place: A Critical Review of Anthropological Theory." *Comparative Studies in Society and History* 20:123–73.

Romans, B.

1775 *A Concise Natural History of East and West Florida.* New York.

Rosaldo, Michelle Zimbalist

1974 "Women, Culture, and Society: A Theoretical Overview." In *Women, Culture, and Society,* ed. Michelle Z. Rosaldo and Louise Lamphere, 17–42. Stanford: Stanford University Press.

Rosaldo, Michelle, and Louise Lamphere, eds.

1974 *Women, Culture and Society.* Stanford: Stanford University Press.

Ross, Alexander

1904 *Adventures of the First Settlers on the Oregon or Columbia River 1810–1813.* Edited by Reuben Gold Thwaites. Cleveland: Arthur H. Clark.

Rothenberg, Diane

1980 "The Mothers of the Nation: Seneca Resistance to Quaker Intervention." In *Women and Colonization: Anthropological Perspectives,* ed. Mona Etienne and Eleanor Leacock, 63–87. New York: Praeger.

n.d. *Property and People: Inheritance and Adaptation.* Unpublished manuscript.

Ruby, Robert H., and John A. Brown

1970 *The Spokane Indians: Children of the Sun.* Norman: University of Oklahoma Press.

Rusco, Mary K.

1989 "Biographical Information about Indian Women in Southern Nevada Mining and Agricultural Communities." Paper presented at the meeting of Southwestern Anthropological Association, Riverside, Calif.

Russell, Scott, and Mark McDonald

1982 "Economic Contributions of Women in a Rural Western Navajo Community," *American Indian Quarterly* 6 (3–4): 262–83.

Sacks, Karen

1982 *Sisters and Wives: The Past and Future of Sexual Equality.* Urbana: University of Illinois Press.

Sahlins, Marshall D.

1971 *Stone Age Economics.* Atherton and Chicago: Aldine.

Saladin d'Anglure, Bernard
1986 "Du Foetus au chamane: La construction d'un "troisiéme sexe" inuit." *Études Inuit Studies* 10(1–2):25–114.

Sandal, L. B.
1921 Letter to the Commissioner of Indian Affairs, 15 April 1921. U.S. National Archives, Record Group 75, Bureau of Indian Affairs, Letters Received, 1907–1937, no. 1921–32221.

Sanday, Peggy Reeves
1974 "Female Status in the Public Domain." In *Woman, Culture and Society*, ed. Michelle Z. Rosaldo and Louise Lamphere, 189–206. Stanford: Stanford University Press.
1981 *Female Power and Male Dominance: On the Origins of Sexual Inequality.* Cambridge: Cambridge University Press.

Sattler, R. A.
1987 "*Siminoli Italwa*: Socio-Political Change among the Oklahoma Seminoles Between Removal and Allotment, 1936–1905." Ph.D. dissertation, University of Oklahoma.

Schaeffer, Claude E.
1965 "The Kutenai Female Berdache: Courier, Guide, Prophetess, and Warrior." *Ethnohistory* 12:193–236.
n.d. Manuscript notes from Blackfoot Informants. Archives, Glenbow-Alberta Institute, Calgary.

Schlegel, Alice Elizabeth
1977a (ed.) *Sexual Stratification: A Cross-Cultural View.* New York: Columbia University Press.
1977b "Male and Female in Hopi Thought and Action." In *Sexual Stratification: A Cross-Cultural View*, ed. Alice Schlegel, 245–69. New York: Columbia University Press.
1977c "Toward a Theory of Sexual Stratification." In *Sexual Stratification: A Cross-Cultural View*, ed. Alice Schlegel, 1–40. New York: Columbia University Press.

Scott, Duncan C.
1911 "Traditional History of the Confederacy of the Six Nations." *Proceedings and Transactions of the Royal Society of Canada*, ser. 3, 5(2):195–246.

Seaver, James E.
1961 *A Narrative of life of Mrs. Mary Jemison.* New York: Corinth.

Seymour, Flora
1930 *Women of Trail and Wigwam.* New York: Woman's Press.

Sharp, H. S.
1975 "Introducing the Sororate to a Northern Saskatchewan Chipewyan Village." *Ethnology* 14(1):71–82.
1976 "Man:Wolf::Woman:Dog." *Arctic Anthropology* 13(1):25–34.
1977a "Bilaterality and Strategies of Caribou Hunting Among The Chipewyan." *Arctic Anthropology* 14(2)35–40.
1977b "The Chipewyan Hunting Unit." *American Ethnologist* 4(2):377–93.
1979 *Chipewyan Marriage.* Mercury Series, Canadian Ethnology Service Paper no. 58. Ottawa: National Museum of Man.
1981 "The Null Case: The Chipewyan." In *Woman the Gatherer,* ed. F. Dahlberg, 221–44. New Haven: Yale University Press.
1982 "Some Problems in Wolf Sociology." In *Wolves of the World,* ed. F. H. Harrington and P. C. Paquet. Park Ridge, N.J.: Noyes.
1986 "Shared Experience and Magical Death: Chipewyan Explanations of a Prophet's Decline." *Ethnology* 25(4):257–70.
1987 "Giant Otters, Giant Fish, and Dinosaurs: 'Apparently Irrational' Beliefs in a Chipewyan Community." *American Ethnologist* 14(2):226–35.
1988a *The Transformation of Bigfoot: Maleness, Power, and Belief Among the Chipewyan.* Washington, D.C.: Smithsonian Institution Press.
1988b "Dry Meat and Gender: The Absence of Ritual for the Regulation of Animal Numbers and Hunting in Chipewyan Society." In *Hunters and Gatherers.* Vol. 2, *Property, Power and Ideology,* ed. T. Ingold, D. Riches, and J. Woodburn, 183–91. London: Berg.
1991 "Memory, Meaning, and Imaginary Time: The Construction of Knowledge in White and Chipewyan Cultures." *Ethnohistory* 38(2):149–75.
1994 "The Power of Weakness." In *Contemporary Issues in Hunter-Gatherer Research,* ed. E. S. Burch, Jr., and L. Ellan, 35–58. London: Berg.
Shepardson, Mary
1963 *Navajo Ways in Government.* American Anthropological Association Memoir no. 96, 65(3):pt. 2.
1982 "The Status of Navajo Women." *American Indian Quarterly* 6(1–2): 149–70.
Shepardson, Mary, and Blodwen Hammond
1966 "Navajo Inheritance Patterns: Random or Regular?" *Ethnology* 5(1): 87–97.
1970 *The Navajo Mountain Community.* Berkeley, Los Angeles, and London: University of California Press.
Sieciechowicz, Krystyna
1990 "Land-Use Rights of Ojibwa-Cree Women." Fairbanks, Alaska: Conference on Hunting and Gathering Societies 6, Precirculated Papers and

Abstracts I: 165–81.

Slobodin, R.

1975a "Without Fire: A Kutchin Tale of Warfare, Survival, and Vengeance." In *Proceedings: Northern Athapaskan Conference, 1971*, ed. A. M. Clark. Mercury Series, Canadian Ethnology Service Paper no. 27, 1:259–301. Ottawa: National Museum of Man.

1975b "Northern Athapaskan Research: Some Comments." In *Proceedings: Northern Athapaskan Conference, 1971*, ed. A. M. Clark. Mercury Series, Canadian Ethnology Service Paper no. 27, 2:786–94. Ottawa: National Museum of Man.

1975c "Canadian Subarctic Athapaskans in the Literature to 1965." *Canadian Review of Sociology and Anthropology* 12(3):278–89.

Smith, D. M.

1973 *Inkonze: Magico-Religious Beliefs of Contact-Traditional Chipewyan Trading at Fort Resolution, NWT, Canada.* Mercury Series, Ethnology Division Paper no. 6. Ottawa: National Museum of Man.

1982 *Moose-Deer Island House People: A History of the Native People of Fort Resolution.* Mercury Series, Canadian Ethnology Service Paper no. 81. Ottawa: National Museum of Man.

1985 "Big Stone Foundations: Manifest Meaning in Chipewyan Myths." *Journal of American Culture* 18(1):73–77.

Smith, J. G. E.

1970 "The Chipewyan Hunting Group in a Village Context." *Western Canadian Journal of Anthropology* 2(1):60–66.

1975 "The Ecological Basis of Chipewyan Socio-Territorial Organization." In *Proceedings: Northern Athapaskan Conference, 1971*, ed. A. M. Clark. Mercury Series, Canadian Ethnology Service Paper no. 27, 2:389–461. Ottawa: National Museum of Man.

1978 "The Emergence of the Micro-Urban Village Among the Caribou-Eater Chipewyan." *Human Organization* 37(1):38–49.

Smithson, Carma

1959 *The Havasupai Woman.* Salt Lake City: University of Utah Press.

Speck, Frank Gouldsmith

1946 "The Delaware Indians as Women: Were the Original Pennsylvanians Politically Emasculated?" *Pennsylvania Magazine of History and Biography* 70(4): 377–89.

Spencer, Robert

1914 The Stefànsson-Anderson Arctic Expedition of the American Museum:

Preliminary Ethnological Report. *Anthropological Papers of the American Museum of Natural History,* vol. 14, pt. 1.

1959 *The North Alaskan Eskimo: A Study in Ecology and Society.* Bureau of American Ethnology Bulletin no. 171.

Spindler, Louise

1962 *Menomini Women and Culture Change.* American Anthropological Association Memoirs no. 91:1–113.

Spiro, Melford E.

1979 *Gender and Culture: Kibbutz Women Revisited.* New York: Schocken.

Spoehr, A.

1942 "Kinship System of the Seminole." Field Museum of Natural History Anthropological Series 33(2):29–113.

Sprague, John T.

1847 *The Origin, Progress, and Conclusion of the Florida War.* New York: D. Appleton.

Stefansson, Vilhjalmar

1914 The Stefansson-Anderson Expedition of the American Museum Preliminary Ethnological Report. Anthropological Papers of the American Museum of Natural History. Vol. 14, pt. 1.

Stewart, Irene

1980 *A Voice in Her Tribe: A Navajo Woman's Own Story.* Edited by Mary Shepardson and Doris Ostrander Dawdy. Socorro, New Mex.: Ballena Press.

Stewart, Omer C.

1942 "Culture Element Distributions." Vol. 18, "Ute-Southern Paiute." University of California Anthropological Records 6:231–355.

Straus, Anne S.

1982 "The Structure of the Self in Northern Cheyenne Culture." In *Psychosocial Theories of the Self,* ed. Benjamin Lee, 111–28. New York: Plenum Press.

Sundquist, Asebrit

1987 *Pocohontas & Co.: The Fictional American Indian Woman in Nineteenth-Century Literature.* Atlantic Highlands, N.J.: Humanities Press International.

Swan, C.

1857 "Position and State of Manners and Arts in the Creek or Muskogee Nation in 1791." In *Historical and Statistical Information respecting the History, Condition and Prospects of the Indian Tribes of the United States,* ed. H. R. Schoolcraft, 5:251–83. Philadelphia: Lippincott, Granbo.

Swanton, John R.

1908 "Social Condition, Beliefs and Linguistic Relationship of the Tlingit Indians." *Bureau of American Ethnology Annual Report* 26:395–512. Washington, D.C.: Smithsonian Institution.

1909 *Tlingit Myths and Texts.* Bureau of American Ethnology Bulletin no. 39. Washington, D.C.: Smithsonian Institution.

1922 *Early History of the Creek Indians and Their Neighbors.* Bureau of American Ethnology Bulletin no. 73.

1928 "Social Organization and Social Usages of the Indians of the Creek Confederacy." *Bureau of American Ethnology Annual Report* 42:23–472.

Swartz, M., V. Turner, and A. Tuden

1966 *Political Anthropology.* Chicago: Aldine.

Tanner, Adrian

1979 *Bringing Home Animals: Religious Ideology and Mode of Production of the Mistassini Cree Hunters.* New York: St. Martin's Press.

Teit, James Alexander

1906 *The Lillooet Indians.* American Museum of Natural History Memoirs no. 4:193–300.

1930 *The Salishan Tribes of the Western Plateaus.* Bureau of American Ethnology, 45th Annual Report, 23–396. Washington: U.S. Government Printing Office.

Terrell, John Upton, and Donna M. Terrell

1974 *Indian Women of the Western Morning.* Garden City, N.Y.: Doubleday.

Thalbitzer, William

1928 Die Kültischen Gottheiten der Eskimos. *Archiv für Religions Wissenschaft* 26, Heft 314.

Thomas, David H.

1971 "Historic and Prehistoric Land-Use Patterns at Reese River." *Nevada Historical Society Quarterly* 14(4):2–9.

Tooker, Elisabeth

1978 "The League of the Iroquois: Its History, Politics, and Ritual." In *Handbook of North American Indians.* Vol. 15, *Northeast,* ed. Bruce G. Trigger, 418–41. Washington, D.C.: Smithsonian Institution Press.

1984 "Women in Iroquois Society." In *Extending the Rafters: Interdisciplinary Approaches to Iroquoian Studies,* ed. Michael Foster, Jack Campisi, and Marianne Mithun, 109–23. Albany: State University of New York.

Trafzer, Clifford E., and Richard D. Scheuerman
1986 *Renegade Tribe: The Palouse Indians and the Invasion of the Inland Pacific Northwest.* Pullman: Washington State University Press.

Turney-High, Harry Holbert
1937 *The Flathead Indians of Montana.* American Anthropological Association Memoir no. 48. Menasha, Wisc.

Uhlenbeck, C. C.
1912 A *New Series of Blackfoot Texts.* Verhandelingen der Koninklijke Akademie van Wetenschappen to Amsterdam, Afdeeling Letterkunde, n.r. 13(1). Amsterdam: Johannes Muller.

United States Congress
1832–61 *American State Papers: Documents Legislative and Executive of the Congress of the United States, Indian Affairs.* Vol. 2. Washington, D.C.

United States, Commission to the Five Civilized Tribes
n.d. *Enrollment Cards of the Five Civilized Tribes, 1898–1914.* Seminole. Seminole Newborn. Washington, D.C.: National Archives Microfilm Publications, M 1186.

Valentine, P. W.
1991 "Hollywood's Noble Indians: Are We Dancing With Myths? *Washington Post,* March 31, 1991.

Van Ball, J.
1975 *Reciprocity and the Position of Women.* Assem/Amsterdam: Van Gorcum.

Van Kirk, Sylvia
1983 *Many Tender Ties.* Norman: University of Oklahoma Press. Originally published 1980.

Vestal, Paul
1952 *Ethnobotany of the Ramah Navaho.* Report no. 4, The Ramah Project, Peabody Museum of American Archaeology and Ethnology, Harvard University 40(4):252, 309, 397.

Wagner Sorensen, Bo
1990 "Folk Models of Wife-beating in Nuuk, Greenland." *Folk: Dansk Etnografisk Tidsskrift* 32:93–116.

Wallace, Anthony F. C.
1947 "Women, Land, and Society: Three Aspects of Aboriginal Delaware Life." *Pennsylvania Archeologist* 17(1–4):1–35.
1952 *The Modal Personality Structure of the Tuscarora Indians as Revealed by*

the Rorschach Test. Bureau of American Ethnology Bulletin no. 150.
1969 *The Death and Rebirth of the Seneca*. New York: Vintage.

Wallace, Paul A. W.
1946 *The White Roots of Peace*. Philadelphia: University of Pennsylvania Press.

Walters, L. V. W.
1938 "Social Structure." In *The Sinkaietk or Southern Okanagon of Washington*, ed. Leslie Spier, 73–99. Menasha, Wisc.: George Banta.
n.d. Field notes. Author's files.

Weaver, Sally M.
1984 "Seth Newhouse and the Grand River Confederacy." In *Extending the Rafters: Interdisciplinary Approaches to Iroquoian Studies*, ed. Michael K. Foster, Jack Campisi, and Marianne Mithun, 165–82. Albany: State University of New York.

Weiner, Annette B.
1976 *Women of Value, Men of Renown: New Perspectives in Trobriand Exchange*. Austin: University of Texas Press.

Weyer, Edward M., Jr.
1932 *The Eskimo: Their Environment and Folkways*. New Haven: Yale University Press.

Whitehead, Harriet
1981 "The Bow and the Burden Strap: A New Look at Institutionalized Homosexuality in Native North America." In *Sexual Meanings: The Cultural Construction of Gender and Sexuality*, ed. Sherry B. Ortner and Harriet Whitehead, 80–115. Cambridge: Cambridge University Press.

Whyte, Martin King
1978 *The Status of Women in Preindustrial Societies*. Princeton: Princeton University Press.

Williams, Walter L.
1986 *The Spirit and the Flesh: Sexual Diversity in American Indian Culture*. Boston: Beacon Press.

Wissler, Clark
1911 *The Social Life of the Blackfoot Indians*. American Museum of Natural History Anthropological Papers, vol. 7, pt. 1, 1–64.
1912 *Ceremonial Bundles of the Blackfoot Indians*. American Museum of Natural History, Anthropological Papers, vol. 7, pt. 2, 65–289.
1938 *Indian Cavalcade*. New York: Sheridan House.

Wissler, Clark, and D. C. Duvall
1908 *Mythology of the Blackfoot Indians.* American Museum of Natural History, Anthropological Papers, vol. 2, pt. 1, 1–163.

Witherspoon, Gary
1975 *Navajo Kinship and Marriage.* Chicago: University of Chicago Press.

Witt, Shirley Hill
1974 "Native Women Today." *Civil Rights Digest* 6:29–35.

1990 "History of Southeastern Alaska Since 1867. In *Handbook of North American Indians.* Vol. 7, *Northwest Coast,* ed. Wayne Suttles, 149–58. Washington, D.C.: Smithsonian Institution Press.

Wolf, Eric R.
1982 *Europe and the People Without History.* Berkeley, Los Angeles, and London: University of California Press.

Wood, C. E. S.
1882 "Among the Thlinkits in Alaska." *Century Magazine* 24:323–39.

Work, Laura
1898 Letter to Commissioner of Indian Affairs, 5 July 1898. U.S. National Archives, Record Group 75, Bureau of Indian Affairs, Letters Received 1887–1907, no. 1898–31787.

Worl, Rosita
1990 "History of Southeastern Alaska since 1867." In *Handbook of North American Indians.* Vol. 7, *Northwest Coast,* 149–58. Washington, D.C.: Smithsonian Institution.

Wright, Anne
1982 "An Ethnography of the Navajo Reproductive Cycle." *American Indian Quarterly* 6(1–2): 52–71.

Wyman, Leland C.
1970 *Blessingway.* Tucson: University of Arizona Press.

1975 *The Mountainway of the Navajo.* Tucson: University of Arizona Press.

Young, James A., and B. Abbott Sparks
1985 *Cattle in the Cold Desert.* Logan: Utah State University Press.

Young, Robert W., and William Morgan
1951 *A Vocabulary of Colloquial Navaho.* United States Indian Service.

1980 *The Navajo Language.* Albuquerque: University of New Mexico Press.

LIST OF CONTRIBUTORS

LILLIAN A. ACKERMAN received her Ph.D. from Washington State University in 1982 and holds the rank of Associate Professor, Adjunct. Her fieldwork has included an Eskimo village in Southwest Alaska and the Tlingit Indians of Alaska, but most of her work has been done in the Plateau. She has published articles in the *American Ethnologist*, the *American Anthropologist*, and other journals. She is currently preparing a book on gender equality in the Plateau.

JOALLYN ARCHAMBAULT, Ph.D., is the Director of the American Indian Program at the National Museum of Natural History, Smithsonian Institution. She supervises the research of fellows and is project manager of the North American Indian Exhibit Project. She also conducts research in the areas of Plains history and culture, the history of exhibits, and gender issues.

JOY BILHARZ received her B.A. degree from George Washington University and her M.A. and Ph.D. degrees from Bryn Mawr College. She is currently Assistant Professor in the Department of Sociology and Anthropology at the State University of New York, College at Fredonia. Her extensive ethnographic research with the Senecas has been funded by the Wenner-Gren Foundation for Anthropological Research.

LEE GUEMPLE is Professor of Anthropology at the University of Western Ontario in London, Ontario. He has written and edited a number of articles and works on the Canadian Inuit (Eskimo), including *Inuit Adoption* and

Alliance in Inuit Society. His other scholarly interests include pragmatic and Taoist philosophy, Tai Chi, and the sociology of industrial communities.

SUE-ELLEN JACOBS received her Ph.D. from the University of Colorado in 1970 and is currently Associate Professor of Women Studies and Anthropology at the University of Washington. She has written numerous publications, based on extensive fieldwork, on the Pueblo Southwest and has recently (1989) coauthored *Winds of Change: Women in Northwest Commercial Fishing.* She is an authority on issues of sex and gender variation and published *Women in Perspective* in 1974.

ALICE B. KEHOE is Professor of Anthropology at Marquette University, where she has taught since 1968. Among her distinguished list of publications are *North American Indians: A Comprehensive Account* and *The Ghost Dance: Ethnohistory and Revitalization.* While maintaining her interest in American Indians, she has also recently worked with the Aymara in Bolivia and has done historical research at the Institute for Advanced Studies in the Humanities, Edinburgh University.

LAURA F. KLEIN received her Ph.D. in anthropology from New York University in 1975. She has done ethnographic and ethnohistorical research with the Tlingit in Southeastern Alaska for over twenty years and has published many articles on the region. She has recently co-edited *The Message in the Missionary: Local Interpretation of Religious Ideology and Missionary Personality* with Elizabeth Brusco for Studies in Third World Societies and is currently working on a project investigating the treatment of tuberculosis among Native Americans before the advent of effective drug treatment. She is Professor of Anthropology at Pacific Lutheran University in Tacoma, Washington.

MARTHA C. KNACK received her Ph.D. in anthropology from the University of Michigan in 1975. She is the author of *Life Is with People* (1980), a study of the social organization of the Southern Paiutes of Utah, and *As Long as the River Shall Run,* with Omer C. Stewart, an ethnohistorical analysis of Pyramid Lake Northern Paiute water rights. She has written more than a dozen articles on Great Basin native women's roles, ethnohistory, interethnic relations, and tribal politics and economies.

284

DANIEL MALTZ is a cultural anthropologist educated at Cornell University and the University of California at Berkeley. Along with his late wife, Ruth Borker, he has done research on contemporary Christianity, gender, and language and is well published in all of these fields. He is presently a researcher in the American Indian Program at the Smithsonian Institution and a free-lance anthropological bibliographer.

VICTORIA D. PATTERSON has lived in Mendocino County, California, the heart of Pomo country, for over twenty years. She has worked with local tribes and schools in a variety of projects ranging from Native language development to economic and technical preparation. She has degrees from the University of Chicago and the Western Institute for Social Research and currently teaches at Mendocino College. She is a contributing editor to *News from Native California*, the author of *Sheemi Ke Janu, Talk from the Past: A History of the Russian River Pomo of Mendocino Country*, and editor of *The Singing Feather: Tribal Remembering from Round Valley* as well as other publications. She is most recently involved in a major museum/college/local history collaboration with the California Council for the Humanities to interpret the 1850 shipwreck of the clipper *Frolic* on the Mendocino coast.

RICHARD A. SATTLER received his M.A. and Ph.D. degrees in anthropology from the University of Oklahoma and has conducted extensive ethnographic and ethnohistorical research on the Seminole and Creek Indians of Oklahoma, as well as more limited research on the Oklahoma Cherokees. His primary research interests are social and political organization and change. He is currently lecturer at Barat College and Assistant to the Director of the Summer Institute in Native American Literature at the Newberry Library, both in Chicago, Illinois.

HENRY S. SHARP received his Ph.D. degree from Duke University in 1973. He has made nearly a dozen field trips to Mission and its outlying bush camps since he began his research among the Chipewyans in 1969 and has published widely on the Chipewyans and to a lesser extent on wolves as well as the symbolic and ecological relations between wolves, caribou, and the Chipewyans. He has held teaching positions at Simon Fraser University, the University of Victoria and Mary, Washington College, and is currently Scholar-in-Residence at the Department of Anthropology of the University of Virginia.

MARY SHEPARDSON'S Ph.D. in anthropology in 1960 from the University of California Berkeley, followed her undergraduate degree at Stanford University by more than thirty years. During those years, she taught and wrote and was an active civil rights worker. During the 1950s, she became increasingly interested in the Navajos and began the anthropological research that has resulted in numerous published works on Navajo men and women, including *The Navajo Mountain Community: Social Organization and Kinship Terminology*, with Blodwen Hammond.

INDEX